DON'T CALL IT THAT

D1564666

Don't Call It That

The Composition Practicum

Edited by

SIDNEY I. DOBRIN

National Council of Teachers of English
1111 W. Kenyon Road, Urbana, Illinois 61801–1096

Staff Editor: Bonny Graham
Interior Design: Jenny Jensen Greenleaf
Cover Design: Frank P. Cucciarre, Blink Concept & Design, Inc.

NCTE Stock Number: 12218

It is the policy of NCTE in its journals and other publications to provide a forum for the open discussion of ideas concerning the content and the teaching of English and the language arts. Publicity accorded to any particular point of view does not imply endorsement by the Executive Committee, the Board of Directors, or the membership at large, except in announcements of policy, where such endorsement is clearly specified.

Every effort has been made to provide current URLs and e-mail addresses, but because of the rapidly changing nature of the Web, some sites and addresses may no longer be accessible.

Library of Congress Cataloging-in-Publication Data

Don't call it that : the composition practicum / edited by Sidney I. Dobrin.
     p.   cm.
Includes bibliographical references and index.
ISBN 0-8141-1221-8 (pbk.)
1. English language—Rhetoric—Study and teaching (Graduate)
   2. Practicums.   I. Dobrin, Sidney I., 1967–
   PE1404.D658 2005
   808'.042'0711—dc22   2005020081

*This one's for
Roy and Stormy*

CONTENTS

ACKNOWLEDGMENTS

I wish to acknowledge a number of individuals for their assistance and support in putting this collection together. First and foremost, I offer sincere thanks to the contributors to this collection for their patience and dedication in writing this book. I would also like to thank Kurt Austin of NCTE for his support for this project and his hard work in bringing it all together. I am particularly grateful for his patience and editorial expertise. Likewise, NCTE Staff Editor Bonny Graham has been a tremendous help in editing and producing this book. Thanks, Bonny.

I offer my gratitude to a number of people who read and offered comments on early drafts of the book, particularly my introduction to the collection: Clay Arnold, Anis Bawarshi, Jeanne Gunner, Linda Howell, Chris Keller, and Sean Morey. I also wish to acknowledge the NCTE reviewers whose substantial commentary provided great direction for revision. I am particularly grateful for the thorough and demanding conversations I had with Joe Marshall Hardin about this book. I value his advice, guidance, collegiality, and friendship well beyond what can be said in an academic acknowledgments page. Likewise, it is the friendship, academic challenge, insight, and collaboration of all of the "Idyots" that encourage me to do the work I do. For that and for them I am grateful: Steve Brown, Julie Drew, Joe Hardin, Merry Perry, Raul Sanchez, Todd Taylor, and Christian Weisser.

Of course, none of this work could be accomplished without the support of my colleagues and friends in the Department of English at the University of Florida. I offer my gratitude to Ira Clark, Kim Emery, Pam Gilbert, Susan Hegeman, Kenneth Kidd, John Leavey, Jack Perlette, and Phil Wegner for their friendship and for the opportunities to talk through my research ideas. I am especially grateful for Program Assistant Carla Blount, who ensures that I have time to get my writing done by making sure it looks like I'm getting my administrative work done.

Finally, I want to thank my best friend and adventure partner, my wife Teresa, without whom there would be no reason for doing any of this. She is my world, my reason. Always.

Finding Space for the Composition Practicum

SIDNEY I. DOBRIN
University of Florida

Practicum: N. Amer. [a. late L. practicum, neut. of practicus, Gr. ΠφάΤΙΚός practical, concerned with action. (Cf. G. praktikum practical training.)]

A practical exercise; a course of practical training.
Oxford English Dictionary Online

It might seem trite to begin this introduction by offering something as simple as a dictionary definition for the key term addressed in this book, particularly when that definition seems so simple, so evident. But as the contributors to this collection explain, in composition studies, defining the graduate-level (or even undergraduate) composition practicum is not such an easy task. The seventeen essays found in this collection consider, in fact, just how problematic the composition practicum has become, not only in terms of definition, but also in terms of its role in composition studies and larger university communities, its function as a training mechanism, and its share in the propagation of composition studies' cultural capital.

The title for this collection, *Don't Call It That: The Composition Practicum*, is taken from the fact that in many institutions, the introductory, graduate-level teacher training class that has traditionally trained new teachers of writing has offered more than simple day-to-day classroom guidance. The "practicum" more often than not serves as an introduction to composition theory, to research methodologies, to pedagogical theory, to histories of composition studies as a discipline, and to larger disciplinary questions about writing, not just to teaching writing per se. In many institutions, compositionists have developed more academically challenging courses than had been expected in a traditional practicum, despite the general impression (most often by those not directly attached to the course) that these intro courses merely teach new teachers of writing how to grade assignments, teach mechanics, oversee classrooms, and the like. Hence, *Don't Call It That* refers to the battle many composition programs have had to fight to identify their introductory graduate-level composition courses as not, in fact, practica, but as more sophisticated introductions to a dynamic field of study, and to identify the role that validation and legitimation have played in the history of the composition practicum. "Don't call it that" refers to the desire for the practicum course not to be perceived as a how-to course, but as a richer, more academically sophisticated and rigorous course.

This collection explores not only the various approaches taken in teaching the introductory graduate course in composition studies for new teachers of writing, but also the debate regarding the role such courses play in graduate-level (and in some cases, undergraduate) curricula in general. By approaching the place and purpose of the practicum both as a subject that should be discussed pedagogically and in terms of curriculum, this collection moves to centralize conversations about the role of the graduate (and in some cases, undergraduate) composition practicum. *Don't Call It That: The Composition Practicum* works to such an end in order that first, composition studies communities have a better idea of how the practicum is addressed at various institutions. Second, it works to bring more scholarly debates regarding the role of the curriculum to the fore in professional conversations so that compositionists better understand not only why this course has become a "universally" offered course, but also why it is—and has been historically—one of the most contested and questioned courses offered in graduate-level English studies.

This collection, unlike other works that address the composition practicum in conjunction with other aspects of teacher training or professionalization, provides a provocative consideration of the scholarly questions that surround the contested site of the composition practicum, rather than simply addressing ways in which to more effectively offer the practicum. The essays in *Don't Call It That* specifically emphasize the central question of the role of theory in the composition practicum. In doing so, the collected essays situate the practicum as one of the most important locations in which composition's "theory wars" or theory/practice debates are played out with very material ramifications. This question of the role theory plays in the practicum is, then, intrinsically enmeshed with the questions of legitimacy that departments, colleges, and universities often ask of the practicum: Should students receive credit for the course since it isn't a "real" course? Should faculty receive teaching credit for teaching the course? These are a few of the major issues that relate to the political positioning of the practicum addressed in this collection.

In addition to these core political questions, the contributors to this collection address the role technology plays in practicum courses. They also consider the direct relationship often found and assumed between the writing program administrator and the course, both in terms of the function of the course in relation to larger programmatic training agendas and methods and in terms of who is assumed to be the faculty member assigned to teach the practicum.

That is to say, then, the chapters in this collection are about more than just how we think about devising the course that gets subsumed under the practicum rubric. They are about the institutional politics of these courses; they are about the subject position of composition studies within departments and larger university structures. The chapters further conversations not just about theory/practice debates but also about the very role and function of theory within the discipline. They consider the professional positions of writing program administrators and the often default association with practicum classes. In fact, one of the greatest strengths of this collection is not just that it addresses the composition practicum as a site of contestation, but that it also addresses the connections that very site has to larger political questions about composition studies, writing program administration, and the role of theory in the discipline, and in doing so, addresses the powerful position of the composition practicum.

For me, the overwhelming attention to the ongoing conversations regarding theory and practice that many of the contributors draw is a crucial facet of this book. For those familiar with my work, it is evident that I am deeply interested in how composition studies negotiates the theory/practice split. The fact that so many contributors to this collection have identified the practicum as a site where this debate is played out, quite literally, on the bodies of new teachers and new scholars—both in and outside of composition studies—is telling. Let's face it, as a device through which ideologies are reinforced and programmatic cultures are created and maintained, the practicum course is a powerful tool not only for guiding the ways new teachers learn to think about their teaching, but also for controlling how and in what ways the very discipline of composition studies is perpetuated. The cultural capital of composition studies is maintained and immortalized by way of the practicum.

Until now there has been little conversation about the composition practicum beyond discussions of how and what to teach in this course. For the most part, conversations about the practicum have been limited to disciplinary lore, and this lore has, in many ways, taken on stereotypical and conventionalized understandings of the practicum. Little attention has been paid to the location of the practicum as a political force in composition. One of the most comprehensive discussions about the practicum appeared in the Fall 1995 special issue of *Composition Studies* titled "A Forum on Doctoral Pedagogy." In this special issue, guest editors Bill Bolin, Beth Burmester, Brenton Faber, and Peter Vandenberg ask a series of critical questions not about the practicum per se but about doctoral pedagogy in general:

> To what extent is the radical diversity of approaches to teaching composition to undergraduates apparent at the graduate level? Just how different can "composition studies" look depending on where one enters the field as a doctoral student? How are theory and practice conceived, differentiated, and/or unified in the training of doctoral students? When doctoral students are introduced to the theory-practice of composition teaching and research, where, how, and why do disciplinary

knowledge and values give way to local or programmatic conditions and expectations? (4)

These are, of course, important questions. The special issue then provides syllabi from seventeen institutions' "first (introductory) or only graduate course in/about rhetoric, writing, composition" (4). Each syllabus is followed by a short critical or evaluative comment from the contributor who submitted the syllabus. These statements are perhaps the best collection of descriptions of why different institutions approach their practica as they do.[1] Under the rubric established by the guest editors, the courses presented in the special issue can each be considered the practicum course for that institution. Inherent in the methodology and questions asked by the guest editors is the recognition that the practicum is the very location—if not the only location—through which composition studies, as a discipline, as theory, as practice, is constructed for the newest members of the field and, perhaps more important, for many who will never identify themselves as compositionists. The titles of these courses are all quite telling:

Seminar in Approaches to Teaching Writing—Catholic University of America

Theory and the Teaching of Writing—University of Connecticut

Teaching Freshman Rhetoric—East Texas State University

Teaching English in College—Florida State University

Teaching Composition—Georgia State University

Introduction to Composition Studies—Illinois State University

Rhetorical Traditions—Indiana University of Pennsylvania

Theory and Research in Professional Communications—Iowa State University

Theory and Practice of Teaching Composition—Miami University

Composition Theory and Practice—University of Nebraska–Lincoln

The Teaching of Composition—University of North Carolina at Greensboro

Teaching College English—University of North Dakota—Grand Forks

Seminar in Teaching Composition—University of Pittsburgh

Approaches to the Teaching of Composition—Saint John's
University

Composition-Rhetoric, 1700–1995—University of Southern
California

Introduction to Scholarship in Composition and Rhetoric—
Syracuse University

The Teaching of Writing—Wayne State University

And to add to this list, I can note that here at the University of
Florida we offer Theories and Practices of Writing. Notice the
recurring notion of teaching, of theory and practice. As I will
show in a moment, neither these course titles nor the approach to
these courses has shifted very much in the past ninety years,
despite remarkable changes within composition studies.

Other studies, too, have made substantial contributions to
how we have come to think about the practicum. Notably, Elizabeth Rankin's *Seeing Yourself as a Teacher: Conversations with
Five New Teachers in a University Writing Program* provides
interviews with five new teachers a year after they have taken the
practicum. The interviews themselves show new teachers struggling with their own attempts to negotiate the theory/practice
divisions of their own teaching, and the interviews manifest the
ways in which the very course designs of practica that negotiate
the theory/pedagogy division affect new teachers' professional
frustrations and development. Similarly, Sarah Liggett's "After
the Practicum" moves toward assessment of how new teachers
move from their practicum training to their classrooms. Liggett
identifies a need to assess the practicum in ways different from
how other graduate courses are assessed, in ways that take into
account the transition from student in the practicum class to
teacher who applies information gained in the practicum class.

In each of these instances, the practicum is painted as a powerful mechanism. In fact, as I will argue, the practicum functions
as a primary purveyor of composition's cultural capital. Before
developing this argument, however, I think it is necessary that we
briefly examine the history of the composition practicum in order
to better contextualize its current position and to clarify that its
history is also the history of the commodification and distribution
of composition's cultural capital.

A (Brief) Historical Look at the Practicum

What I offer here is by no means a comprehensive history; it is merely an attempt to provide a general overview of how conversations about the practicum course have been constructed. I offer this with the intention of identifying when and how the very idea of teacher training courses entered into English department conversations, of examining the ways in which those conversations were resisted, and finally, of contending that though more institutions now offer such courses, and though the content of such courses may have changed over the years, the political arguments that surround such courses have changed very little.

The question of how to train new teachers of composition has been asked for a good while. Raymond MacDonald Alden, in his 1913 "Preparation for College English Teaching" published in the *English Journal*, examines the relationship between a graduate student's course work and his [sic] training for a career in teaching. He does not call for a particular course in teaching, but emphasizes the role of teaching as part of professionalization and the need for strong connections between graduate course work/ research and classroom preparation. In the same volume of *English Journal* is a printed version of a talk and responses given before the College Section of NCTE on November 29, 1912, by Chester Noyes Greenough. Greenough reports that

> for some time the department of English at Harvard has felt that the equipment of the men whom it has been sending forth to teach English has been inadequate on the side where beginners are most likely tested, namely, in their ability to teach elementary English composition. This inadequacy has been perceptible both in the very moderate skills displayed by most graduate students in writing theses and reports, and in the dismay with which even the best of them have approached the unfamiliar task of teaching Freshmen to write. (109)

To remedy these "inadequacies," Harvard in 1912 established English 67, a course officially described as "English 67—English Composition. Practice in Writing, in the Criticism of Manuscript, and in Instruction by Conferences and Lectures. Discussion of the Principles of Composition and of the Organization and Management of Courses in English Composition" (109). Even in this early experimental manifestation of a practicum-type course, Greenough is quick to note that the course is "one in English Composition more than in methods of teaching" (110). Because the course is taken for credit, the appearance of validation and legitimation is apparent. This is not a teaching methods course; such courses would not rate as valid in English departments, we hear Greenough suggest. Despite this, Greenough's introduction of the composition teacher training course initiates a call for the need for such courses. In response to Greenough's talk, M. Lyle calls attention to "the present glaring need of courses for English instructors—not necessarily teachers' courses as we ordinarily know them, but courses for teachers, nonetheless. . . . I am convinced that a specific need exists for courses for English teachers" (Greenough 116). He goes on to explain that "in composition this need for adequate training is even more glaring than in the language and literature courses" (117).

Likewise, J. M. Thomas calls again for specific training for teachers of composition courses as different from training for teaching literature courses in his 1916 article "Training for Teaching Composition in Colleges." In this article, Thomas notes Greenough's call for specific courses in training composition teachers, but unlike Greenough, he is not willing to commit to the method as useful: "whether the plan of establishing special courses in method will solve the problem remains to be seen. It may be that we cannot expect successfully to combine graduate study with instruction in pedagogy" (450). But, like other early discussions of the development of training classes, Thomas does specify that any training of composition teachers must be presented in a multifaceted way that includes a number of training mechanisms.

Two years following Thomas's skepticism of Greenough's experiment in offering graduate courses for training teachers of composition, J. V. Denney published "Preparation of College Teachers of English," in which he examines the professional value of such training courses. He identifies two primary classifications of such classes:

> (1) Courses that aim to supply elements that have been omitted in the previous education of the student and that are

deemed essential to professional equipment; (2) courses that deal directly with the educational problems involved in the teaching of English and that appeal directly to the student as a prospective teacher. (322)

What Thomas contends is that very few of the content-driven courses in English graduate programs "have a distinctively professional intention" (324). Thomas also argues, however, that much of what is taught in graduate courses—particularly those in linguistics and historical English grammar—is necessary for the college English teacher to know and to transfer into teaching strategies. Ultimately, Thomas calls for the development of specific teacher training courses:

> [T]here is a need of at least one directly professional course for the prospective teacher, and it is highly desirable for those who have experience in teaching, as well as for those without such experience. I mean a course in which attention is given specifically to the problems of teaching that center in the Freshman composition work and in the first college course in English literature. (326)

Yet, even in such early discussions of the practicum course, Thomas identifies prevailing concerns that must be addressed:

> the specific aims of the elementary course; the necessity for such courses[;] . . . the proper content of such courses; the order of topics; the best basis of differentiating students into groups for instruction; the use of the conference period; co-operative schemes among departments; the grammar question; oral composition; the measurement of results. (326)

By the mid 1940s, some programs had begun to adopt Greenough's experiment. The University of Illinois, for instance, developed Rhetoric 480, The Theory and Practice of English Composition. The UI catalog listed the course as "A study of the problems facing the writer and the teacher of writing at the college level." Yet Charles Roberts in "A Course for Training Rhetoric Teachers at the University of Illinois" notes that there was confusion as to what the course should offer. Roberts explains that in the first eight years of the course, he essentially taught sixteen different classes under the same title (191). It "is not really a course in writing at all but a teacher training course," he explains (191). Part of Roberts's frustration grew from the fact that there was no successful connection between the course and the PhD program in which his students were enrolled (192). For Roberts the central goal of the Illinois practicum course was to address teaching specifically:

> [W]hat, I asked myself, is the biggest problem which all teachers of English everywhere have in common? It is the young person seated at a desk, with a blank piece of paper before him, and gnawing on a pencil, whole ideas tumble over one another in his mind. Our job is to help him get those ideas arranged in his mind and recorded on that sheet of paper. (192)

Roberts even notes the discrepancy between compositionists (writing teachers) sitting at conferences such as the Conference on College Composition and Communication (CCCC) quibbling "about the relative merits of composition and communication programs or the latest developments in the upper stratosphere of linguistic research" while students struggle to write (193). In this, I hear not only early rumblings of composition's theory/practice debates and questions of composition's disciplinary agendas, but also direct links between the development of the composition practicum and those very debates. In many ways, the early practicum courses became the very site in which questions of pedagogy and theory as valid pursuits within composition began to get played out. The question, of course, must be posed as to what extent, then, the practicum was responding to those debates, fueling those debates, or engaging in a mixture of both activities.

In 1950 the University of Kansas introduced its teacher training course, Rhetorical Background of Written English, under the direction of Albert Kitzhaber. "We must help [graduate students] to know what to teach; for though such young teachers usually have an abundance of enthusiasm and the best will in the world, they are often at a loss to know just where and with what to begin," explained Kitzhaber (195). Kitzhaber saw the importance of training teachers of writing, even though some would likely go on to work in more literary areas:

> We would like to give the students in this course something
> that will be of use to them as long as they are teaching com-
> position, whether on our campus or elsewhere. And, even
> after they have served their novitiate and have been trans-
> planted to the headier regions of the teaching of literature, we
> hope they will have gained a perspective that will cause them
> to show more understanding of the problems of composition
> work, and a keener appreciation of its importance, than I am
> afraid many literary scholars do now. (195)

Of course, Kitzhaber is talking about more than teaching skills
here; he is addressing the propagation of cultural capital, of teaching a particular view of composition in the practicum in order to
propagate a disciplinary understanding of what is done in composition teaching. He is working toward spreading an understanding of composition designed to infiltrate traditionally
resistant populations. I will address this notion of the practicum
as purveyor of composition's cultural capital in detail in a
moment. For now I want to note that even in the early inceptions
of the composition practicum, compositionists recognized the
power such a course had for disseminating a particular (political)
view of what teaching composition is. That is, by training students who did not intend to pursue composition (teaching) as a
career choice to recognize that teaching composition is a difficult
and legitimate endeavor, Kitzhaber hoped to perpetuate a more
professionally amiable view of composition work through
(future) literature faculty.

The KU course was established to emphasize day-to-day
operations of a composition classroom. Yet, even in this early
development of practica agenda, Kitzhaber explains, "We had no
wish to standardize, to impose teaching methods or teaching
philosophies" (196):

> We wanted, rather, to put our young teachers in the way of
> ideas that would stimulate them to think seriously about the
> teaching of compositions. We wanted to help them develop
> ideas of their own and organize these ideas into some sort of
> coherent system. And, finally, we wanted to give them the
> opportunity to put their ideas to the test in their own class-
> rooms. (196)

In the second volume of *College Composition and Communication* (*CCC*) (1951), in which workshop proceedings from the first CCCC Convention were reported, Workshop 16, "Teacher-Training for Composition or Communication" (attended by ten participants and chaired by Albert H. Marckwardt of the University of Michigan), reports that "[t]hough some favored a specific graduate curriculum for future teachers of composition or communications, predominant opinion favored, as practical minimum, a single course supplementing the present curriculum" (31).

Even with these early courses, the understanding that there needed to be a curriculum of theory and practice is evident:

> The two-hour class meeting is divided equally between lecture and discussion—a lecture during the first half of the period on whatever topic is being considered that week, followed by a discussion that aims to work out some of the practical applications of the theoretical material presented in the lecture. (Kitzhaber 196)

"In this way," Kitzhaber goes on, "we try to avoid the unreality of the purely theoretical course, and at the same time offer enough *legitimate* subject matter to distinguish the course sharply from courses in educational method" (196, my emphasis). What is interesting here isn't just that the issue of theory/practice splits was evident from the earliest moments of composition practica, but that how theory and practice were valued and how theory was to be delivered to student teachers are underwritten implications. Here we see Kitzhaber clarifying that the theory portion of the course was set as lecture, as a delivery of information, information that he denotes as more legitimate than the practical, but that the practical applications of such theories could be more collaborative, dialogic. I also read a hierarchy in Kitzhaber's statement that devalues the students/teachers' ability to engage the theoretical aspect of pedagogy as more than information provided them, and that if they are to engage such material in any substantial way, it necessarily must be by way of finding practical application for those theories. I suppose, in this way, Kitzhaber is clearer about what he means by putting "young teachers in the way of ideas that stimulate them to think seriously about the teaching of composition" (196). He later notes,

> Certain things, though, we have intentionally excluded from
> the course and will probably continue to do so. Except for
> incidental discussion in the second hour of the meetings, we
> do not take up routine matters such as how to handle assign-
> ments, what to do about late themes, how to take care of pla-
> giarism, etc. It is not that we think these matters unimportant;
> we simply believe there are other and better ways of attending
> to them. (198)

He specifically notes that discussions of teaching methodologies
are deliberately not included in the course: "We have done this
not alone because we wish to distinguish our course from one in
Education, but mainly because we believe that specific teaching
methods are a perishable commodity" (199).

Kitzhaber also seems to be making a statement of legitimation, of what would legitimize such a course in the eyes of both
English programs and universities in general. He writes that at KU
the practicum course (though he doesn't use that term) was not
regarded as "a course in how to teach, but as one in what to
teach; it is, in other words, a course which we may validly claim
to be one in English" (196).

In the same issue of *CCC* in which Kitzhaber details the KU
course, Joseph Schwartz addresses Marquette University's English
208: Seminar in the Teaching of College Composition. Schwartz
notes that it is a responsibility of English departments to have
teacher training courses since teachers of composition cannot be
assumed to know how to teach composition based solely on their
experiences in having taken composition. Unlike the KU program
Kitzhaber describes, the Marquette course is entrenched in "how-
tos." It introduces rhetoric and linguistics. Its ultimate goal is to
make "beginning teachers more conscious of their teaching"
(204). When the course at Marquette was developed, the dean of
the Graduate School resisted the class, questioning whether there
was sufficient course content to be able to offer credit for it (201).
Similar questions and arguments, I'm sure, are familiar to many.
In fact, one of the prevailing discussions, though often handled
briefly, in early conversations regarding the practicum is the question of awarding credit for the course. More often than not, in
their early history, graduate teacher training courses were not
given for credit, because they were seen as courses in "education"

or "professionalism," not in substantive scholarly disciplines; more to the point, many of the early courses were devised specifically to avoid appearing to be education or training courses, but instead to appear as legitimate subject area courses in order to be credit worthy, in order to be institutionally validated.

It is crucial that these kinds of resistance be noted and that we pay attention to the push not just to develop such courses, but also to identify the ongoing resistance from institutions to such courses, despite the evident push from course developers to make the courses "legitimate." For instance, in his 1951 *CCC* article "A Training Course for Teachers of Freshman Composition," Robert S. Hunting contends that "insofar as a graduate student or beginning instructor spends time with a training course and gives more than the minimum required time to teaching freshman composition, he is doing hurt to his professional career. Willfully to do such hurt is manifestly foolish" (3). Of course, by "professional career," Hunting refers to the study of literature. Yet Hunting recognizes that most colleges and universities have to have first-year composition and, therefore, until such conditions can be "fixed" (Hunting's language throughout this article is quite telling), some bare-minimum training programs should be established: "if, under such conditions in most universities, there is really no solution, one can at least offer some plan which would permit us to muddle through less aimlessly than we have in the past" (3). Hunting goes on to describe the content for such a course that "should not be vaguely directed at any sort of college teaching" (4). Hunting describes how to develop such a course and manage to keep it away from legitimate graduate study. What is critical here is that, following a rather vague outline of the course, Hunting is clear that "the amount of work demanded by this training course should not seriously interfere with the *normal* pursuit of graduate studies. Those studies should still come first" (5, my emphasis).

In his final paragraphs, Hunting makes clear that this program outline must not interfere with the real work of English departments. In response to the claim made in Blegen and Cooper's *The Preparation of College Teachers* that "the curriculum for college teachers must include professional subject matter" (qtd. in Hunting 5), Hunting is adamant that he is "in emphatic disagreement. The curriculum for college teachers must not, of necessity, include any professional subject matter at all" (5). He goes on to explain as well that no credit should be given for the course because

> it really involves extra-curricular work. A graduate school of liberal arts is not, and should not pretend to be, a trade or pro-fessional school. To give credit for training in a trade or profes-sion would betray its purpose. Such training must always be a felicitous, but incidental, increment to graduate studies. (6)

This sentiment is echoed in Harold B. Allen's 1952 *CCC* "Prepar-ing the Teacher of Composition and Communication—A Re-port." In this piece, Allen recounts numerous department chairs who questioned his motivations in inquiring about how graduate students were trained as teachers. One such chair

> suddenly leaned forward and asked suspiciously, "Did you say you were a professor of education?" "No," I replied, "my field is English Linguistics." "Huh!" he grunted, "I didn't know that anyone but a professor of education thought you had to train a scholar in order to make him a teacher." (4)

Allen's report goes on to show that a majority of the campuses he visited did little to prepare graduate students in the teaching of composition; only in a few departments did he find courses offered specifically for training in composition pedagogy. According to his observations, Michigan had offered the course since 1925; Indiana added one in 1950 (when Philip Wikelund moved from Michigan to Indiana); NYU ran such a course in 1949 but abandoned it; Illi-nois (as I noted earlier) offered Theory and Practice of Composi-tion; and several programs at other institutions offered courses specifically in the teaching of communication that were rarely attended by English graduate students (6–7).

In "The 1956 Conference on College Composition and Com-munication Workshop Reports," published in *CCC*, Workshop 9, "Preparation of Composition/Communication Teachers: Toward a Comprehensive Program," conference participants offer a five-point program that integrates the work of graduate students in English with their training as composition teachers. Because this

DON'T CALL IT THAT

report recounts work done in the five previous years' workshops on preparation, four of the five points offered had been addressed by previous workshops: that adequate professional preparation in composition be offered; that the training of composition teachers be the responsibility of English departments, not education programs; that changes in graduate curriculum should be made to improve teacher training; and that there should be more latitude in allowing graduate students to do research in composition areas. The remaining point, however, and the focus of the 1956 report, includes a detailed examination of the development of inservice training programs, including "a special course in the teaching of composition/communication" (138). Though the report does not outline what the course should entail, it does identify the course as a necessary requirement. Interestingly, Kitzhaber chaired this session.

In 1963, CCC published a series of statements regarding training graduate students as teachers. These statements, organized by institution, represent Pennsylvania State University, Loyola University, Arizona State University, and the University of Illinois. Of these, all but Penn State report offering a teacher training course. James D. Barry details Loyola's English 404: Studies in Methods of Language Analysis, which operates on five premises: (1) "Beginning graduate students have little background in the study of language"; (2) "Our graduate students pursue a set of courses which are predominantly literary"; (3) "Our graduate assistants acquire very good preparation in literature through their graduate studies and a good to very good preparation in composition through their teaching and the conferences dealing with this important matter"; (4) "Graduate assistants who plan to go into high-school teaching and those who plan to stay in college work need not be in separate groups for their training in language"; (5) "A graduate course like 404 should not degenerate into a methods course. It should be predominantly—in the ideal order exclusively—academic" ("Training Graduate Students" 76–77). In contrast, Arizona State University offered a required course in which "practical matters rather than theory dominate course content" (79). The course addressed issues of plagiarism, classroom management, spelling, and grading themes. By 1962 the University of Illinois had revamped its TA training program into a three-part inservice training system involving regular staff meetings, a mentor program identified as a "big brothers" program, and a requirement that "assistants with less than one year of college teaching experience take Rhetoric 480, a course in the teaching of college composition" (81).

One of the things I find interesting in looking at the historical development of the practicum is that the earliest incarnations of the course (Greenough, for instance) made the argument for a course heavy in theory. In the 1940s and 1950s, the debate became more vocal, and proponents of both sides of the theory/pedagogy argument developed courses that emphasized varying positions. While this history is intriguing, what I find more interesting is the manner in which lore has evolved about the practicum course, casting its history as one of a tradition of a practically focused class. Scholars who address the practicum in their work have been quick to associate the course with a history of pedagogical focus and to account for the desire to move toward theory as a recent maneuver. Stephen Wilhoit, for instance, makes the common assessment that "while early in-service practica focused on pedagogy, the trend lately has been to place more emphasis on theory" (18). The fact is that the emphasis on theory—and the subsequent questioning of that emphasis—has existed since the inception of the idea of composition practica. Of course, much of this history can be reconsidered through the simple fact that it was not until the late 1960s and the 1970s that writing scholars had developed any theory of writing that attended to practical and pedagogical approaches. That is, the advent of cognitivism and process approaches to writing provided writing teachers with specific methodologies of how to teach writing students how to write. Hence, training new teachers how to teach the writing process allowed the practicum course to shift to a more fully practical focus. By the 1970s and 1980s, the push to include theory in graduate-level teacher training was as dominant as ever but now stood in opposition to conventional wisdom grounded in the process paradigm. Scholars such as Frank D'Angelo, Richard Gebhardt, and John Ruszkiewicz all called for theory-integrated training. Certainly, this debate carries through in contemporary conversations of the practicum, and we see much insistence on a theory-based graduate training from a variety of well-respected composition scholars, including many in this collection. Yet I want to be clear that this debate is not new. More recent manifestations of these debates are evident in the program descriptions provided in Betty P. Pytlik and Sarah Liggett's excellent collection *Preparing College Teachers of Writing*, a collection that provides one of the most substantial examinations of composition practica in conjunction with other aspects of teacher preparation prior to this collection.

Likewise, the resistance to theory that has also plagued the field (particularly since the advent not only of cognitivism but also specifically of expressivist rhetorics) has been manifest in resistance to inclusion of theory in the practicum. Wendy Bishop's 1997 book *Teaching Lives: Essays and Stories* stands as a recent example of the ongoing struggle against theory in graduate programs. Rather than rehash all of Bishop's argument here, I want to note her position that "most of us have failed to consider how the 'theory' in our graduate student (teacher)s complicates any changes we hope to introduce to the culture of English studies" (194). What Bishop argues is that new graduate students come to courses like the practicum or other teacher training programs already invested in particular theories and cultures of teaching and learning. In reference to one student, she writes, "clearly, theory was already in the student" (195). Ultimately, Bishop argues that because students come to graduate programs with their own theories and because the theories we often throw at them are contested by other theories, the very introduction of theory can confuse new teachers as they try to negotiate their own ideas about teaching (I am still trying to understand why this would be thought of as a bad thing). Similarly, in 1993 in "Teachers as Students, Reflecting Resistance," Doug Hesse examines the frustration and resistance many new graduate students demonstrate in relation to the introduction of theory in their first composition course. Though the course Hesse describes is not cast as a practicum course directly, it is a course populated by new composition teachers—many of whom are literature students—trying to make connections between their teaching and their work as graduate students. The course, Introduction to the Composing Process, is described as a site in which theory and practice are placed in conflict, if not by Hesse himself, then certainly by his students.

I don't want to rehash all of composition's "theory wars" or the "new theory wars" (Olson 25) here, though discussing the history of the composition practicum would seem to lead to such a discussion. What I want to emphasize (again) is that historically, little has changed in terms of how we perceive the role of the practicum course. Certainly, in many programs the content of how we achieve these goals has shifted over the last fifty years, yet historically the course's position has shifted little. I note this not to make some progressive argument that in fifty years the course's position *should* have changed, but to clarify that as a field composition studies has done little to consider that location of the course. Look for instance at the titles of such courses and the ways in which these titles have been maintained over the past ninety-plus years. This is not to suggest that such course titles should change; in fact, I think departments have been quite savvy in maintaining the titles, because their ambiguity allows faculty flexibility in course design. What needs to be noted is that throughout the history of the composition practicum (one which I admittedly offer only a sketch of), the prevailing questions have been posed in regard to the content of the course, its role within graduate curricula, and the validity of the course as an academic course.

The Power of the Practicum

As a primary component in teacher professionalization,[2] the practicum serves multiple ends, many of which are in no way central to providing teaching methodologies to new teachers of writing per se, but rather are more broadly conceived in terms of overall professionalization of graduate students and introduction to composition studies. In other words, the practicum, since its inception, has developed not just into a course about teaching methods and theories, but also into a general introduction to composition studies, to teacher professionalization, to research methodologies in graduate-level English, to theory (to specific theories), to writing, and so on. Rosemary Winslow explains about the practicum course at the Catholic University of America, "as this is the only course in composition theory, research, and practice the majority of them will ever take, the course must provide an overview of knowledge in the field and make available resources with which to pursue further study on their own" (9). Donna Dunbar-Odom makes a similar point about the East Texas State University practicum when she explains that "because many of the teaching assistants come here as literature majors, I also want them to have a solid sense of process pedagogy and at least a fast contextual grounding of composition as a discipline with a history and different branches" (19). Numerous other descriptions of practica make similar claims (see the critical statements in the special issue of *Composition Studies* mentioned earlier). My own Theories and Practices of Writing course, which I have now taught and revised twice at the University of Kansas and more than ten times at the University of Florida, covers in the fifteen-week semester the following subjects: history of composition studies as a discipline; introduction to English studies as a profession (in this segment we rapidly cover the MLA job search system, credentialing, publications, graduate research, etc.); introduction to classical and contemporary rhetoric; history of first-year composition (FYC); writing research in composition studies; computers and composition; using MOO spaces; online research in English studies; and introductions to various theoretical positions (these vary semester to semester), including cognitivism, expressivism, social constructionism, feminisms, resistance pedagogies, postcolonial theory, theories of public spaces, spatial theories, philosophies of language, alternative discourse theory, literacy theory, new media theory, postprocess theory, ecocomposition, and so on. All of this is set within an agenda of asking students to think not about how to teach, but about how they think of themselves as teachers and as writers. But, ultimately, to be honest, what I teach in this class is of less consequence in terms of how my students think of themselves as teachers than it is in terms of what version of composition studies and the profession of academic work in English that I present. That is, the course stands more as an introduction to thinking about how and why teachers of writing find themselves in the institutional positions in which my students find themselves. The course, then, becomes a conveyor of a particular cultural capital of composition studies, one that I personally forward and one that falls in line with departmental agendas (to some extent).

Based not on this anecdote of my own teaching experiences, but on the limited, published accounts of the composition practicum (research) and the prolific, less-formal conversation about the practicum nationally (lore), one of my primary arguments in this introduction is that the practicum—no matter how it is presented, no matter in what institution it is presented—is the largest, most effective purveyor of cultural capital in composition studies. I forward this claim since the practicum is often the first contact with and initiation into composition studies that graduate students face and because it reaches professionals who do not identify themselves as compositionists specifically. More often than not, too, it is specifically these noncomposition specialists for whom the practicum is the sole experience in composition studies, and thus the sole defining mechanism for them. How the practicum is presented, then, defines for the noncomposition specialist what composition is. The course, generally speaking, is not merely a space in which new teachers are "trained" or even professionalized, but one in which they are encultured into the cultural ideologies of composition. This, I argue, makes the practicum one of the most powerful and important spaces of occupation in composition studies. And if that is the case, a number of issues need to be addressed in terms of the composition practicum, and while I introduce those subjects here, I do so not to wrap up those discussions in neat little dispensable packages, but to unwrap some seriously problematic issues that composition studies needs to address.

The first issue that I see as needing further examination is the manner in which the practicum course is often conflated with an introduction to composition studies course. Such conflations stand to create the image that (a) an introduction to composition studies is an introduction to teaching, that composition is centrally identified as a teaching subject, and (b) that all graduate students who teach composition classes and/or who take the course should have an introduction to composition studies. While I like the idealistic, discipline-promoting idea that all English graduate students should take this intro course, I'm not so certain this is the case. Although I admit this is how we attract/convert many of our comp/rhet graduate students—by introducing new graduate students to a field many of them were not introduced to as undergraduates—I am bothered by the disciplinary maxim that no matter what area of study one pursues in English, one *will end up teaching composition*; hence, all graduate students *should be* trained to teach composition. This traditional understanding, not about English but about teaching composition as something everyone "must do," seriously demonizes composition into a subordinate and servile position—the very position scholars such as Susan Miller and hosts of others have fought against for nearly as long as composition has claimed disciplinary status. Catherine Latterell, for instance, in "Training the Workforce: An Overview of GTA Education Curricula," surveys different training programs around the country and concludes not only that the practicum is the primary method for professionalizing graduate teaching assistants and for initiating them into teaching disciplines, but also that the construct of the practicum supports the very struggles composition has had to face in developing its professional identity:

> Teaching writing is not valued, even by the rhetoric and composition field. By dispensing "training" in one- or two-hour doses once a week for one (possibly two) terms, this model encourages the passing out of class activities and other quick-fixes—an inoculation method of GTA education. We need to examine the message we are sending GTAs and our colleagues in English studies by maintaining such practices. (20)

In addition, numbers of us in composition would argue that composition studies is not a "teaching subject," or at least not only a teaching subject. As the practicum appears to be the only standard required course for graduate students in English nationally, it is the one course that conveys that a particular branch of English—composition—must be covered by all students, no matter their area of study, because it is the course in which graduate students are initiated into the cult of teaching—not scholarship, but teaching.

I think it is also important to note that when the English maxim says that everyone in English will teach composition, what is meant is that everyone will likely teach FYC. Two problems grow from this: first, a minor point, is that composition, in general, is equated with FYC, and second, part of the overall issue of professionalism, as understood to be the goal of the practicum and as integrated with other teaching English models/methods, is the idea that training to teach composition is training to teach FYC. This is manifest in the fact that more often than not (I'd be tempted to say "always" but have no quantitative evidence to support my assertion) the practicum is taught by the writing program administrator or by another composition faculty member who is being groomed for the position or has served in that position before. The question, then, must be asked: does the practicum teach only pedagogical methods that are to be used only in FYC, or does the course address methods for English studies (or even pedagogy) in general? Of course, the answer to this question is one of economics, both in terms of the ability to afford to offer practica for multiple kinds of courses and in terms of the economics of moving graduate students through their degree programs efficiently (in terms of both their funding and the efficiency of granting regular degrees). Or, we might ask, why doesn't that class rotate to other faculty? The answer here can be articulated with two more critical questions: would those faculty choose to teach the course that appears to have been cast as the graduate version of FYC, a course not necessarily granted the same legitimation as other graduate seminars, and, second, would we trust them to do so? I assume that in the same breath that I and the other contributors to this collection question the very space of the practicum, we would also not want to relinquish control of that space. After all, the practicum is a site of control. It is a location that allows composition to maintain hold of the small bit of territory composition is permitted to occupy, despite the fact that the course curriculum is perhaps the most contested graduate curriculum.

In many ways, I have come to think about the composition practicum in the same light as FYC as Sharon Crowley positions it in larger institutional goals. Crowley, in one of the most important books in composition studies in the past ten years—*Composition in the University*—argues that FYC courses are universally required as an institutional disciplining function. Because the practicum is so directly linked with the FYC requirement (itself often the only graduate English requirement, just as FYC is often one of the only "universal" undergraduate requirements), Crowley's critiques of FYC can be applied to the practicum as well. For

Crowley, FYC is a course that sees first-year students as a homogeneous audience, all with the same needs as writers. Hence, it is assumed that general, universal pedagogies—those then taught to new teachers in the practicum—can be applied to these classes wholesale. While I agree with Crowley's argument about FYC courses, her arguments about the disciplinary function of FYC also give me pause to consider the role the practicum plays in the very problems she notes about the introductory required course; the practicum, it seems, is one of the primary institutional disciplining mechanisms for FYC. After all, it is through the practicum that new teachers are molded into the taskmasters that oversee the FYC classes. It is, despite the good, critical, liberating intention of any practicum instructor, a function of the practicum to bring order to the approaches of teaching FYC. Just as Crowley criticizes the tradition of the FYC class for being put in place to teach taste and convention—terms which imply standardization and approval—so too can the practicum be seen as an ideology-shifting control mechanism.

Other scholars have noted the ideology-shifting agendas of the teacher professionalization process as well. Wendy Bishop, for instance, in her book *Something Old, Something New: College Writing Teachers and Classroom Change*, introduces the idea of "convergent theory." Bishop argues that the very structure of teacher professionalization programs that incorporate workshops, orientation programs, practica, and so on presents idyllic versions of what teaching is and can be, thereby driving new teachers toward an image of the ideal pedagogy in order that the new teachers pursue such a pedagogical vision. Likewise, Nancy Welch, in her 1993 *College English* article, "Resisting the Faith: Conversion, Resistance, and the Training of Teachers," examines how the religious metaphors of conversion apply to such professionalization programs and how resisting such moves to conversion can be more empowering than blind-faith following. What each of these scholars notes is that the very idea of teacher professionalization, when manifested in institutional structures such as a practicum, is an idea of ideological conversion, an attempt to bring new members into line with a particular culture, to show them the righteous path and ask them (rather forcefully and often deceptively) to follow its teachings. Even Welch's resistance to such religious conversions and her attempts to provide a location for resistance within the conversion process must operate within the confines of the culture; a new teacher can only resist so much before she or he is excommunicated.

We must recognize that the manner in which the practicum disseminates cultural capital is a means of control; call it a means of conversion or even enculturation. By professing a particular cultural capital through the practicum, the program itself is able to maintain control over what can and should be taught not just in FYC classes but also in any other class students then teach. The very curriculum of the practicum course initiates new teachers into the realm of what might even be considered "pedagogy" and provides them with the vocabularies with which to name their pedagogical worlds. Certainly, new teachers rely heavily on previous classroom experiences such as modeling on past teachers, but the practicum takes those experiences and does more than name them for student teachers; those courses codify, critique, validate what can be considered good teaching methodologies. As Kitzhaber notes of the continuing role of the practicum in the teaching lives of students, "We have been able, in other words, to exercise a necessary measure of control over their teaching, yet have done it, we hope, tactfully and without resorting to strictures" (199).

The practicum, then, is one of the most powerful policing tools in English. Even in contemporary attempts to use the practicum as a site of TA empowerment, we see issues of control not-so-quietly demarcating the agendas of particular programs. Often we see the inclusion of theory to suggest a critical, questioning position, but the practicum also provides a site where theory can be used coercively as well. Note for instance the professionalization program at the University of Louisville as described by Katrina M. Powell, Peggy O'Neill, Cassandra Mach Phillips, and Brian Huot in "Negotiating Resistance and Change: One Composition Program's Struggle Not to Covert." Basing their program agendas on Welch's notion of convergence and Hesse's understanding of potential student resistance to theory, the Louisville program is "theoretically 'open' to any method of teaching" because of the thorough professionalization provided in the practicum (English 602) (124). Students in English 602 are encouraged to explore a range of kinds of theories in order to develop their own theories about language and teaching. While I agree in theory with the Louisville approach, I want to note two issues of control that occur in the program as Powell and colleagues describe it. First, the English 602 curriculum provides a particular set of readings for the graduate students enrolled in the course. By doing so, the course, despite its "open" intentions, paints a particular picture of what teaching is, of what writing is, and of what composition is, no matter what reading is assigned. Likewise, and perhaps more important, I wonder whether the new teachers that experience this open approach to developing their own theories then translate such openness to their own FYC classes. That is, does the open approach to teaching methodologies then translate to an open approach not to how teachers teach, but to what they require of FYC students? Are those students given an "open" training in writing? Likewise, even an "open" approach purveys a particular (read politicized) version of what teaching is and is not, what writing is and is not. I say this not to criticize the Louisville program or even to question the program as Powell and colleagues have described it, but to note that even in TA-empowering/open programs, we must begin to seriously consider the power of the practicum as a disseminator of cultural capital and a policing mechanism. Nor am I arguing for the removal of such control mechanisms in favor of anarchist pedagogy, but I am calling for attention to the manner in which such mechanisms function and their larger institutional operations. For instance, Christine Hult and Lynn Meeks, in describing the practicum at Utah State University, make the savvy point that "the curriculum of the Writing Practicum (and therefore the Writing Program) is based on collaborative learning, literacy learning, social linguistics, and discourse theory" (186). Here they distinctly make the point that the practicum is the very mechanism that defines the culture of writing programs. Practica give shape and formula to the identity of programs. This notion of program identity is important because it carries cultural capital through to first-year students and what it means "to write."

Likewise, examinations of various practicum descriptions reveal that practica perpetuate larger programmatic agendas, which in turn propagate the very identity of what composition studies is. For instance, the graduate program here at the University of Florida Department of English emphasizes theory, both in composition/rhetoric and in other fields within English. As a result, the practicum course is primarily a theory course. Graduate students who come to the UF English department generally come specifically because of our overall focus on theory (the notable exceptions to this are the graduate students who come to the department to pursue an MFA in creative writing; we have recently released this population from the requirement of taking the practicum). Conversely (but by no means in opposition to), the program and practicum at Florida State University emphasize the teaching of writing, as Ruth M. Mirtz explains:

> [S]ince the graduate program in composition and rhetoric at Florida State emphasizes research in the teaching of writing, rather than historical research or other areas, the teacher-training course can function as an introduction to composition studies because it points future composition specialists toward an agenda for studying the teaching of writing. (24)

Hence, graduate students who take the practica course at FSU and UF are given rather different ideas as to what the discipline of composition studies is, and those disseminating these images of the discipline maintain a position of authority in determining what composition is for a particular population. I point this out not to give value to one program over the other, but to show how a single semester's introduction to composition studies at two different programs can forward distinctly different cultural capitals. I think that it is important not to ask which is the correct cultural capital to be forwarding, but to ask about the very politics of the practicum as purveyor of cultural capital.

As a follow-up, I must also point out that the cultural capital and programmatic identity that is purveyed through the practicum often can be traced to the cultural capital/program identity of the WPA's own practicum experience—should he or she have had one. Hence, a single semester practicum has the power to affect the culture not only of that one classroom but also of large numbers of institutional identities around the country.

Finally, I would like to observe that part of the power of practica comes from the fact that the identity of those who take the practicum is an oddly contested space: on the one hand, they are cast as students learning a skill/trade/pedagogy or taking an introduction to a "discipline," and on the other hand, they are the teachers passing on a likeness of those same skills/trades/pedagogies and disciplinary knowledges to students of their own. This past semester in my own course, one graduate student asked, "In this class, are we students or are we teachers?" Unlike other graduate classes in which student identities tend to be set primarily in the role of student, the practicum confuses student/teacher identity. The very names we assign to participants in the practicum are quite telling: student, student teacher, graduate assistant, graduate teaching assistant, and so on. These labels create a system in which participants in the practicum are given identities—identities, first, that are foisted on them and that carry historical and institutional baggage, and second, that demarcate an "us" and "them" division, reinforcing the control mechanism.

What I hope this section has demonstrated is not that the practicum is a negative space, one that controls identities—programmatic and individual—in improper ways, but that we need to become more cognizant of the implications of that power and begin to see the practicum not as merely the required course in professionalization, but also as one of the most powerful sites in composition studies and English studies.

The Essays in This Book

Having made my argument about the history and power of the practicum, I want to end this rather long introduction by turning to the essays found in this collection. As I mentioned early in this introduction, one of the prevailing issues that arises in the selections in this book is the purpose of the practicum in terms of what should be taught. Through this focus, the course becomes a site in which the discipline's continued theory/practice contestation gets played out; as Mary Lou Odom, Michael Bernard-Donals, and Stephanie Kerschbaum note in their contribution, "many practica seem to dwell so heavily on either the theory *or* the practice of teaching writing." There is little doubt that the question of the position of theory and practice is predominant in the essays. The question seems to carry an undercurrent of issues of validation, of making the course a legitimate intellectual pursuit, not just a how-to course. I say "not just" because as the essays in this collection contend, for many, separating the how-to from the theory is not a possibility, in terms of curriculum, content, or theoretical understanding of the relationship between practice and theory. In terms of the role of the practicum as purveyor and controlling mechanism of cultural capital, I am interested here, too, that in many essays practice often gets cast as "teaching" in the ways that the theory/practice debate gets played out. Because such divisions are prominent in curricular design of practica, such parameters of what theory/practice (read theory/pedagogy) is and can be ultimately move to set up the larger disciplinary debates, relegating practice to teaching. As Joe Marshall Hardin explains in his contribution to this collection, "The claims that practice make on the field are unusually strong, perhaps because the roots of rhetoric and composition as a contemporary field of study were planted by a group of academics, mostly trained in literary studies, who were driven by a quest to find better ways of teaching writing— a practice for which they had no theory." The result of this quest, then, has been manifest through the practica and in turn disciplinary definitions that pit not practice against theory, but specifically one kind of practice—pedagogy—against theory. While many of the pieces in this collection maintain such a vision of practice as teaching, most do so in an effort not to play out the theory/practice debate, but in an attempt to better understand the role of that debate in the construction of the practicum and vice versa.

Likewise, one of the more striking similarities between many of these pieces is how often the contributing authors turn to the personal/the experiential. That is, more often than not, contributors ground their discussions of practica in the experiences and practices of their home institution's practicum. I, of course, have done so several times in this introduction. I read this reliance on local experience as displaying two key facets of the ways in which practica have been discussed professionally and publicly: First, the conversations about the practica have been so limited that there is little context in which to discuss such courses (and problems) other than in the personal/experiential. Second, even in a course that is apparently (as these essays seem to indicate) a central site in which the theory/practice debates get played out, and because these are still teaching sites, notions of teacher–student relationships still maintain a strong hold over the very discourses in and through which we can discuss teaching. That is, as Hardin suggests, because composition as a field developed as a means to discover better ways of teaching, those same teaching approaches that grew to see writing as centered in personal and experiential methods maintain an advantage over how composition can discuss issues of teaching. How we can talk about the practicum, because it is a teaching space, is regulated by the vocabularies with which we have surrounded it. To talk about a kind of class is to talk about the experiential; "here's what we do." Please don't misread me here: I am not faulting the contributors to this collection for taking the experiential approach to addressing issues of the practicum. What I am faulting is composition in general and specifically the ways in which composition has failed to address the very idea of the practicum in more theoretical/political ways (prior to this collection) that would have opened the spaces for conversations other than the individual experience.

The selections in this collection begin to open doors to reconsider not just what is and can be done in specific practica classes, but also the role those classes play in larger conceptions of what composition studies is and can be. For instance, another prevailing theme that appears in many of these contributions is the relationship, often assumed and required, between practica and writing program administrators. As Kelly Belanger and Sibylle Gruber note, the practicum course is often designed and taught by the WPA, the same person who designs and maintains course agendas for the FYC course that the practicum serves. Noting both the favorable and problematic issues that come into play when a single administrator oversees these key components of a writing program, Belanger and Gruber ask us to think seriously about how the relationship between the practicum and the WPA becomes a critical point of contact in forwarding local programmatic agendas and well as larger disciplinary motives. Similarly, Juan Guerra and Anis Bawarshi consider the political shifts that occur during transition periods from one WPA to another, noting that "periods of transition within writing programs too often become figured as changes in WPAs, as changes from so and so's program to so and so's program. Such a cult of personality distracts us from recognizing these periods of transition as opportunity spaces, not for the enactment of another personality, but for thinking about the institutional and intellectual place of a writing program and its relationship to the discipline that informs and is informed by it." In this claim I hear echoes of Jean Baudrillard's explanation that "[f]rom a political point of view, that a head of state remains the same or is someone else doesn't strictly change anything, so long as they resemble each other" (25). In terms of the programmatic culture of writing programs and the impact individual WPAs have on individual programs, it is crucial that we consider the relationship between WPAs and practica.

Ultimately, what this collection provides are attempts to answer some of the questions about the role of the practicum that have been asked since English departments and writing teachers began thinking about, teaching, and taking composition practica. In providing these answers, the contributors also identify the need for further speculation and further questions about the practicum. For me, this collection stands as a call to research, as a call to ask and answer more questions about the politics and power of the practicum.[3]

Notes

1. In my initial conception of this book, I envisioned the collection divided into two parts: the first providing syllabi of composition practica from as many programs as I could gather, and the second consisting of critical essays about the practica. My original call for papers requested both kinds of submissions. By the deadline for submissions, however, I had received only three syllabi contributions and more than twenty critical essays. I'm glad this happened and that the book has come together as it has. The 1995 *Composition Studies* special issue did a remarkable job of gathering examples of how and why different programs approach their practica as they do. There was no need to duplicate that project,

but there is a need for serious discussion of the politics surrounding the very idea of the composition practicum.

2. I want to note a specific shift here in how I address issues of professionalization. In the section prior to this, in which I sketch a loose outline of the practicum's history, I refer to teacher "training," not professionalization. For the rest of this introduction, however, I use the term *professionalization*, not *training*. In his foreword to Pytlik and Liggett's collection, Richard Fulkerson makes an important point regarding the differences between training and professionalization. Fulkerson reminds us that "training" refers to "the rote behavior for which one can be trained with some sort of Skinner-like stimulus/response conditioning." "Trained" teachers, Fulkerson says, would know *the* correct answer all of the time. "One *trains* animals. One *educates* people," he explains (xi). I agree wholeheartedly with his assessment and will refrain from using the term *training*. The only exceptions to this are instances in which "training" refers to the historical view of teacher preparation.

3. I want to thank Anis Bawarshi and Joe Hardin for comments on early drafts of this introduction.

Works Cited

Alden, Raymond MacDonald. "Preparation for College English Teaching." *English Journal* 2.6 (1913): 344–56.

Allen, Harold B. "Preparing the Teacher of Composition and Communication—A Report." *College Composition and Communication* 3.2 (1952): 3–13.

Baudrillard, Jean. *Simulacra and Simulation*. Trans. Sheila Faria Glaser. Ann Arbor: U of Michigan P, 1994.

Bishop, Wendy. *Something Old, Something New: College Writing Teachers and Classroom Change*. Carbondale: Southern Illinois UP, 1990.

———. *Teaching Lives: Essays and Stories*. Logan: Utah State UP, 1997.

Bolin, Bill, Beth Burmester, Brenton Faber, and Peter Vandenberg. *A Forum on Doctoral Pedagogy*. Spec. issue of *Composition Studies/Freshman English News* 23.2 (1995): 1–132.

Crowley, Sharon. *Composition in the University: Historical and Polemical Essays*. Pittsburgh: U of Pittsburgh P, 1998.

D'Angelo, Frank J. "Strategies for Involving Graduate Students in the Teaching of Composition." *ADE Bulletin* 54 (1977): 34–36.

Denney, J. V. "Preparation of College Teachers of English." *English Journal* 7.5 (1918): 322–26.

Dunbar-Odom, Donna. "East Texas State University." *Composition Studies/Freshman English News* 23.2 (1995): 15–20.

Fulkerson, Richard. "Foreword: Preparing the Professors." Pytlik and Liggett xi–viv.

Gebhardt, Richard C. "Balancing Theory with Practice in the Training of Writing Teachers." *College Composition and Communication* 28.2 (1977): 134–40.

Greenough, Chester Noyes. "An Experiment in the Training of Teachers of Composition for Work with College Freshmen." *English Journal* 2 (1913): 109–21.

Hesse, Doug. "Teachers as Students, Reflecting Resistance." *College Composition and Communication* 44.2 (1993): 224–31.

Hult, Christine, and Lynn Meeks. "Preparing College Teachers of Writing to Teach in a Web-Based Classroom: History, Theoretical Base, Web Base, and Current Practices." Pytlik and Ligget 184–93.

Hunting, Robert S. "A Training Course for Teachers of Freshman Composition." *College Composition and Communication* 2.3 (1951): 3–6.

Kitzhaber, Albert R. "The University of Kansas Course in the College Teaching of English." *College Composition and Communication* 6.4 (1955): 194–200.

Latterell, Catherine. "Training the Workforce: An Overview of GTA Education Curricula." *WPA: Writing Program Administration* 19.3 (1996): 7–23.

Liggett, Sarah. "After the Practicum: Assessing Teacher Preparation Programs." *The Writing Program Administrator as Researcher: Inquiry in Action and Reflection.* Ed. Shirley K. Rose and Irwin Weiser. Portsmouth, NH: Boynton/Cook, 1999. 65–80.

Mirtz, Ruth M. "Florida State University." *Composition Studies/Freshman English News* 23.2 (1995): 20–26.

"The 1956 Conference on College Composition and Communication Workshop Reports: 9. Preparation of Composition/Communication

Teachers: Toward a Comprehensive Program." *College Composition and Communication* 7.3 (1956): 138–40.

Olson, Gary A. "The Death of Composition as an Intellectual Discipline." *Rhetoric and Composition as Intellectual Work*. Ed. Gary A. Olson. Carbondale: Southern Illinois UP, 2002. 23–31.

Powell, Katrina M., Peggy O'Neill, Cassandra Mach Phillips, and Brian Huot. "Negotiating Resistance and Change: One Composition Program's Struggle Not to Convert." Pytlik and Liggett 121–32

Pytlik, Betty P., and Sarah Liggett. *Preparing College Teachers of Writing: Histories, Theories, Programs, Practices*. New York: Oxford UP, 2002.

Rankin, Elizabeth. *Seeing Yourself as a Teacher: Conversations with Five New Teachers in a University Writing Program*. Urbana, IL: National Council of Teachers of English, 1994.

Roberts, Charles W. "A Course for Training Rhetoric Teachers at the University of Illinois." *College Composition and Communication* 6.4 (1955): 190–94.

Ruszkiewicz, John J. "Training Teachers Is a Process Too." *College Composition and Communication* 38.4 (1987): 461–64.

Schwartz, Joseph. "One Method of Training the Composition Teacher." *College Composition and Communication* 6.4 (1955): 200–204.

"Teacher-Training for Composition or Communication: The Report of Workshop No. 16." *College Composition and Communication* 2.4 (1951): 31–32.

Thomas, J. M. "Training for Teaching Composition in Colleges." *English Journal* 5.7 (1916): 447–57.

"Training Graduate Students as Teachers." *College Composition and Communication* 14.2 (1963): 73–84.

Welch, Nancy. "Resisting the Faith: Conversion, Resistance, and the Training of Teachers." *College English* 55.4 (1993): 387–401.

Wilhoit, Stephen. "Recent Trends in TA Instruction: A Bibliographic Essay." Pytlik and Liggett 17–27.

Winslow, Rosemary. "Catholic University of America." *Composition Studies/Freshman English News* 23.2 (1995): 6–10.

CHAPTER ONE

Writing Theory and Writing the Classroom

Joe Marshall Hardin
Western Kentucky University

In "The Death of Composition as an Intellectual Discipline," Gary A. Olson describes the history of rhetoric and composition as a hegemonic struggle over the heart and soul of a discipline (30). While some of the participants in this struggle and the various ideological camps they represent are identified in Olson's essay, the quickest way to get at what is often at the center of this struggle is to refer to what Jasper Neel describes as "an intractable conundrum, the theory versus praxis split" (3). There is, of course, more to the field of rhetoric and composition than the struggle over whether theory or practice will dominate, and most compositionists would, no doubt, object to the easy dichotomy suggested by Neel. Still, both theory and practice camps have made strong claims on the disciplinary territory of rhetoric and composition. The claims that practice makes on the field are unusually strong, perhaps because the roots of rhetoric and composition as a contemporary field of study were planted by a group of academics, mostly trained in literary studies, who were driven by a quest to find better ways of teaching writing—a practice for which they had no theory. Additionally, the field first began to grow in the 1960s and '70s—when higher education faced a need to develop new pedagogies to address the needs of a more diverse student body. On the other hand, the place of theory in rhetoric and composition is also strong. Many of its emerging scholars saw the limitations that would ensue if rhetoric and composition identified itself primarily as a pedagogical project, especially if it were to become a subject of graduate study. As such, scholars began to develop a theoretical base that partook of the various emerging postmodernisms. The claims of theory on rhetoric and composition were also strengthened by the fact that the field began to develop much of its theory in the1980s, when the debate over the value of postmodern theory and theory in general raged in the so-called theory wars. Ironically, the theory/praxis split may be particularly embedded in rhetoric and composition precisely because both theory and practice are so much a part of how the field identifies itself.

My primary argument in this chapter is that the tension between theory and practice in rhetoric and composition has produced an unfortunate confusion among compositionists, English departments, and universities about the content of rhetoric and composition courses, especially at the graduate level. Further, I argue that while composition scholars and teachers have quarreled about whether theory or practice will guide the field, the department and the university have in many cases co-opted basic graduate courses in rhetoric and composition in the service of teacher training and have constructed a primary role for the composition scholar as administrator, teacher trainer, and manager of contingent faculty and graduate teaching assistants.

What's also interesting about Olson's argument in "The Death of Composition as an Intellectual Discipline" is the idea that rhetoric and composition is—not could be, but is—a discipline. In spite of the certainty implied by Olson's title, however, rhetoric and composition at this time looks more like a "subdiscipline" or, perhaps, an "interdiscipline." Part of the problem is, of course, that the idea of disciplinarity is itself problematic. As Paul Prior notes,

> Our usual notions of learning a discipline are grounded in metaphors of entering a discourse community. Everyday references to "going into" a field, metonymic expressions like "psychology has explored," and more specialized analyses of disciplinary discourse communities have been grounded in images of disciplines as unified social territories or abstract systems of codified knowledge. Such accounts, however, become difficult to sustain under situated examination. (xi–xii)

Among those who write and read its theory, rhetoric and composition might seem to possess a distinct discursive formation that would, in fact, set it off from other discourse communities. However, outside of the academy and the field of English studies—perhaps outside of a small group of composition scholars—most people would not have much reference at all for the signifier "the discipline of rhetoric and composition." There is much to be gained from using that phrase for those who wish to see rhetoric and composition attain genuine disciplinary status; however, the idea that rhetoric and composition can now claim the kind of disciplinary recognition that is afforded other disciplines is doubtful. For most academics, rhetoric and composition would seem to be either a subdiscipline of English or an interdisciplinary activity that might, at best, warrant the status of academic "program." Not all would agree that rhetoric and composition is or should be an academic discipline, of course, but the persistence of the theory/praxis split among compositionists and the perception that composition at the graduate level is primarily concerned with teacher training have unfortunately made the issue of disciplinarity largely irrelevant.

The same impulses that drive some compositionists to argue against what has sometimes been called "theory for theory's sake" and to link the field of rhetoric and composition to the practice of teaching writing are, I think, the same impulses that lead many of the same compositionists to worry about what full-fledged disciplinary legitimacy might mean to the field. Make no mistake about it: the road to disciplinary status would be a difficult and dangerous one for a field that originated, at least in part, in the search for a sensible teaching practice. Despite the fact that the struggle over direction within rhetoric and composition has largely been driven by the theory/praxis split, the truth is that rhetoric and composition—as discipline, subdiscipline, interdiscipline, or program—is in a unique position regarding pedagogy. I hope that it is more than what Kenneth Burke might call occupational psychosis to think that rhetoric and composition could bring something new to conceptions of what both theory and pedagogy can mean to an academic discipline. After all, the impulse to ground the teaching of writing in theory and to make pedagogy an integral part of scholarship has been useful to the creation and dissemination of pedagogical methods that are among the most progressive and informed in all the disciplines.

Still, too many compositionists have confused the idea that practice must always be informed by theory with the idea that all composition theory must be linked to teaching to be useful. Even if the connection between theory and praxis is accepted as axiomatic, there is more to the idea of praxis than teaching. The theory–praxis link may also refer to the need to link composition theory to the act of writing itself, a need that is important to those who may need or want to study how people write without studying how to teach it.

A quick survey reveals that in too many universities the composition theory course is also the training course for teaching assistants—or perhaps the training course for teaching assistants is also the composition theory course. In other universities, the composition theory course stands apart from the teaching practicum, but the practicum is a noncredit course or a noncredit seminar for new teaching assistants held before classes begin and run by the writing program administrator. In very few places are there three courses: a teaching practicum, a composition pedagogy course, and a course in composition theory, although the goals of these three courses are obviously quite different.

Composition is in a unique position to highlight the link between theory and practice—between disciplinary content and discipline-specific pedagogy—but compositionists need to be very clear about the very different goals of teacher training seminars, courses in composition pedagogy, and courses in composition theory. Without a clear distinction, courses in composition will continue to function primarily in the service of teacher training. I'd like to indulge here in a vision of graduate studies in rhetoric and composition in which composition pedagogy and composition theory are both valued as scholarly pursuits worthy of separate courses of study, and in which the teaching of classroom practices within a specific writing program is not the responsibility of either the composition pedagogy or the composition theory course. Surely the attention that compositionists have given to developing theoretically driven writing pedagogy warrants a content-heavy, theoretically rich, credit-bearing course in composition pedagogy, and I believe that composition theory that is not always linked to the teaching of writing is also worthy of its own course. Trying to crowd a practicum for new teaching assistants, a survey of composition pedagogy, and a survey of composition theory into one course is certainly not practical, nor is it good for the field of rhetoric and composition.

First, I suggest that any instruction on teaching within the local context should not take place in a practicum at all, but should be accomplished in a collaborative environment in which new teaching assistants are not isolated from the other faculty who teach in the writing program. In fact, the primary function of this project should be to ensure that all teachers who work in the writing program—new and returning—orient their teaching within a program that they have helped to define. Issues such as the content of courses in the program, development or renewal of goals and objectives and evaluation and assessment guidelines, the selection of textbooks, the use of computer environments, and new policies and procedures specific to the writing program should be discussed each year by *all* the teachers who will teach within the program. Although the writing program administrator may be ultimately responsible for guiding the program and its teachers, he or she should not be solely responsible for training new teaching assistants. If the department is to rely on the labor of graduate assistants and contingent faculty to teach composition courses, then the department should help shoulder the responsibility for orienting the new teachers in the program. Instead of having a writing program administrator instruct new teaching assistants in a practicum dedicated to explaining what the department expects of them as teachers, new teachers should be invited to become equal stakeholders in the process of developing and maintaining a cohesive program that is responsive to the needs of the students, the teachers, the department, and the university. New teaching assistants should work with returning teachers to make sure the program is as coherent as possible in light of the various levels of experience, techniques, and interests of the teachers. The focus of such a project is on orientation and development rather than on instruction, although new teachers will obviously learn from interaction with the returning and experienced teachers. Such a brief seminar, requiring as it would the participation of returning faculty, would obviously not be sufficient training for new teachers, even when coupled with one-on-one mentoring throughout the new teaching assistants' first semester; so this arrangement would also call for an intensive, for-credit course in composition pedagogy for teaching assistants. Ideally, they might have the opportunity to take the composition pedagogy course before they begin to teach, but I believe that a well-designed course in composition pedagogy can actually accompany the new teaching assistants' first semester in the classroom.

Considering the depth and breadth of pedagogical theory in rhetoric and composition, the composition pedagogy course is also not the place for training new teachers. Composition pedagogy is much more than the nuts and bolts of classroom management, syllabus design, textbook selection, and assessment and evaluation techniques. Pedagogical theory in rhetoric and composition has developed into an amazingly rich body of knowledge that relies on social theories as varied as cultural studies and post-colonial theory; psychological theories drawn from cognitive, behavioral, and developmental psychology; and educational theories from thinkers as varied as Isocrates and John Dewey. Scholars in composition pedagogy have developed and pioneered sophisticated assessment and evaluation theories specifically for writing and have originated complex theories of classroom authority and student resistance. Composition pedagogy is also informed by studies of how gender, class, and race affect academic enculturation. Scholars in composition pedagogy have turned their attention to how texts are made in the disciplines, culture, and the workplace, and they have pioneered theories of how technology affects both the teaching of writing and education in general. Surely this is enough content to warrant a credit course in composition pedagogy.

A course that includes an introduction to the preceding list of issues in composition pedagogy would still not constitute an introductory course in composition theory, as it would not sufficiently cover the range of language and writing theory that is not directly related to the teaching of writing or is related primarily by extrapolation. There is a vast body of knowledge about composition that is not specifically related to teaching, and that body of knowledge deserves its own course. After all, is composition theory useful only for teachers? My own composition theory course this semester is at least one-third filled with professional writing majors whose intentions are not to teach at all but who instead hope to become technical or creative writers, to work in the publishing industry, to attend law school, or to work in some other field besides teaching. What does composition theory have to offer these students if it construes the theory–practice link only as a link between theory and teaching and ignores the opportunity to provide theory for other kinds of writing praxis? Surely there is enough content to warrant a course in composition theory that is separate from the course in composition pedagogy.

Regardless of individual stances toward the theory–praxis question, compositionists must resist the urge to collapse teacher training, composition pedagogy, and composition theory into one or even two courses. Can any one course, regardless of what it might be called, possibly hope to present a survey of pertinent contemporary theories about what it means to make a text, a survey of theories about how students might best be taught to write, and a survey of the best teaching practices within a local context?

Part of the problem is, of course, that too many English departments arrange instruction in composition based on the material needs of the department to staff and fill courses and to train teaching assistants quickly. Still, the tendency to conflate the body of knowledge that constitutes what we know about how writing is best taught with the body of knowledge that constitutes what we know about what it means to make text may be at least partially responsible for the fact that composition theory, pedagogical theory in composition, and teacher training are often collapsed into one course, or one course and a teaching practicum. I believe that the time has come for compositionists, whether or not they support the idea of disciplinarity, to set aside the age-old struggle between theory and practice—at least as that struggle is represented in course design. Instead of letting the needs of the institution and misunderstandings about the content of rhetoric and composition guide the structure of our courses, we need to put aside our fears that theory might be separated from practice and set the agenda for our own courses, and I believe the first step is to separate once and for all the training of new writing teachers from the teaching of composition pedagogy and the teaching of composition pedagogy from the teaching of composition theory. Left as it is, rhetoric and composition may simply become a convenient way for universities and colleges to administer writing programs and manage contingent faculty and teaching assistants. It must be made clear that composition pedagogy is much more than training teachers to teach in the local writing program, just as composition theory is much more than how to teach writing, and neither of these courses should be saddled with the additional requirement of preparing teaching assistants. It's time to shift the responsibility for teacher training away from compositionists and composition courses and to make the distinction between composition pedagogy and composition theory clear.

Works Cited

Neel, Jasper. "Reclaiming our Theoretical Heritage: A Big Fish Tale." Olson, *Rhetoric and Composition* 3–11.

Olson, Gary A. "The Death of Composition as an Intellectual Discipline." Olson, *Rhetoric and Composition* 23–31.

———, ed. *Rhetoric and Composition as Intellectual Work*. Carbondale: Southern Illinois UP, 2002.

Prior, Paul A. *Writing/Disciplinarity: A Sociohistoric Account of Literate Activity in the Academy*. Mahwah, NJ: Lawrence Erlbaum, 1998.

CHAPTER TWO

Managing Transitions: Reorienting Perceptions in a Practicum Course

JUAN C. GUERRA AND ANIS BAWARSHI
University of Washington

Over the course of the last fourteen years, as successive writing program administrators (WPAs) have been granted responsibility for running the Expository Writing Program (EWP) in the Department of English at the University of Washington at Seattle, the practicum course has evolved from one that strictly focused on practical matters to one that took into more serious consideration theoretical issues that inform the teaching of writing. In 2003, as one of us was beginning his tenure as the new director of the EWP and the other anticipated taking over the task in three years,[1] we were faced with what has become a pronounced tension in writing programs across the country: to what extent do we need to balance the need of new teaching assistants (TAs) for a grounded and pragmatic understanding of how best to teach writing while simultaneously ensuring that whatever practices they do learn are theoretically informed? This chapter describes our latest attempt,[2] during this time of transition between program directors, to manage the theory/practice tension in our practicum course. But while part of our purpose here is to provide a generalizable perspective that WPAs in other programs may want to consider, we must also admit that much of what we end up describing in terms of how we have decided to structure the practicum course is informed by contextual circumstances that may be applicable in very few other writing programs.[3]

What may be more generalizable, however, is a consideration of what such times of transition mean, in terms of both the strategic opportunities they allow for reflecting on, developing, and (re)articulating a writing program's philosophies and practices, as well as the research opportunities such transitions allow for examining the study and teaching of writing within the disciplinary, institutional, political, and material conditions in which it takes place. In short, we can learn a great deal about the discipline of composition studies and how it gets activated locally during these moments of program transition. And the practicum course is one of the sites in which such reflection and articulation can take place.

Indeed, as we argue at the end of the chapter, the practicum course, in its various manifestations, functions as a key site for the articulation of composition studies. It may be useful, in fact, to understand the practicum course in terms of what Charlotte Linde has called a "coherence system." Linde describes a coherence system as

> a system of beliefs that occupies a position midway between common sense—the beliefs and relations between beliefs that any person in the culture may be assumed to know (if not share) and that anyone may use—and expert systems, which are beliefs and relations between beliefs held, understood, and properly used by experts in a particular domain. (163)

While the practicum course is more a site than a system of beliefs as Linde describes them, it nonetheless plays an important role in both providing "a means for understanding, evaluating, and constructing accounts of experience" and guiding "future action" (Linde 164–65). To the extent that it brings into contact new teachers of writing and specialists in composition studies, the practicum course serves as a site for the continuous articulation and deployment of beliefs and practices about the study and teaching of writing. At the same time, it contributes to the creation of coherence (the relations between beliefs) between scholarship within composition studies, the TA orientation, and first-year writing courses (FYCs) within writing programs.

In this chapter, we examine how we intervened in this site of articulation at the University of Washington. First we explain how we worked together to address the various tensions between the fall orientation, the first-year writing course that our new TAs are being trained to teach, and the practicum course that TAs take at the same time they teach their first writing course. We then describe the new version of the practicum course that we developed in our effort to address this tension. Finally, we reflect on the importance of making sure that WPAs take advantage of the opportunities a transition period affords them to undertake modifications in consultation with others, and we suggest ways in which we can think about the practicum course as an important scholarly site for thinking about and articulating our discipline.

Laying the Groundwork

In March 2003, three tenure-track faculty members of our composition and rhetoric program—George Dillon and the two authors of this chapter—interviewed a group of graduate students who had submitted applications for the two vacant assistant director (AD) positions in the EWP. For several years now, the EWP has employed three ADs hired for two-year terms to assist the program director in managing the day-to-day affairs of the program. Once Spencer Schaffner and Lisa Thornhill were hired and joined Amy Vidali, the senior AD in the program, we were ready to engage in discussions about how we wanted to go about modifying the three major components of the program: the two-week fall orientation for new teaching assistants, the English 567 practicum course they would be required to take in the autumn quarter, and the first-year composition class they would be teaching.

Over the course of the preceding six years, Gail Stygall, the former director, had transformed the first-year comp course into a rigorous program with three sequenced, cumulative assignments and a final portfolio specifically designed to introduce first-year students to academic discourse. In addition to developing the aforementioned course, Stygall revamped the two-week autumn orientation so that it would reflect the shift to academic writing. Over the years, Stygall and her various teams of ADs revised the orientation materials used in the past to reflect the dramatic shift in focus. Finally, Stygall revised the readings and the assignments for the practicum course so they would reflect a sharper interest in theorizing the teaching of writing. By the time we entered the picture and took on the task of rethinking these three elements as part of the transitional moment that informed our work, Stygall had a firmly grounded apparatus in place that was as well conceived as any writing program in the country. As a consequence, our own task was genuinely simplified; instead of having to begin from the ground up, we would have the luxury of tinkering with aspects of a program that was already doing an outstanding job.

In late April 2003, Juan called a meeting of the EWP staff to review the three key elements of the program and to talk about ways to modify them so that they would address what would become the expressed needs and goals of the new administrative body. In his e-mail message to the group, Juan made the following observations:

> Since this is a transitional year, I'd rather that we spent [our time] reconfiguring the orientation itself [instead of revising different sections of the orientation manual]—which of course means that we will want to revise [certain aspects of the orientation manual] to reflect that. From what you've all said—both privately and in interview situations—one of the main things that you'd all like to see is less of a talking heads approach and more of an interactive, workshop approach during the training period. . . . I'm [also] interested in having the 567 practicum be more closely integrated into and be a continuation of the orientation itself. . . . Because we need to focus our energies on the fall orientation and the 567 practicum (which is already a whole lot of work), we're going to put off talking about the curriculum for 131 for now. (e-mail communication, 29 April 2003)

As the new director of the EWP, then, Juan laid out a specific set of goals for the team to address. During its first meeting the following month, the group reviewed the orientation schedule from the previous year and brainstormed various modifications that would increase the number of opportunities participants would have to interact with one another over the course of the various sessions. While some of the orientation materials were also revised and different workshops and activities were reorganized, the overall orientation was not very different from the one that the former director had developed and fine-tuned over the preceding six years.

In June 2003, the group was ready to meet to focus its energies on the practicum course. In an e-mail to the group, Juan offered the following guidelines:

> I've attached a copy of last year's syllabus and would like to ask each of you for suggestions about revising it—especially in light of the changes that we've made in the fall orientation. To begin with, focus your attention on the list of topics and readings on pages 6 to 8, and respond to the following questions: Are there topic categories that you would like to add, delete, revise, keep as is, or reorganize?
>
> In light of your recommendations for reframing the course, what specific readings would you like to add, delete, or recategorize according to topic?
>
> I'd also like to get your feedback on the assignments that we have used in the past: the responses, the grammar activity, the midterm, and the final. What would you change? What would you leave as is? Why?
>
> Finally, I'd also like to have us think about how we want to deploy assistant directors in 567. (e-mail communication, 10 June 2003)

On the basis of feedback he received from Anis, Amy, Spencer, and Lisa, Juan put together a revised version of the topics and readings and later that month convened a meeting where the group discussed it. Once the topics and readings were in place, the group met again to decide on the kinds of writing assignments that would effectively connect the reading we were doing with the TAs' experiences in the autumn orientation and their work in their English 131 classrooms. The following two sections describe the readings and the assignments we developed and the reasons why we did it.

Selecting the Readings

While we decided to drop two of the topics—contemporary and historical literacy and educational reform—from the previous syllabus and replaced them with two other topics—the politics of access and developing literacy tasks—the biggest changes we undertook involved the ordering of the topics and the readings themselves. Most of these changes were in response to the general consensus among the EWP staff that, as Spencer put it, "567 should have more of a focus on 'how to teach writing' (in a very practical sense) than on an 'introduction to the field of comp/ rhet.'" More-over, Spencer argued, "the topics and readings in 567 should line up with key classroom practices: structuring curriculum, assess-ment, conferencing, peer review, in-class writing, revision, respond-ing to student papers, collaborative learning, differences in student learning styles, differences in teaching styles, etc." (e-mail commu-nication, 11 June 2003). Lisa concurred: "The biggest thing that I see in 131 is that [TAs] still seem to be grappling with how to effec-tively and efficiently teach all of the parts of the UW 131 experi-ence" (e-mail communication, 23 June 2003). In her response, Amy warned us against moving too far to the practical end of the con-tinuum and forgetting about theory:

> Clearly, 567 needs to be more practical for the reasons well stated by my fellow ADs. However, perhaps because no one else has done so, I'd like to stand up for the theory a bit as well. While it is clearly important to make sure that teachers can deal with practical/everyday issues, I think it is also important that they examine their role as teachers, and I think that theory importantly achieves this. Otherwise, I fear that [567] students will jump past questioning their role as teach-ers and the role of composition in the university in order to get to the "now that we're teachers what do we do?" (e-mail com-munication, 24 June 2003)

In the end, we agreed that the tension between theory and prac-tice would have to inform everything we did in the practicum course; more important, we decided that effectively and produc-tively integrating all three elements—the autumn orientation, the practicum course, and the teaching of English 131—would need to be the driving force behind helping to reorient the perceptions of the new TAs we were training.

On the basis of that information and his own extended research over several weeks of the latest published work related to preexisting topics, Juan eventually proposed a set of topics that he had realigned with a particular logic in mind and a set of readings that seemed to address the group's need for a syllabus that was more practice oriented but still acknowledged the importance of theory. In the course of his research, Juan also identified a range of new essays that he felt would theorize more directly and explicitly the renewed focus in the syllabus on specific pedagogical strategies that had been introduced in the autumn orientation and that TAs would now be able to revisit and reconsider through the various theoretical lenses the readings would provide. As a consequence, over 80 percent of the readings in the revised syllabus were new.

Whereas the previous syllabus began the course by having TAs reflect on "our choice of academic writing over purely personal writing," the revised syllabus begins by locating students in the midst of the current controversy over whether FYC courses should even be taught. After posing the logic that informs the new abolitionist movement's concerns about first-year writing in the form of Richard Larson's essay (see the appendix for the course syllabus and bibliography), we decided to problematize that logic by acknowledging both the national view in favor of the FYC course as it is embodied in the WPA Outcomes Statement and the more local view of a committee on writing appointed by the dean of arts and sciences at the University of Washington that justified its inclusion in the context of the committee's proposal for an interdisciplinary and multiyear writing requirement. Two chapters from Lee Ann Carroll's longitudinal study of the writing of a group of students over the course of their four years in college provided a segue from the controversy to the specific needs of students confronted with the task of learning how to handle academic writing in a variety of contexts. Carroll begins by acknowledging the inherent limitations but necessary inclusion of first-year writing instruction in university settings.

Once we established a framework for our TAs that would provide them with an opportunity to locate themselves in the midst of the ongoing controversy, we sharpened the focus on the roles students are often asked to take as writers in the first-year writing classroom. Here, our goal was to highlight the complications that a poststructural understanding of student agency and authorship has introduced in recent years. We then made an effort to examine the conflicts that emerge when students resist disciplining as a consequence of their efforts to challenge the teacher's authority and privilege in the context of their own limited power when they come to the university from marginalized communities.

We also thought it was important for new TAs to be aware of the ways in which some students are kept out of the university because they do not possess the necessary credentials to gain admission in the first place. Because Amy, one of our ADs, specializes in disability studies, we were persuaded to include material that makes certain students who would otherwise remain invisible visible to our TAs.

Having established a broad set of parameters that would help TAs establish a grounded understanding of the larger culture of the university, its influence on first-year writing, and the various challenges that both students and teachers face when we acknowledge difference, we then shifted the focus to particular pedagogical strategies TAs would need to enact in their work with students in English 131. We began with the broader question about how the readings that TAs assigned their students must be deployed in the service of writing—that is, how the readings can be used rhetorically, to teach students about writing choices and effects, rather than hermeneutically, to search for meanings. Because the course is academic in orientation, we then proceeded to familiarize TAs with the teaching of a particular kind of argumentation in their classes. The rest of the readings revisited several activities TAs had already engaged in over the course of the autumn orientation: developing and deploying assignments; responding to student writing through marginal and end comments and conferencing; organizing students so that they can engage in collaborative work in groups. Once TAs got a final opportunity to revisit the role of portfolios in their classrooms, we concluded the quarter with a set of readings that closed the circle by reminding them of the ways in which FYC programs tend to exploit graduate students who produce much of the necessary labor in FYC courses yet are often not adequately compensated. We concluded the course by encouraging them to reflect on and discuss the difficulties that all graduate students in English studies are likely to encounter in a job market that has changed dramatically in recent years. While we made every effort not to dwell on the negative aspects of our profession, we decided that it was important for new TAs to be aware as soon as possible of the consequences of their decision to join a profession under siege, and to examine the role of FYC in that controversy.

Developing the Assignments

Because we all agreed with Lisa that "any 567 assignments should be directly linked and applicable to the teaching experience that students are having" (e-mail communication, 23 June 2003), members of the EWP staff elected to replace the four- to six-page midterm essay (an analysis of a teaching artifact) and the ten- to twelve-page final paper (an empirical study of writing) that the previous syllabus had stipulated. Early on, Spencer recommended that we have TAs develop "a teaching portfolio" and "a micro-ethnography project in which [they] either observed a classroom, shadowed a student around for a day, or observed a set of writing conferences" (e-mail communication, 11 June 2003). While both of these ideas met with enthusiastic responses, neither survived our brainstorming session in their original form. After extensive discussion, it dawned on us that the best approach was to develop a series of shorter assignments that would give TAs a series of opportunities both to revisit most of the pedagogically oriented tasks we had given them in the autumn orientation and to reconceive them in light of their actual experiences in the classroom as well as through the various lenses the assigned readings would provide. This idea made even more sense once we realized that we could have TAs mirror the work their English 131 students would be doing by requiring TAs to revise two of these assignments and submit all of them as part of a final teaching portfolio (for a description of the assignments and portfolio, see the appendix).

In addition to keeping the workshop on teaching grammar from the previous syllabus, we decided to add a second workshop, this one on strategies for teaching argument. Our goal here was to have the TAs develop various activities they could then share with their colleagues. In the course of reviewing the topics and related readings we had negotiated by that point, it became clear that there were several junctures along the way that would allow us to develop the series of three-page assignments. Very early in the autumn orientation, we had asked TAs "to decide on and write up a set of goals" that would eventually become part of the course description for their classes. Once we had spent the first two weeks in 567 immersed in a conversation about the controversy surrounding the teaching of first-year writing and our students' roles as writers, we asked them to reconsider their original goals and reflect on how they would revise them in light of what we had read and our in-class discussions about those readings. For their second assignment, we asked them to shift their attention from their students to themselves as they wrestled with the ways in which they were either being asked or electing to position themselves in light of the complicated political and ideological circumstances of their work. In both cases, the TAs ended up trying to locate themselves and their students in the midst of the tensions and conflicts emerging from having to teach a course that was literally under fire. Our hope was that they would be able to use their writing for these first two assignments as a point of departure for their evolving philosophies as teachers.

The next four assignments asked the TAs to reconsider a specific set of pedagogical practices—teaching close reading, sequencing assignments, commenting on student writing, and student conferencing—that we had discussed in the autumn seminar and that they had enacted or would be enacting in their English 131 classrooms over the course of the quarter. Because the academic essays their own students would be reading in the FYC classes were challenging (among them, Michel Foucault's "Panopticism," Roland Barthes's "The Death of an Author," Joan Didion's "Sentimental Journeys," Lisa Lowe's "Imagining Los Angeles in the Production of Multiculturalism"), TAs were encouraged to train their students in close, critical reading. For this particular assignment, then, TAs are asked to review a reading assignment they had used in their classes and to critique it in the context of the readings and discussions we had had in 567 about reading in the service of writing. One of the most important tasks that TAs undertook during the autumn orientation was to develop a three-part cumulative sequence of assignments for one of the readings they had elected to teach. The fourth assignment we gave them provided them with a midquarter opportunity to reflect on how their first or second assignment sequence worked and then to use that newfound knowledge to formulate the final assignment sequence for their classes.

Not surprisingly, one of the most time-consuming tasks that TAs are expected to undertake in their 131 classes involves giving their students feedback through student–teacher conferences and through both marginal and end comments. Assignments 5 and 6 were therefore designed to have them reflect on the actual work they had done or were doing in both these contexts. After reading some theoretical and research-based work that problematized written response, the TAs were asked to examine the comments they had made on two of their students' essays and to think about ways in which they would want to revise their strategies. For assignment 6, they were encouraged to observe one of their colleagues conferencing with a student, in an effort to see firsthand and in meta-terms the social and discursive practices in which students and teachers engage over the course of one of these sessions. The final assignment asked them to review the previous six assignments and to begin to draft a discursive representation of what they saw as their emerging teaching philosophy. As we note in our description for this assignment, this "narrative [could] serve as an initial piece for the teaching portfolio [they] will want to develop" over the course of the next several years.

As a final project for the class, the TAs were asked to mimic the kind of work they would be asking their own students to do at the end of the quarter. As such, they were required to select and revise two of the seven assignments they had generated during the quarter. Like their students, they were asked to write a cover letter in which they could explain the logic behind their decision to revise the two assignments they had selected. In so doing, we expected that the TAs would gain some valuable insights into both how the work their students were doing in 131 was disciplined by the expectation that they must generate a portfolio and what it feels like to be on the receiving end of such a requirement. Taken together, the readings and written assignments TAs were asked to do in 567 were self-consciously designed to help them integrate the preparatory work they initiated in the autumn orientation with the day-to-day work they had been doing in the 131 classes. Moreover, these activities become an occasion for praxis: TAs were not simply asked to undertake a series of practical projects that would help them become better at putting certain pedagogical practices into play; in the course of revisiting these practices, they were encouraged to reorient themselves by seeing them again in the context of the theoretical texts that we as a

group had read and discussed in class in relation to these specific
activities in and of themselves.

Making the Best of Opportunity Spaces

Periods of transition within writing programs too often become
figured as changes in WPAs, as changes from so-and-so's program
to so-and-so's program. Such a cult of personality distracts us from
recognizing these periods of transition as opportunity spaces, not
for the enactment of another personality, but for thinking about
the institutional and intellectual place of a writing program and
its relationship to the discipline that informs and is informed by it.
We conclude this chapter first by examining how the practicum
course, as an important site of articulation, helps enact and reproduce what gets defined as composition studies, and second, by
speculating on ways WPAs can use the practicum course to examine critically their writing programs and the disciplinary tensions
articulated within them.

To describe the practicum course as a site of articulation is to
understand it both and at once in local, material terms as a site
that prepares new TAs to teach FYC (thereby actualizing disciplinary theories about the study and teaching of writing) and in ideological terms as a site that confirms and reproduces disciplinary
theories about the study and teaching of writing. Anthony Giddens, in *The Constitution of Society: Outline of the Theory of
Structuration*, describes this process of articulation as the "dual-
ity of structure," in which human beings, through their various
activities, reproduce the very structures that subsequently make
their activities necessary, possible, recognizable, and meaningful,
so that their practices reproduce and articulate the very structures
that consequently call for these practices. For Giddens, social
structures function on two simultaneous, homologous levels: the
conceptual and the actual. On the one hand, structures are concepts, virtual rules and resources that exist ideologically and that
dwell in memory traces regardless of whether we are conscious of
them (25). They function on the level of ideology, as what Pierre
Bourdieu calls "predispositions" that frame the ideological and

epistemological boundaries of what we assume to be knowable, doable, or at least possible in any given situation. On the other hand, structures do not just have a conceptual existence, but are actualized as social practices that "comprise the situated activities of human agents, reproduced across space and time" (Giddens 25). According to Giddens, social practices, manifested as certain technologies, conventions, rituals, institutions, tools, and so on, materialize structures. These practices are the social means (the tools, resources, conventions) by which we enact and reproduce ideology as everyday social action. In short, we reproduce structures as we articulate them through various practices.

Within composition studies, the practicum course constitutes one such site of practice, with those involved in it—WPAs, other faculty, ADs, TAs—participating in this process of disciplinary production and reproduction. For at least this reason, we argue, the course can and should be recognized as a legitimate and rich research site both for examining, locally, the values, assumptions, and goals of the writing program at one's institution and for examining the larger disciplinary dispositions that support these values, assumptions, and goals. As we described earlier, we at the University of Washington tried to take advantage of the current period of transition to begin to do just that. First, we reflected on the accomplishments of previous WPAs and the important work they did in legitimizing the study and teaching of writing at the University of Washington. Then we considered ways in which we could build on their work in light of our current institutional context (which includes the ongoing development of a collegewide writing initiative) as well as more recent developments in the discipline, such as the publication of the WPA Outcomes Statement for First-Year Composition and the tension between FYC and writing in the disciplines over the question of transferability. It was crucial that we conducted these discussions as a group so that we were able to create an intellectual conversation around the practicum course, a conversation that ranged from the state of composition studies to the state of writing instruction at the University of Washington to the summer orientation to the FYC course. Our practicum course took shape as a result of these pragmatic, strategic, theoretical conversations.

We could have done more. Treating the practicum course as a site of research could also involve gathering more artifacts and conducting interviews with previous and current WPAs, ADs, and TAs who participated in recent practicum courses. Such interviews, for example, might explore agreements and/or miscommunications between the WPA's stated or unstated goals for the practicum and the TAs' understanding of these goals. More specifically, such interviews could involve examining existing artifacts such as practicum course syllabi, assignments, and so on and gauging how they are perceived by the WPA who designed them, the ADs who help administer them, and the TAs who are their audience. More ethnographic research could also include examining the extent to which TAs in the practicum course apply what they learn to their own FYC courses, as well as how student learning in FYC is affected by what TAs learn in the practicum course. In short, there is a great deal more we can learn about the practicum course by conducting research such as this. But what we can learn would be relevant to more than the practicum course itself or even the writing program it helps support; by recognizing the practicum course as an important site of articulation, what we can learn would contribute not only to how we think about and articulate our discipline to ourselves and others, but also to how we orient ourselves and others, pragmatically and theoretically, within the study and teaching of writing.

Appendix

Modified Version of English 567 Syllabus Theory and Practice of Composition (Autumn 2003)

COURSE DESCRIPTION:

In this course, we will explore some of the theories and practices that guide the teaching of writing in the context of pertinent essays written by scholars in the field of composition and rhetoric. In the process of examining the "best practices" that some of you are going to have your students enact in English 131, we will make every effort to help you understand the "why" behind the "what we do" and "how we do it" when we teach writing.

Many of you come to this course without ever having taken the course you are teaching and most of you have never had a course in the field of composition studies. Because of that, this course is in many ways a survey course, rather than focused on any area of specialization in rhetoric and composition. In conducting this survey, we want you to become aware that the teaching of writing has been intensively researched in the past thirty years and that you can make use of that research in what you do in the classroom. We also want to make you aware of how to find additional resources after you leave this course. If you are in the program for a full five years as a TA, you will be teaching writing for at least three of those five years, and often for four or five years. And even when you teach literature, the writing that students do is central to their learning and evaluation. The more you know about how to support your students' writing, the better they will be able to perform and the less frustrating teaching will be.

Knowing why you ask your students to perform particular tasks and what those tasks might mean in a broader, social framework should mean more thoughtful, more enjoyable teaching. And realistically, you *will* be asked about your teaching practices and philosophy when you go on the job market. There are only a handful of jobs in English that don't require teaching, and they are always senior positions. Many positions now require that you submit teaching evaluations or a teaching portfolio or require you to submit a statement of teaching philosophy—even at Carnegie Research-Extensive institutions. So in your first job, your ability to articulate what you do in the classroom becomes critical in the search. But even before that, we want you to be able to explain to your students, your peers, to us, and most of all to yourself why you have chosen particular strategies for your classroom and the ideological implications of those strategies.

One final note on the course: you can expect that your workload— amount of readings and the total length of written assignments—to be similar to any other five-credit, graded graduate seminar you might take in the department. If you are trying to take three courses this quarter based on the assumption that English 567 is a "practicum" with no readings or graded assignments, you may want to reconsider your course load. We will spend some time in each class session talking about what has been happening in your English 131 classes, but we will tie it back to the materials we are reading for this course.

COURSE REQUIREMENTS:

Because we want to encourage you to integrate your work in the autumn orientation, in the English 131 class you're currently teaching, and in this practicum course in ways that will prove most beneficial for you, the assignments and workshops we have developed will revisit many of the issues we discussed in the orientation and in turn will inform much of what you do in English 131. For these reasons, instead of asking you to do the mid-length midterm and long final papers that many graduate courses require, we will ask you to participate in a couple of workshops in class and to undertake a series of shorter assignments that will give you an opportunity to reflect and build on the work you're doing as a teacher. Because we also want to partly mimic what many of you are asking your own students to do, we have decided to ask that you submit a final portfolio for this class as well. We hope that the cumulative effect of these activities will give you a better idea of how you can respond to the needs of your students in the various classes that you will be teaching over the course of your tenure with us here in the English Department.

Class Participation:

Although we will be lecturing on occasion, most of our in-class activities will be interactive in nature. For this reason, we expect everyone to participate in our class discussions on a regular basis. It is important to note, however, that participation is best measured in qualitative, and not quantitative, terms. In other words, what you say and how you say it is often more important than how much you say. Moreover, some individuals feel very comfortable engaging classmates in conversation right away, while others need time to establish a comfort zone. These differences are both personal and cultural; let us all, therefore, be sensitive to one another's needs. Above all, keep in mind that regular class participation is required because it is essential for the successful operation of our problem-posing approach to classroom activities.

Assignments:

Reviewing Goals for English 131. During the autumn orientation, we asked you to decide on and write up a set of goals for your writing class. This set of goals then became part of the course description for your class. Based on the assigned readings for the first two weeks of this course, reflect on these goals and write about how the readings supported or challenged them. In other words, use the theory we're reading to locate and re-articulate your goals: Which of your goals do you find reinforced in the theory? Which now seem problematic, and why? Finally, how would you need to revise your goals so that they more accurately reflect what you hope students can and will manage to learn in your class? (3 double-spaced pages)

Situating Yourself and Your Students. By the time this assignment is due, you will have been in your English 131 classroom for more than three weeks. Using what you've learned about your students in social, cultural, and linguistic terms and what you've learned about students in general from the readings we've covered thus far, situate yourself and your students in the complex matrix of physical, political, and pedagogical constraints that influence your work as a teacher and their development as writers. How have the particular characteristics they share affected how you've decided to teach the course? And how has your own sense of who you are as a teacher been changed, especially in light of how your original expectations compare with the actual circumstances you've encountered? (3 double-spaced pages)

Teaching Reading. By this point in the quarter, you have faced the task of helping your students understand the importance of developing particular strategies for reading challenging texts in order to write about and in relation to them. Review an assignment that you've developed specifically to help students address this need, then, based on the readings for the unit on "Reading in the Service of Writing," analyze it and discuss the assignment's strengths and weaknesses. Knowing what you know now about the tensions between reading and writing, how would you revise this assignment for future use? Be sure to include the reading assignment (as an artifact) along with your written analysis. (3 double-spaced pages)

Sequencing Assignments. At this point in the quarter, you're probably preparing the sequence of assignments for the last essay that your students will be writing. (If you're not far enough in developing the final sequence at this point, please feel free to use the assignment sequence you developed for your students' second essay.) In light of what you have learned in the course of developing your first sequence (and second sequence, if you choose to do the final one), as well as what you have learned from the readings for the unit on "Developing Literacy Tasks," think about the underlying logic informing the assignment sequence. How does each succeeding assignment build on the one that came before? To what extent are they integrated? Are students using each preceding assignment as a building block for those that come next, or is each assignment in the sequence distinct? Explain. Be sure to include your assignment sequence (as an artifact) along with your written analysis. (3 double-spaced pages)

End Comments: The Hows and The Whys. There are few tasks more time-consuming than responding to student writing. Anything we can do to become more efficient and still provide our students with adequate feedback is likely to grant us more time to address other equally important tasks. In preparation for this assignment, we encourage you to keep a few examples of the kind of written feedback you've provided your students. Select a couple of the student papers you've collected (you'll probably want them to be contrasting in one way or another—either in terms of the quality of student writing or the kinds of feedback you provided), then analyze them looking in particular at the quantity and quality, as well as the underlying patterns, of your feedback. Did you, for example, provide both marginal and end comments, as well as make markings at the word, phrase, or sentence level? What is the nature of these comments? Develop your analysis in the context of what you have learned from the readings for the unit on "Response to Student Writing: Commenting." Be sure to include the student essays (as artifacts) along with your written analysis. (3 double-spaced pages)

Observing a Student–Teacher or Peer Group Conference. Some time during the quarter, make arrangements to observe one of your colleagues engaged in a conference with one of his or her students, or to observe a peer group discussing an essay draft among themselves. Take notes on your observations, paying careful attention to seating arrangements, turn-taking, the amount of talk produced by the participants, the quality of their comments and observations, and the underlying logic of the activity itself. Once you read the material for the units on "Response to Student Writing: Conferencing" and "Working in Groups: Addressing Issues of Reading Comprehension, Invention, and Revision," review your notes and analyze various aspects of the activity that you observed, paying special attention to the role of power and authority, as well as the quality of the activity itself. Be sure to submit your notes (as an artifact) along with your written analysis. (3 double-spaced pages)

Developing a Teaching Philosophy. After you review what you wrote for the preceding 6 assignments, write a brief description of your philosophy at this point in your development as a teacher. What are the broad pedagogical goals that you aim for when you are teaching? How do you situate yourself and your students in light of the subject matter and the issues of power and authority that inform any teaching moment? Finally, what theoretical imperatives inform how and why you do what you do in the classroom? This narrative can then serve as an initial piece for the teaching portfolio you will want to develop over the next several years to send along with your curriculum vita when you're ready to apply for a teaching job. (3 double-spaced pages)

Workshops:

Teaching Argument. The Toulmin approach to analyzing an argument is often as challenging as the professional essays we expect our students to read. Nevertheless, it has proven to be quite a useful tool in helping our students understand what qualifies as acceptable evidence, especially in terms of how evidence differs from personal opinion. Select an assignment that you have used/developed to demonstrate some aspect of the Toulmin model (or some other aspect of argument) to your students, and bring it to class. The goals of this workshop activity will be to have you discuss these assignments with each other in groups of 3 or 4, to acknowledge the different ways you may want to revise the assignment, and to report your conclusions to the other members of the class at large. You may want to take notes during the workshop discussion for your own edification, but you will not be required to submit any written material for assessment.

Teaching Grammar. Even more challenging for most of us than the Toulmin model and the professional essays we assign is the teaching of grammar. While we think of this as a particular problem that we face when we work with second-language learners, a recent "SAT summary report for the entering class of 2004 suggests an alarming decrease [at the high school level] in composition and grammar instruction over the last 10 years" (Tim Washburn, Executive Director, Admissions & Records, University of Washington). Our own continuing practice of de-emphasizing grammar in our writing classes—based on years of research which suggests that the explicit teaching of grammar contributes little to the improvement in student writing—complicates matters further. For this workshop, each of you will be grouped with 2 or 3 other students and will develop a grammar assignment or activity that addresses a problem of prominence that you have witnessed in your students' writing. After you develop the assignment or activity, you will share it with and provide a handout to the class at large so that others can use them in their own teaching. While each group is expected to develop a handout to share with the rest of the class, you will not be required to submit any written material for assessment.

Final Portfolio:

Your final portfolio will consist of the following materials: a 2- to 3-page single-spaced cover letter, 2 revised assignments (each followed by the earlier draft and artifact), and the original drafts of the 5 remaining assignments (along with their respective artifacts) in the order in which you produced them. The cover letter should be construed as an argument that develops and supports a claim about your development as a teacher, especially in light of your readings in composition theory and your experiences this quarter. You will want to explain how and why the two assignments you selected to revise reflect this development. You're encouraged to use quotations from and references to particular parts of your assignments as evidence. The criteria you use to select the 2 assignments for revision are up to you. You may select them because you thought they represented your best work in the class, because they were among the least fulfilling assignments you wrote, or because they gave you an opportunity to revisit a couple of issues that you consider central to your teaching. Please be sure to submit the materials in a notebook that will allow us to review them efficiently and productively.

Readings for English 567 in Chronological Order

1. Disciplinarity and Academic Writing
Larson, Richard L. "Enlarging the Context: From Teaching Just Writing, to Teaching Academic Subjects with Writing." In *Composition in Context*. Eds. W. Ross Winterowd and Vincent Gillespie. Carbondale: SIU Press, 1994. 109–125.

Steering Committee of the Outcomes Group. "WPA Outcomes Statement for First-Year Composition." *College English* 63.3 (January 2001): 321–325.

UCWC. "Transforming Writing: Final Report of the Undergraduate Curriculum Writing Committee." College of Arts and Sciences, University of Washington at Seattle, 2003. 1–24.

Carroll, Lee Ann. "A Preview of Writing Development" and "A Concluding Look at Development." *Rehearsing New Roles: How College Students Develop as Writers*. Carbondale: SIU Press, 2002. 1–28, 118–148.

2. Understanding Our Students' Roles as Writers
Halasek, Kay. "Redefining the Student Writer." *A Pedagogy of Possibility: Bakhtinian Perspectives on Composition Studies*. Carbondale: SIU Press, 1999. 27–51.

Horner, Bruce. "Students, Authorship, and the Work of Composition." *College English* 59.5 (September 1997): 505–529.

3. Challenges in the Classroom for Teachers and Students
Miller, Richard E. "Fault Lines in the Contact Zone." *College English* 56.4 (April 1994): 389–408.

Stygall, Gail. "Resisting Privilege: Basic Writing and Foucault's Author Function." *College Composition and Communication* 45.3 (October 1994): 320–341.

4. The Politics of Access
Soliday, Mary. "Ideologies of Access and the Politics of Agency." In *Mainstreaming Basic Writers: Politics and Pedagogies of Access*. Ed. Gerri McNenny. Mahwah, NJ: Lawrence Erlbaum, 2001. 55–72.

Horner, Bruce, and John Trimbur. "English Only and U.S. College Composition." *College Composition and Communication* 53.4 (June 2002): 594–630.

5. Diversity Matters

Kleege, Georgia. "Disabled Students Come Out: Questions and Answers." In *Disability Studies: Enabling the Humanities*. Eds. Sharon L. Snyder, Brenda Jo Brueggemann, and Rosemarie Garland-Thomson. New York: MLA, 2002. 308–316.

Brueggemann, Brenda Jo, et al. "Becoming Visible: Lessons in Disability." *College Composition and Communication* 52.3 (February 2001): 368–398.

Marshall, Margaret. "Marking the Unmarked: Reading Student Diversity and Preparing Teachers." *College Composition and Communication* 48.2 (May 1997): 231–249.

6. Reading in the Service of Writing

Miller, Susan. "Technologies of Self-Formation." *Journal of Advanced Composition* 17.3 (1997): 497–500.

McCormick, Kathleen. "Closer Than Close Reading: Historical Analysis, Cultural Analysis, and Symptomatic Reading in the Undergraduate Classroom." In *Intertexts: Reading Pedagogy in College Writing Classrooms*. Ed. Marguerite Helmers. Mahwah, NJ: Lawrence Erlbaum, 2003. 27–50.

Bartholomae, David. "Introduction." In *Ways of Reading* (5th edition). Eds. David Bartholomae and Andrew Petrosky. Boston/New York: Bedford/St. Martin's, 1999. 1–14.

Smith, Frank. "Reading, Writing, and Thinking." *Understanding Reading* (5th edition). Hillsdale, NJ: Erlbaum, 1994. 167–182.

7. Argumentative Writing

Gage, John T. "The Reasoned Thesis: The E-Word and Argumentative Writing as a Process of Inquiry." In *Argument Revisited; Argument Redefined*. Eds. Barbara Emmel, Paula Resch, and Deborah Tenney. Thousand Oaks, CA: Sage, 1996. 3–18.

Freedman, Aviva. "Genres of Argument and Arguments as Genres." In *Perspectives on Written Argument*. Ed. Deborah P. Berrill. Cresskill, NJ: Hampton Press, 1996. 91–120.

Fulkerson, Richard. "The Toulmin Model of Argument and the Teaching of Composition." In *Argument Revisited; Argument Redefined*.

Eds. Barbara Emmel, Paula Resch, and Deborah Tenney. Thousand Oaks, CA: Sage, 1996. 45–72.

8. Developing Literacy Tasks
Rankin, Elizabeth. "From Simple to Complex: Ideas of Order in Assignment Sequences." *Journal of Advanced Composition* 10.1 (January–February 1990): 126–135.

Speck, Bruce W. "Constructing Writing Assignments." *Grading Students' Classroom Writing: Issues and Strategies*. Washington, DC: Graduate School of Education and Human Development, The George Washington University, 2000. 11–26.

9. Response to Student Writing: Commenting, Grammar, and Conferencing
Horvath, Brooke K. "The Components of Written Response: A Practical Synthesis of Current Views." In *The Writing Teacher's Sourcebook* (4th edition). Eds. Edward P. J. Corbett, Nancy Myers, and Gary Tate. New York: Oxford University Press, 1999. 243–257.

Smith, Summer. "The Genre of the End Comment: Conventions in Teacher Responses to Student Writing. *College Composition and Communication* 48.2 (May 1997): 249–268.

Weaver, Constance. "Teaching Grammar in the Context of Writing." *Lessons to Share on Teaching Grammar in Context*. Ed. Constance Weaver. Portsmouth, NH: Boynton/Cook, 1998. 18–38.

Kolln, Martha. "Cohesion and Coherence." In *Evaluating Writing: The Role of Teachers' Knowledge about Text, Learning, and Culture*. Eds. Charles R. Cooper and Lee Odell. Urbana: NCTE, 1999. 93–113.

Black, Laurel Johnson. "Conversation, Teaching, and Points in Between." *Between Talk and Teaching*. Logan: Utah Sate University Press, 1998. 11–37.

10. Working in Groups: Addressing Issues of Reading Comprehension, Invention, and Revision
Gere, Anne Ruggles. "Theories of Collaborative Learning" and "Practical Directions." *Writing Groups: History, Theory, and Implications*. Carbondale: SIU Press, 1987. 55–76, 99–112.

Trimbur, John. "Consensus and Difference in Collaborative Learning." *College English* 51.6 (October 1989): 602–616.

11. Portfolios in the Classroom

Elbow, Peter, and Pat Belanoff. "Reflections on an Explosion: Portfolios in the '90s and Beyond." In *Situating Portfolios: Four Perspectives*. Eds. Kathleen Blake Yancey and Irwin Weiser. Logan: Utah State University Press, 1997. 21–33.

Huot, Brian, and Michael M. Williamson. "Rethinking Portfolios for Evaluating Writing: Issues of Assessment and Power." In *Situating Portfolios: Four Perspectives*. Eds. Kathleen Blake Yancey and Irwin Weiser. Logan: Utah State University Press, 1997. 43–56.

12. Professional Issues

Aronowitz, Stanley. "The Last Good Job in America." *The Last Good Job in America: Work and Education in the New Global Techno-culture*. Lanham, MD: Rowman & Littlefield, 2001. 29–44.

Sledd, James. "Disciplinarity and Exploitation: Compositionists as Good Professionals." http://www.fredonia.edu/department/english/simon/workplace/sledd/html

Notes

1. Before his first year as WPA ended, Juan was appointed co-director of a Carnegie-funded project at the University of Washington called Teachers for a New Era and Anis took over as WPA. In retrospect, our decision to work together from the beginning of Juan's tenure as WPA proved fortuitous.

2. Since Anis took over as WPA, the Expository Writing Program has gone through a number of additional changes, especially in the English 131 curriculum. To see the shape these changes have taken, please visit the EWP Web site at http://depts.washington.edu/engl/ewp.

3. Among the more important issues for us, for example, is the fact that we have the option of teaching a parallel and nonpracticum composition theory course for graduate students who are not TAs and who want to learn more about composition studies outside the context of our writing program.

Works Cited

Bourdieu, Pierre. *The Logic of Practice*. Trans. Richard Nice. Stanford: Stanford UP, 1990.

Giddens, Anthony. *The Constitution of Society: Outline of the Theory of Structuration.* Berkeley: U of California P, 1984.

Linde, Charlotte. *Life Stories: The Creation of Coherence.* New York: Oxford UP, 1993.

Chapter Three

Practica, Symposia, and Other Coercive Acts in Composition Studies

Bonnie Lenore Kyburz
Utah Valley State College

What happens when there is no practicum? What happens when your institution offers no such forum—or scant provision—for teacher training and preparation? At many smaller colleges and universities, such is the case. Nevertheless, even minimal forums for professional development at small colleges function in ways that resemble large university practica.

Despite important differences, small college and large university practica manifest similarly disenchanting effects. At one level of disenchantment, both practica function to render explicit relations of power. This is not necessarily wicked, for most college writing programs function by relying on adjuncts or teaching assistants (TAs) who may or may not have had appreciable training in writing instruction; many adjuncts come with training that is somewhat dated. Thus, such a program seems to call for *support* if it is to cohere and gesture toward particular kinds of work; I am here talking about *leadership*, a loathsome term we associate with corporate culture, a precision-oriented term that wants to disambiguate the real experience of working together with variously prepared teachers toward a massively difficult task that presumably requires the delineating action of a "mission statement" or set of desired "outcomes." Clearly, in this theoretical space, I am contemptuous of this language; I have in my role as a writing program administrator (WPA) called forth such language often enough. Perhaps my contempt derives from my less than idyllic experience as a small college WPA, which entailed leading our small college version of the practicum. This work and its disenchanting effects have compelled me to imagine new ways of theorizing "quality" as progressive, *emergent intensities* within college writing programs.

For two years, I directed the writing program at Utah Valley State College, an institution that evolved rapidly from a technical to a community to a two-year/four-year college hybrid. My charge was to *streamline* the program, to *coerce* it into alignment with prevailing practices in composition studies; we wanted to mimic other national models, a key concern among local administrators with eyes toward future state university status. With (then) some fifty adjuncts and twenty-three faculty members teaching our core writing courses, the "program" was a program in name only. I had to discover ways of encouraging us to (1) adopt shared goals and curricula, (2) develop awareness of key theories and practices that might shape our work, and (3) make sure that we got along. I was told that such goals had been previously accomplished through occasional "symposia" offered by the former writing program coordinator and available faculty (note that as with "practicum," we resort to the archaic Latinate lexicon for our title, a particularly Literary trend, one that holds Composition Studies clearly within the domain of the defining force in most English departments, Literary Studies, problems for perhaps another essay). In these symposia, leaders would discuss various topics of relevance, which were often related to specific classroom practices, and then much time was given over to general conversation, which often resembled a "bitch session" for adjuncts. Food and drink were always provided as an enticement to attend, and, given that our adjuncts are severely underpaid, they were remunerated for attendance at their normal hourly rate of service.

On the surface, our symposia operated primarily to provide a common space in which to discuss our problems as teachers of writing. I do not want to deride this purpose, for it clearly helps teachers of writing sense shared goals and values even as it gives them an outlet for purging frustrations associated with the work. But surely there can be much more to the teaching practicum. Knowing Sid Dobrin's work, I feel certain that in generating this collection he is motivated by a desire to see practica become less clearly practice oriented (perhaps limiting time devoted exclusively to "bitching") and more obviously integrated in terms of the mutually informing domains of theory and practice (promoting thinking that gestures toward imaginative work regarding potentially progressive and kinesthetic classroom scenarios). Such integration may in fact be necessary if composition studies is to ultimately survive as a field of inquiry and be recognized as a "deadly serious"[1] academic discipline. Aligning too neatly with the view of composition studies as the field devoted to a radically limited notion of "good" (i.e., "correct") writing, the practice-oriented conceptualization of the practicum implies that most anyone can teach writing with a bit of "training" (note again the corporate lexicon and the practices it describes, echoing in composition studies/in the contemporary academy). This view limits composition studies and impoverishes our potential to think about the field as rich, as historically situated and complexly progressive, as informed by vast bodies of research and knowledge, as anything more than a field devoted to the teaching of elementary courses defined by diligent work on correctness, grammar, punctuation, usage, and spelling. As well, this feeble view of the field refuses to embrace writing expansively, as "central to living in the world" (Olson 11) or as capable of "enacting the numerous freedom projects of resisting systems of domination—whether in the very uses of discourse itself or in the multiple discourse systems that comprise and constitute our social institutions and academic disciplines" (Olson 11). Against the implications of "training" and narrow conceptualizations of the roles of composition courses, we find that an invitation to create a more expansive theoretical space entices our experience of thinking about what the practicum might be(come). My charge as WPA was far less attractive, although I advocated passionately for a more intensive relationship with theory for our teaching population (adjuncts and contract faculty).

   Working against considerably thin notions of composition studies, I attempted to shape a program through the newly formed professional development forums (PDF) I created at UVSC. And while I am at this point in time rather appalled at the name I chose for this work—so clearly a function of the corporate sensibilities shaping academic life (and I was, after all, an "administrator")—the work extended to incorporate both theoretical and pedagogical purposes. I wanted to encourage our teaching population to

engage with scholarly texts on writing, writers, and writing instruction (again, many have English—or other—degrees that are
dated, some granted nearly twenty years ago). I desired their
agreement on shared goals and assumptions and believed that we
could discover them together even as I *imposed* the "WPA Outcomes Statement" as a strong document with national support
(again, I see my monstrous desire for control only in hindsight). I
wanted these teachers to feel valued and valuable (but was surely
overeager to settle in with my beliefs and practices and to institute
them). Not surprisingly, as with the practicum at larger institutions, our PDFs left much to be desired. We could not escape the
sense of ominous presence, of immanent "leadership." Despite
attempts at "community,"[2] we could not shake off the notion that
the PDF functioned in order to *control* the group with benevolent
albeit sincerely desperate measures (food, drinks, money). "Community" functioned as a disambiguating screen through which we
could enact the strange alliance(s) we pretended toward, but
everyone understood that our "community" actualized, as Joe
Harris describes the workings of most *real* communities, "at a
vague remove from actual experience" (100). In the end, adjuncts
seemed to attend as a nod to their subordinate status rather than
out of a sincere or even genuine-in-appearance-only desire to
"develop." What's more, many were concerned first and foremost
with *practice*, seeking little in the way of theoretical knowledge
that might shape their work (theory can seem a luxury when you
must teach multiple sections, sometimes on two or three different
campuses, in order to support families—the case with many of
our adjuncts). Not only did many of our adjuncts evade critical
theory broadly conceived, but they also seemed perfectly happy to
continue to avoid research on writing (we need them; they know
this; what's the point in creating the illusion that the situation is
not so clearly cut?). Some did more than avoid engaging with
scholarly texts and research on writing; some openly resisted
prominent concepts deriving from the literature (now this is
arguably just nasty business; I have no parentheticals to excuse
this social and professional faux pas). For example, after my second PDF, in which I discussed the roles of grammar instruction in
first-year composition (informed by Hillocks, Hartwell, and others who proclaimed that formal grammar instruction had delete-

rious effects on student learning), one longtime adjunct reported to our department chair (my boss): "Bonnie Kyburz says that grammar doesn't matter." What had happened to my subtly nuanced discussion on the roles of formal grammar instruction and/versus immersion in literate practices? What had happened to our respectful and collaborative atmosphere? Where was the joy in discovery regarding the political nature of certain literate practices (i.e., grammar instruction and usage)? I simply cannot imagine such a scenario playing out in the context of a graduate writing program practicum. But why is this the case? Might the PDF have better succeeded were it a practicum? A required course? Costly professional training? Had my "students" been working not only to gain confidence, community, and professional status but also for *grades*, might they have responded differently to my teaching and/or encouragement? I wonder about the nature of the "reward" for engagement with the concepts I was promoting. Specifically, could the small college context have shaped a desire among our adjuncts to continue to operate as they had for years without the intervention of a theoretically minded mentor-leader-coordinator (i.e., me)? Had their longtime experience of working at UVSC been so impoverished? Had their experience been so profoundly marked by the shared goal of getting students to write *clearly* (at the level of simple sentences, correctly punctuated and formatted) that they could not conceive of new work that would prepare students to write both clearly and *complexly* (evolving to exploration, inquiry, critique, and so on)? Given that our college has been emerging and expanding for some years now, our adjuncts might have foreseen the need to enlarge their repertoire, but the PDF clearly would not provide adequate space for this work.

Turning back to the first level of disenchantment I am exploring here, I suspect that many adjuncts sensed a shift in the power structure of the program; no previous writing program coordinator had held a terminal degree in rhetoric and composition. The move to bring one in had been part of a project to validate the work of our writing program and to make it contemporary, to render it "normal" in terms of current theory and practice. Adjuncts suspecting a shift to a new and perhaps more pervasive power structure attempted to exert their force by rejecting the imposition of "new" thinking; thus, many rejected the practices I was seeking to bring to the program. At one level, this is hurtful, but on another level altogether, I see adjunct resistance as a clearly useful response to change. In fact, I saw this at the time, but because I was asked to resign from my position as the program's leader, I was not able to discover ways of theorizing this understanding sufficient to enable further change in the program (change *was* happening despite resistance; there was a small core of adjuncts and many contract faculty members who were "with me," very happy to read suggested essays, try new classroom practices, and adopt new pedagogical orientations). My time away from my former role as program coordinator has allowed me the luxury of discovering ways of theorizing this resistance; emerging theories on both silence and affect are aiding me in efforts to think about framing a successful anti-forum for teacher preparation.

Theorizing the Anti-Forum

We can worry the question from a variety of perspectives, but we desire singular answers that are responsive to singular approaches; we do not have the luxury of time, and few of us have resources sufficient to enable the wealth of approaches that may actually provoke new scenarios for preparing teachers and ensuring the quality of our programs. Like petulant children, we want to know: Why are practica so limited/limiting? I will continue to explore this question, to worry a variety of concerns, but I will attempt to confine my critique to issues involving power and coercion, (in)effectiveness, and impoverished theoretical experience in light of the practice-oriented nature of most practica. Throughout this exploratory work, I hope to negotiate a new concept for teacher training, one that does not coerce or bill its members, one that does not obediently accept and promote each and every prominent theoretical and practical concept but instead explores, questions, and critiques current theories and practices. Perhaps most important, I want/we need to imagine scenarios that will enable us to avoid the easy tendency to sever theory from practice. Thus, I imagine the anti-forum, space(s) in which we can elide the presence of clearly defined hierarchies of power—even if this elision operates only in an imaginary field of desire—in order to theorize what we do and what we might do as teachers of writing. Experiencing our work together as infinitely complex and varied, and rejecting the ostensible need to impose strictures that function with and against particular normative statements, mandates, and dicta that are both imposed and received as "rules," we might theorize more effectively toward the generation of a functioning cooperative of dedicated teachers of writing. Clearly, such a utopia requires that we privilege theorizing as central to our work together. The anti-forum operationalizes theory as always already a manner of practice; that we should have to signify this "always-alreadiness" with the term *practice* suggests the dominance of practice-oriented ideologies at work in our conversations about the teaching of writing in its programmatic iteration(s). How do we feel about this? I ask because I want later to argue that theories of affect may be useful for articulating the value of the emerging anti-forum I am imagining.

Dialogic Silence in the Anti-Forum

The anti-forum wants to privilege ambiguity and curiosity in our work. Such moves oblige us to engage an understanding of "theory and practice" similar to contemporary considerations of "art and life," as James Zebroski would have it. He argues that theory and practice "need to be in a kind of dialogue with each other, though at the same time the differences between the two must be preserved" (2). Zebroski's dialogue that clearly articulates key terms seems a reasonable proposition even as I cannot fully imagine what he means when he differentiates between theory and practice. More fulfilling is his suggestion that "we must allow for the moments when of necessity silence passes between them" (2). Such reflective moments seem to me to be the stuff of the (ideal) practicum, the work of professional development in the anti-forum space(s) I imagine.

Taking up such imaginative and contemplative work may encourage us to resist the totalizing logic of writing program administration, which often though not always wants to regularize, normalize, and routinize certain practices in ways that clearly privilege the practical and pragmatic and even the corporate over the theoretical, the exploratory, and the reflective (this desire is not wholly descriptive of our Ultimate Goals—most WPAs I know yearn for greater programmatic complexity—yet the goal of simplicity and ease obtains within the economy of "efficacy" that holds most WPAs accountable for programmatic "success"). For some, rethinking the practica beyond conceptualizations of writing programs as controlled or routine or streamlined may seem counterproductive. This may be good. Can you see it?

Turning back, then, to the question that opens this chapter: What happens when there is no practicum? Logistics notwithstanding (a massive mental aside, I realize), can we imagine this postapocalyptic terrain for a moment, Baudrillard's "Desert of the Real"? Can we Reload? Think about it: with no practicum, we may recognize that we must do the one thing many of us are now exquisitely unable to do: *hire responsibly out of need*. Absent a teaching practicum, we see ourselves without "opportunity" to engage in coercive work that wants to routinize teaching and classrooms. Hiring responsibly—even at the level of adjunct hiring, which clearly needs our attention and responsible care—we may find ourselves working with invested and interesting colleagues with whom an ongoing dialogue about teaching seems always possible, even *natural*. In taking up Zebroski's contemplative dialogic silence, for instance, we may avoid the temptation to see our work in reductive categories of experience, thereby essentially saying to a new hire, "we trust and respect your particular expertise." Building a writing program from such a foundation of refreshing respect, we may then engage—formally, informally, virtually, in hallways and offices and parks and coffeehouses and bars and whatnot—and "vibe out" on our insights in a variety of productive ways (these vibrations may gesture toward the achievement of shared goals, for those of you/us who cannot shake this compulsion). This, as opposed to the coercion to attend social functions through which the laws are decreed (rather like the functions of theater in ancient Greece). We may work together—professors, adjuncts, TAs, research assistants, etc.—to teach writing generously, effectively, creatively, even if this means that we resist institutional strategies to force compliance with certain models, and even if it means that we bring a dizzying array of strategies to bear on our complex work in the complex present.

Such moves require a good deal of mental contortion for those of us who are responsible for a program's success; we have been conditioned to believe that streamlining and routinizing writing program practices will manifest the desired effects (simplicity and ease). And because such moves hint that we will not be able to hire sufficiently to teach the many sections we are required to fill, we may have to generate increasingly complex theories and practices that account for this reality (we defend smaller classes, but at what cost?). Such ideational moves insist that we open ourselves to possibilities inclusive of confusion and anxiety. Such moves encourage us to resist discourses of mastery and regular practices in discursive disambiguation. Such moves find expression in the chaosmos of theory. As Zebroski argues when tracing the emergence of theory in composition studies,

> The very impetus to composing theory seems to have been institutional, disciplinary control, while present theory would appear to seek to break out of such restraints. What began as a move for control ends as a call for release. What started as a search for an underlying order has (re)turned full circle to the dialectical other, to a quest for generativity and chaos. (4)

Assuming hopefully with Zebroski that "present theory" really does want to destroy boundaries that would control and enforce the ways in which theory functions (practically), I want to argue that we (re)integrate theory into the work of the practicum—in an idealized anti-forum—as a form of appropriately expansive (liberatory?) rather than exclusively disciplinary or managerial administrative practice. What I really want to do is free first-year composition. And as we are talking about the teaching practicum that is usually constrained to the teaching of first-year composition—that which so often and problematically "defines" composition studies—I want to talk about a move to free composition studies in part by creating a new form of professional development and/or practica that engage Zebroski's contemplative dialogic silence and other rhetorics of silence, such as Cheryl Glenn's, currently enjoying an audience in composition studies. Such a model respects both teachers of writing (in training) and the students with whom they interact. It resists static meanings as received "truths," "isms," or rigid taxonomies. It does not seek to coerce or overtly control. It does not want to routinize any particular practice but instead delights in encouraging excitement and exploration for those willing to live with the ambiguity that comes from accepting (embracing) complexity and an absence of overt managerial presence. In imagining the absence of a practicum we find an emergent "dialogic silence" model within the space(s) of the anti-forum, a model that resists the specifically damning functions of managed experience we must almost certainly critique.

Postpracticum Silence of the Anti-Forum

Theorizing the anti-forum that thrives in dialogic silence, we must begin to revalue the roles of silence in our professional lives. Such work requires a shift in our languishing epistemological orientations regarding what we are about in composition studies. Such work wants us to resist "a discourse of mastery and assertion" as we move "toward a more dialogic, dynamic, open-ended, receptive, non-assertive stance" (Olson 14). This work may find promise in silence.

Advancing rhetorical acts of resistance we find in rhetorics of silence, Cheryl Glenn argues that such work "can resist disciplinary pigeon-holing, embrace political resistance, and refuse the discipline (or 'correct training') of sociopolitical culture and power" (262). This potential becomes important for thinking about teaching in composition courses and forums for ensuring good teaching within an increasingly conservative, corporatized academic context. Glenn makes clear that "silence and language work together" (263), arguing that "whether it is a forced position or a tactical choice, it [silence] carries meaning" (263). Considering the ways in which silence functions as either a sociopolitical (or other) imposition or a rhetorical move to privilege a kind of absence, we may imagine the value of the anti-forum that does not operate according to the logic of the lecture regarding "best practices" or even via narratives of grief and woe from what are often called the "front lines" or "trenches" (military metaphors really must go). Instead, we may see a new community of knowledgeable peers who communicate insights not only by speaking with and against the dominant interests of the program/school/college/ university/culture/current administration but also by *listening*, by *enacting silence* in ways that encourage further reflection, by avoiding the temptation to resolve problems in a Q&A format that cannot fully account for the various aspects of a teacher's concern or problem (which register as theoretical, practical, affective, emotional, visceral, and psychological problems, to name only a few complicated domains of experience that often render the "solution" unavailable within the economy of "problem solving" and constrained by the (re)productions of power that define current practica). We may also think of practicum scenarios in which a particular teacher narrative emerges as scapegoat for a larger problem that is perceived by the "leader," who then silences the (teacher) narrative in order to render the moment "teachable" (appropriating the moment of articulation/reflection in service to Ultimate Goals). As Glenn insists, "silence and silencing can be sites of disciplinary resistance . . . [and they] can also work to resist the correct training of sociopolitical culture" (281). Olson might agree that such resistance enables and supports theoretical work that "speculate[s] productively about how writing is deeply implicated in structures of power and domination, how writing can never be disconnected from ideology, how writing as traditionally conceived is driven by a discourse of mastery and a rhetoric of assertion" (14).

Can the anti-forum sustain speculation of this kind *and* function in ways that respond to the demands of programmatic accountability? I am able only to provoke the question in the space I have here. This aggravating work, however, seems essential to our work in the complicated present, as programs are increasingly underfunded and assessment schemes persist in imposing limited views on writing upon our hopeful composition spaces. Our resistance clearly requires increasingly radical thinking, beyond the scope of the "gods" Geoff Sirc names and rejects as no longer relevant to our project(s):

We erect temples to language, in which we are the priests among the initiates (of varying degrees of enthusiasm), where we relive the rites of text-production for the *n*th time, despite the sad truth that the gods have fled so long ago that no one is even sure that they were ever there in the first place (in Composition, the gods are called, variously, *power, authentic voice, discourse, critical consciousness, versatility, style, disciplinarity, purpose, etc.*). (2)

If the gods have truly fled, if we are without recourse to stabilizing truths (we are without stabilizing truths), then we might revalue the roles of theoretical and literal silence; we must take up the mammoth task of privileging theorizing as critical work in the life of writing teachers, be they adjuncts, TAs, or professors. How can we theorize the roles of silence in the anti-forum in order to reveal both the potential in and faults of the practicum? Naturally, practical concerns arise in the context of such theorizing, but it seems likely that by *privileging* theory we create spaces for analysis and critique of our work that far exceeds what we have in the speaking, controlling, certain spaces of many current practica.

Eroticizing the Anti-Forum

If it seems I am overly critical of the practicum, understand that I am in many ways aligning the aims of such forums with an increasing corporatization of higher education, moves to ensure that colleges and universities are preparing workers for corporate life beyond their educational experience. A certain privileging of the practical obtains in this economy, and so my resistance speaks my attempt to disrupt this imbalance. Discussing ways in which we might return composition classrooms (and the professional development that prepares or more enchantingly *sustains* its teachers) to the conceptual domain of the *humanities* and thus return it to the human(e) in all of its earthly unruliness and carnality (as opposed to the clarity and mission-driven objectives of corporality), Jenny Edbauer argues for what she calls "Big Time Sensuality" (23), a sensibility and intense "thinking-feeling" that demands a disposition toward expansive and dynamic potential. A dialogic silence might prepare space(s) for such potential, for the anti-forum. Writing this space seems desirable, and I hope that my writing gestures toward these spatial possibilities.

As I have, it is likely that you have engaged in a dialogic exchange as you have read what I've written thus far; you have probably moved with and against my imaginary postpracticum space. It is also likely that you return frequently to the safety of the practicum. But resist the urge for a moment longer so that I might engage your growing sense of dis-ease. Resist the compulsion to patrol the body's sensation of pleasure that comes from imagining the possibilities of freedom and/in silence.

Toward such possibilities, Edbauer insists that our work matters beyond the ideological, beyond the control of our hermeneutic impulse: "the critical impulse to de-value a bodily sensation in the rush to uncover ideological meaning is a destructive act" (25). With T. R. Johnson, Edbauer compels us to consider pleasure in our work, not simply the pleasures we associate with "a job well done" as we order and regiment writing instruction, as we strain toward "effectiveness" across the imaginary domains of our imaginary control; she wants "for us to recognize the pleasures that already exist for our students and all textual users" (25). Here, I want to suggest that we imagine "students" not simply in terms of matriculating students in composition courses, but, as we always already do, we might consider the teachers in our programs (including ourselves) as "students." We all *use* (here, the drug metaphor is pleading for our reflective silence).

Edbauer reads critical responses to film in ways that uncover ideological critiques that aspire to pedagogy. Beyond these critiques, which easily become rigid within the sometimes-stultifying air of pedagogy, Edbauer worries about the unaided response to the film as text: "what happens to the intensities of pleasure that surround them?" (28). We might similarly worry the divide between a teacher's response to a particular classroom scenario and our "reading" of it within the practicum. As Edbauer argues, "how a text means does not determine how it matters" (30). Perhaps our exchanges with teachers in our programs could matter more, could provoke contemplative reflection in dialogic silence? Edbauer considers the value of "a pedagogy that embraces the body's thinking-feeling" as a kind of desire; she wants to engage what she calls the "overspill" (31). How might we enable such pleasure to inform our work without making familiar moves to "incorporate" such profound experiences as "the body's thinking-feeling"? Edbauer continues to wonder about such questions when she argues that "affective intensity embarrasses us as an uncritical remnant of what writing studies *used* to be before we got our act together," realizing that our work now functions to shift the experience of writing "from pleasurable engagement to discipline" (31). Such shifts have generated new vocabularies of meaning and experience within the teaching practicum, and they have sometimes (often?) conceptualized sensual pleasure and the affective intensities associated with our work as a kind of pornography. But, as Edbauer argues in terms of first-year composition pedagogy, we might see that teaching and learning may evolve a kind of "sensual textuality" that demands a material pedagogy responsive to the real spaces of teaching and learning that exist in and between "community" (35).

Can we feel a potential sensuality associated with our experience of the anti-forum? If so, we must sense that to do so is to eroticize our work within and without classrooms, absent rules and leaders, coercion and punishment. And that this is good. But can such eroticism exist within an economy of correctness that is dominated by conservative ideologues? I want to argue that we must first desire and then seek to answer this question affirmatively, to reappropriate "practical" action in a Third Wave gesture that moves beyond identity, beyond professional signification or "status," beyond the "safe" spaces of most college and university practica. I want to develop a reverence for the anti-forum that imagines pedagogy as lived experience rather than as instructional tools and "lessons." Here, as Edbauer might have it,

> pedagogy is teeming with bodies that care less for the symbolic than the material. It is materiality with a vengeance. . . . We must begin to transform and revise our pedagogies with/in the places that matter. . . . [S]uch pedagogy can be as much about shutting up as inventing new lessons. (35)

Can we shut up?

Notes

1. See Donna Haraway's *Simians, Cyborgs, and Women: The Reinvention of Nature*. Haraway argues that "writing is deadly serious" (175).

2. Joseph Harris critiques impoverished and disingenuous conceptualizations of "community" in composition studies. See *A Teaching Subject: Composition since 1966*.

Works Cited

Edbauer, Jenny. "Big Time Sensuality: Affective Literacies and Texts That Matter." *Composition Forum* 13.1–2 (2002): 23–37.

Glenn, Cheryl. "Silence: A Rhetorical Art for Resisting Discipline(s)." *JAC: A Journal of Composition Theory* 22.2 (2002): 261–91.

Haraway, Donna J. *Simians, Cyborgs, and Women: The Reinvention of Nature*. New York: Routledge, 1991.

Harris, Joseph. *A Teaching Subject: Composition since 1966*. Upper Saddle River, NJ: Prentice Hall, 1997.

Hartwell, Patrick. "Grammar, Grammars, and the Teaching of Grammar." *College English* 47.2 (1985): 105–27.

Hillocks, George, Jr. *Research on Written Composition: New Directions for Teaching*. Urbana, IL: ERIC Clearinghouse on Reading and Communication, National Institute of Education, 1986.

Olson, Gary. "Toward a Post-Process Composition: Abandoning the Rhetoric of Assertion." *Post-Process Theory: Beyond the Writing-Process Paradigm*. Ed. Thomas Kent. Carbondale: Southern Illinois UP, 1999.

Sirc, Geoffrey. *English Composition as a Happening*. Logan: Utah State UP, 2002.

Zebroski, James Thomas. *Thinking through Theory: Vygotskian Perspectives on the Teaching of Writing*. Portsmouth, NH: Boynton/Cook, 1994.

CHAPTER FOUR

The Composition Practicum as Professional Development

SUSAN KAY MILLER AND ROCHELLE RODRIGO
Mesa Community College

VERONICA PANTOJA
Chandler-Gilbert Community College

DUANE ROEN
Arizona State University

When first-year graduate teaching assistants in composition arrive on campus in July or August, they often have had little or no formal teaching experience; they also often have had little or no formal preparation to teach at any level. Because of their relatively slight grounding in teaching writing, teaching assistants anxiously—and often eagerly—seek skills and knowledge that will support them during the first semester or two in the composition classroom.

Although the composition practicum certainly needs to support first-year teaching assistants so that both they and their students succeed in the composition classroom, the practicum must do much more than that. In particular, the practicum needs to be conceptualized more broadly as an early foundation for lifelong professional development. A crucial goal for the practicum is to encourage teaching assistants—regardless of the focus of their degree program (literature, creative writing, technical writing, rhetoric and composition, theoretical and applied linguistics, English as a second language, English education)—to view all of their work in the academy as scholarly.

For graduate students preparing for a career in university teaching, the practicum can encourage them to consider their work in the academy as Michael Crow, president of Arizona State University, has conceptualized it:

1. Teaching is our prime directive. We are teachers. I am a teacher; you are teachers; the institution is a teacher. I can't think of anything more important than that. That is the prime directive.

2. Scholarship is our pathway to better teaching. Scholarship, in whatever form each of us takes it, is essential to the quality of our teaching. There's a whole range of things that scholarship means, but all of us must be creatively engaged in pushing back the edges of whatever it is we do if we hope to be great teachers.

3. If teaching is our prime directive, creative expression in all forms is our highest goal. We have a responsibility to be creative.

4. We must be an institution built around openness and access to our learning environment for all. Whatever we're doing, the energy we create, the creativity that we stimulate, the teaching we do, if we sequester it, hold it inside, or wall it off, it's greatly diminished.

Crow's goals echo what Ernest Boyer provided the foundation for in his broad definition of scholarship more than a decade ago. In Boyer's scheme, the *scholarly* work of the professoriate has four interrelated functions: discovery, integration, application/engagement, and teaching. The scholarship of *discovery* is essentially what academics traditionally consider to be research. In the scholarship of *application/engagement*, the scholar asks, "How can knowledge be responsibly applied to consequential problems?" (21). The scholarship of *integration* involves "making connections across the disciplines, placing the specialties in larger context, illuminating data in a revealing way, often educating nonspecialists, too" (18). The scholarship of *teaching* involves publicly scrutinizing our work with students—to share it with others and to make it better in the future.

At the very least, every teaching assistant should complete the practicum with a lifelong commitment to "effective teaching"—teaching that results in student learning. Effective teaching is the contractual, ethical, social responsibility of everyone who works with students at any level. Further, the practicum should provide an opportunity for most teaching assistants to develop a commitment to "scholarly teaching," which Lee Shulman, president of the Carnegie Foundation for the Advancement of Teaching, defines as "teaching that is well grounded in the sources and resources appropriate to the field" (49). Additionally, the practicum should encourage many teaching assistants to engage in the "scholarship of teaching and learning," which Shulman defines as that which occurs "when our work as teachers becomes public, peer-reviewed and critiqued, and exchanged with other members of our professional communities so they, in turn, can build on our work. These are the qualities of all scholarship" (49).

Furthermore, the practicum should equip teaching assistants with the tools for evaluating their work as teachers *and* in the three other arenas of scholarship that Boyer defines. Glassick, Huber, and Maeroff provide such tools in *Scholarship Assessed*. In particular, they offer six powerful criteria for evaluating all four kinds of scholarly work in the academy: (1) clear goals, (2) adequate preparation, (3) appropriate methods, (4) significant results, (5) effective presentation, and (6) reflective critique. Table 4.1 presents some of the questions that each of these criteria and each of the four scholarly activities suggests.

These questions are not exhaustive. Rather, they are meant to suggest the kinds of thinking that can guide teaching assistants' work throughout their careers in the academy. Teaching assistants will continue to develop professionally throughout their lives in academe if we encourage them to view their work through the aforementioned lenses. Such perspectives also benefit teaching assistants' students, as well as their departments, colleges, institutions, disciplines, and the community.

In addition, the criteria and model for assessment that we offer should not be limiting. These categories and questions can manifest themselves in many ways and lead to multiple paths for rethinking how we teach the composition practicum, how we characterize the practice of teaching writing, and how we assess what we do. In the remainder of this chapter, we offer some practical suggestions for designing a composition practicum that

TABLE 4.1. Example Questions Suggested by Boyer's Four Categories of Scholarship and Glassick, Huber, and Maeroff's Six Criteria for Assessing Scholarship

	Discovery	Application/Teaching	Engagement	Integration
Clear Goals	How will my research or creative activity add something of value to the discipline?	How can I apply my disciplinary knowledge and skills to solve consequential problems?	How can I draw on other disciplines to enhance my skills and knowledge?	How can I maximize student learning and continuously improve my teaching?
Adequate Preparation	What skills and knowledge do I need to acquire or develop to do research or creative activity most effectively?	What skills and knowledge do I need to acquire or develop to most effectively solve consequential problems?	What interdisciplinary skills and knowledge do I need to acquire or develop to more effectively solve consequential problems?	What teaching skills and knowledge do I need to acquire or develop to maximize student learning and continuously improve my teaching?
Appropriate Methods	From among all my sets of skills and knowledge, which ones are most appropriate for the research or creative activity that I wish to pursue?	From among all my sets of skills and knowledge, which ones are most appropriate for solving the problems that I have identified?	From among all my sets of interdisciplinary skills and knowledge, which ones are most appropriate for solving the problems that I have identified?	From among all my sets of teaching skills and knowledge, which ones are most appropriate for enhancing student learning and improving my teaching in this course?
Significant Results	What counts as an important contribution to my field?	What constitutes a solution to a consequential problem?	What constitutes a solution to a consequential problem?	What kinds of learning are important for my students?

continued on next page

Table 4.1 continued

	Discovery	Application/Teaching	Engagement	Integration
Effective Presentation	How can I most effectively write this research report or short story?	How can I explain this solution so that it will be useful to those who can benefit from it?	How can I explain this solution so that it will be useful to those who can benefit from it?	How can I interact with students (e.g., lecture, discussion, online chat) so that they will learn most effectively?
Reflective Critique	How do I know that I have made contributions to my field?	How do I know that I have solved consequential problems?	How do I know that I have solved consequential problems?	How do I know that my students have learned and that I have improved as a teacher?

encourages teaching assistants to value these perspectives and to employ these perspectives in their work.

Part I: Developing the Practicum

Designing and teaching a composition practicum is in itself an opportunity to engage in and model effective teaching, scholarly teaching, and the scholarship of teaching and learning. The act of teaching a composition practicum can be scholarly. We are, for example, engaging in the scholarship of teaching and learning by writing, theorizing, and reflecting on teaching the composition practicum in this volume. As we practice effective teaching, reflect on our teaching, and share the results and lessons learned with our colleagues in our discipline, we model for our graduate students what it means to engage in the scholarship of teaching and learning.

As Glassick, Huber, and Maeroff mention, scholarship often has numerous goals (26), and indeed, the goals of a composition practicum are multiple. The first priority is supporting and preparing first-year teaching assistants so that they and their students experience success in the writing classroom. In addition to this goal, the composition practicum can be designed to encourage teaching assistants to view all of their work in the academy as scholarly, encourage their commitment to that scholarship, and give them tools for evaluating their own work in the four areas of scholarship as defined by Boyer.

The criteria outlined by Glassick, Huber, and Maeroff—clear goals, adequate preparation, appropriate methods, significant results, effective presentation, and reflective critique—offer a useful framework both for developing the composition practicum and for evaluating its overall effectiveness. These criteria are not discrete categories, however; they overlap and intersect and are best used in a holistic manner. They are applicable to all four areas of scholarship (as demonstrated in the previous questions and as discussed later in this chapter), but applying them in the context of the composition practicum can result in an engaging meta-analysis of teaching. We can discuss these criteria with graduate students in the composition practicum as a useful framework for analysis and assessment of their own scholarship while we model using the criteria to reflect on our own practice and also ask graduate students to evaluate the results of the practicum with the criteria.

Using these criteria to design and assess the effectiveness of the composition practicum itself offers the opportunity to engage graduate students in a discussion of *why* they do what they do in the classroom. The suggestions we offer in this chapter for implementing the criteria in a composition practicum are most likely methodologies many of us use already, but the criteria offer a way to segue into a discussion of the theoretical rationale behind our methodologies in the composition practicum and the graduate students' methodologies in their first-year composition classrooms. In other words, designing and evaluating a practicum with these criteria encourages us not simply to model what to do but also to discuss why we do it, giving graduate students the tools to develop their own methodologies in their writing classrooms, to evaluate those methodologies, and to evaluate *our* methodologies in the practicum itself. In this section, we offer suggestions for how these criteria could be used to design a composition practicum.

Clear Goals. As is mentioned earlier, the composition practicum has multiple goals, and these goals shift according to the context of the practicum, the graduate students participating in the practicum, the faculty member teaching the practicum, and the institution in which it is offered. One thing is clear, however—the goals of the practicum itself should be clearly articulated by the teacher(s) to and with the graduate students in the course. In addition, we argue that graduate students should be encouraged to question these goals and to articulate their own goals in the practicum, whether or not they are parallel with the goals of the instructor, especially because graduate students will immediately encounter similar conflicting goals and expectations in the highly political arena of the first-year composition classroom. A discussion of goals could also include a dialogue about the goals of teaching writing in general, opening the opportunity to discuss theories of teaching writing and why certain goals are considered to be important in specific contexts. For an example of multiple perspectives on the goals of first-year composition courses, see the first section of Roen, Pantoja, Yena, Miller, and Waggoner's edited collection *Strategies for Teaching First-Year Composition*. That section, Contexts for Teaching Writing, includes perspectives from diverse faculty and administrators at a range of postsecondary institutions.

Adequate Preparation. When addressing adequate preparation, teachers can begin by questioning whether they are "adequately prepared" to teach the composition practicum. Not all teachers of the composition practicum are trained in the field of rhetoric and composition, and we often come to this field from other disciplines. This opens the door for discussion of the history and context of the first-year composition course itself, the influence of other disciplinary perspectives, and the preparation that writing teachers have historically had (not to mention discussion of how we define and measure *adequacy*). Such a discussion could also include the development of various theories of teaching writing as well as dialogue about whether taking the composition practicum is "adequate preparation" for the teaching of first-year composition.

Appropriate Methods. Teachers of the composition practicum should, of course, model how to choose methods that are appropriate to learning goals, and we should also discuss with graduate students how to make those choices. In addition, we should include a discussion of various methods for and approaches to teaching writing, including those theories and approaches that might not resonate with our own. We can demonstrate that choosing methodologies is a recursive process; we make pedagogical choices, we determine whether those choices were appropriate by assessing the results, and then we revise our pedagogical choices based on what we have learned.

Significant Results. We should also model for graduate students the multiple ways to measure results and examine the various results that can be measured. When assessing the effectiveness of our instruction, we can look at direct measures of learning, students' perceptions of learning, and even our own perceptions of and reflections on what happened in the classroom. We should ask ourselves whether we achieved our original goals for our students' learning and for our own learning and development, encouraging graduate students to ask these questions of themselves.

Effective Presentation. When we teach the composition practicum, we model for graduate students how to effectively communicate and present material to their students. We should ask them to assess the effectiveness of our presentation and to offer feedback for improvement. Also, we can discuss with graduate students other elements of and venues for effective presentation, including presenting the results of the practicum (or first-year composition course) to students, colleagues in the department, and colleagues in the discipline, among others. This discussion offers the opportunity to encourage graduate students to be engaged in other scholarly activities.

Reflective Critique. Finally, we should model in the composition practicum how to engage in reflective critique as an assessment tool. We should engage in self-reflection ourselves, even overtly with the graduate students in the practicum course, and also discuss how we share our work with colleagues and ask for critique. We might even consider having a colleague come into the composition practicum class one day to observe and offer feedback, and we can model what teachers could do with such feedback to improve their own teaching. Finally, we can ask graduate students to participate in reflective critique on the results of the composition practicum, offering suggestions for improvement and critiquing their own scholarly activity in the class.

Part II: After the Practicum

Just as these criteria offer a useful lens through which to view and effectively assess the outcomes of a composition practicum, they also serve as a framework for modeling how teaching assistants might structure their own courses. As teaching assistants reap the benefits of their first TA practicum for immediate use in their first-year composition classes, they can also continue to develop and refine their methodology for designing effective courses and refining their teaching methods once they are teaching classes on a more independent basis. The criteria described by Glassick, Huber, and Maeroff can provide graduate teaching assistants a model with which to continue enhancing their teaching, especially if the framework is discussed and modeled within the practicum itself. As described in the previous section, the criteria—clear goals, adequate preparation, appropriate methods, significant results, effective presentation, and reflective critique—can be implemented in multiple ways for meta-analysis about teaching and for introduction into the scholarship of academic work. In most cases, first-time graduate teaching assistants of first-year composition are given a syllabus to use; however, once those teachers are teaching more independently, lessons learned from their practicum truly come into play. The criteria can be adapted on a more fundamental level to structure courses and develop syllabi with a focus on scholarly teaching and the scholarship of teaching and learning.

Clear Goals. Designating clear goals not only allows teachers to construct more effective syllabi, but it also encourages teachers to determine what their overall purposes are in teaching. Understanding what's possible in their own courses is important to ensure student success, as well as in determining how learning is assessed and represented. Explicitly stating goals in a syllabus can also be important for students as they work toward your goals with a clearer understanding of the sequence of assignments and activities that work in concert with the intended final goals of the course.

In addition, understanding and stating clear goals entails recognizing the context of the course within the department, the college, the institution, and the local area, even beginning to recognize that the instructor's own personal context in relation to the course changes over time. Staying aware of the course context can help a teacher maintain scholarly attention to the subject matter and his or her teaching methods.

Adequate Preparation. Just as leaders of a composition practicum should be well versed in theories of teaching and learning as well as in the various theories of teaching writing, so too should new teachers assess their own skills and knowledge regarding the topic/issue of their courses, no matter the subject matter. Adequately prepared teachers know their content and know the most effective ways of presenting information to students, reflecting the interconnectedness of the criteria. Adequate preparation also involves continuing to keep up-to-date with current pedagogical methods and participating in scholarly discussions about teaching and learning.

Appropriate Methods. Combining clear goals and adequate preparation encourages teachers to seek out the appropriate methods to achieve their learning goals in the development and design of the course. Teachers should consider the various pedagogical methods available to them, including the various forms of active, cooperative, and computer-assisted learning strategies. Seeking out the appropriate methods also suggests that teachers should be able to adjust their pedagogical approaches as they need to.

Significant Results. When designing a course and syllabus, teachers will also make choices about the most effective methods for asking students to demonstrate their learning. Just as teachers have many pedagogical choices for presenting information, so do they have many choices in determining and assessing student learning. Again, keeping in mind the context, assignments, and pedagogical approaches used in the course, teachers can best determine the most appropriate ways to ask students to demonstrate significant results in their learning. Moreover, teachers maintaining a scholarly approach to teaching can gauge student success to continue revising and developing their pedagogy.

Effective Presentation. Effective presentation of course and syllabus design entails an awareness of the audience, the students in the course. What methods has the teacher employed to focus on his or her students effectively? Even if goals are in place and methods are explored and carefully chosen, students may not be reached if the presentation of information is not in line with student needs. Furthermore, effective presentation of teaching methods is important in a teacher's scholarly development. One way of illustrating effective presentation is through a teaching portfolio (or professional portfolio) that highlights innovative strategies and activities. In some employment opportunities, a teaching portfolio is crucial. Other ways to ensure effective presentation are through attending and presenting at conferences, participating in professional e-mail listservs, making presentations at the institution's center for faculty development, and conducting and participating in peer reviews with fellow teachers.

Reflective Critique. As teachers are asked to reflect on their own teaching and learning both in a practicum and as teachers, so too should they ask students to reflect on their own learning. Space should be made in a course and syllabus for students to engage in reflective critique of their own work. Asking students to assemble a portfolio of their work is one way to encourage reflection; the process itself is a chance for students to think about their writing and what changes they've made. Students could also be asked to share their critiques with one another or conduct peer reviews. Finally, students' critique of the course provides material with which to work through the assessment criteria again, starting with revised, clearer goals for the next section of students.

Part III: The Well-Rounded Professional Scholar

As demonstrated, Glassick, Huber, and Maeroff's assessment criteria not only help teachers participate in the scholarship of teaching and learning but also facilitate a critical attention to professional development as teachers. If we follow their original intent, the six assessment criteria developed by Glassick, Huber, and Maeroff also work to document other scholarly activities: discovery and integration (research) and application (service).

    Novice scholars benefit greatly from conducting all scholarly activities in a systematic and well-documented manner. Setting clear goals for, adequately preparing for, applying appropriate methods to, achieving significant results from, effectively presenting on, and reflectively critiquing research and service activities not only demonstrates professionalism and prepares for outside evaluation, but it also ensures growth and improvement. For many novice scholars, it is a challenge to think outside of the required graduate program of study. Working through the assessment criteria can help them to see the bigger picture of their scholarship and discipline(arity). Shulman calls for a scholar's lifelong commitment to individual scholarly "improvement" as well as "significant improvements" to the activities in which the scholarly assessment is being performed (49). In other words, critically assessing one's research and other scholarly activities already functions as a professional development opportunity, as Schön claims in *Educating the Reflective Practitioner*.

Although it appears that the scholarship of discovery, traditionally referred to as research, already has a well-developed method of assessment, peer review, and publication, it is primarily summative assessment—assessment conducted at the conclusion of the activity. By also including Glassick, Huber, and Maeroff's first three criteria of assessment (understanding goals, preparing, and applying appropriate methods), researchers also would begin to conduct formative assessment that would allow for a more robust research process. Explicitly articulating, sharing, and possibly revising research goals and methods as well as dialoguing with other members of the discipline about them as a form of research preparation, *before* conducting research itself, builds robust assessment and revision activities into the research activity early. Clearly this is already recognized as a professional development activity for beginning researchers in the academy because it parallels the thesis/dissertation proposal process. Ideally, researchers would make all six assessment criteria explicit throughout their research process, throughout their career.

Research does have a well-developed example of Glassick, Huber, and Maeroff's sixth assessment criteria of reflective critique: publishing. Since publishing is one of the areas that most graduate students are just beginning (equivalent to their position as new teachers in the TA practicum), helping them to understand their publication practices as explicit social reflection and research assessment gives them an edge in the publication process. In "Making the Gesture: Graduate Student Submissions and the

Expectations of Journal Referees," Richard McNabb claims that it is exactly this connection to the broader scholarship of the discipline as a whole that makes graduate student journal submissions stand out to journal referees. In other words, graduate student journal submissions need the explicit "social reflection" section that connects their work to other works and researchers in the discipline. Ultimately, it is also this explicit reflection that allows scholars to make meaningful connections between Boyer's four scholarly activities.

And whereas research activities have always had some of Glassick, Huber, and Maeroff's assessment criteria built into the academic process, and the current trend in making teaching scholarly has associated many of their assessment categories with teaching, not much has been published to suggest the systematic assessment of service beyond Ernest Lynton's *Making the Case for Professional Service*, a critical work on scholarly service. Like teaching and research, scholarly service—service related to the scholar's research, not institutional or civic service—can incorporate Glassick, Huber, and Maeroff's assessment criteria to construct a more meaningful and scholarly rich service experience. One space, outside of the TA practicum, to introduce the concept of scholarly service is in the graduate research methods course. Having students consider the design, development, and assessment of research-related service projects while also designing, developing, and assessing their research projects would engage them in the clear goals and reflective critique categories of scholarly service assessment. Some graduate programs might also include service learning and graduate assistant administrative positions as a chance for graduate students to develop their scholarly service skills. Presenting Glassick, Huber, and Maeroff's assessment criteria as applicable and useful in service activities not only allows graduate students to consider themselves as scholar citizens, but it also prepares them to present and publish their service activities in a detailed, scholarly manner.

In "From Minsk to Pinsk: Why a Scholarship of Teaching and Learning?," Shulman states that teachers should pursue teaching and learning as a scholarly activity for three reasons: professionalism, pragmatism, and policy. Professionalism refers to the "obligations and opportunities" scholars are responsible for as members of a discipline and as educators (49). Most scholars would agree that a more explicitly designed, developed, and publicly accessible assessment process would strengthen their research and teaching. Pragmatism refers to the need for a scholar's work to be "constantly improving and meeting its objectives" (49). Clearly, many institutions design their faculty evaluation plans based on Shulman's idea of pragmatism. Again, preparing new scholars to more explicitly reflect and document their scholarly practices would meet these goals. And, finally, policy refers to the "capacity to respond to the legitimate questions of legislatures [and] boards" (49).

With the current financial crisis of most state and private institutions of higher education, many state legislatures and school government boards are requiring more details on how and why money is being spent. In other words, these governing bodies are asking that faculty members justify (all of) their scholarly practices. Implementing the exploration and application of a systematic assessment system into the TA practicum, and briefly explaining how and why it also applies to research and service, will not only make new teaching assistants better scholars, but it will also prepare them for a more demanding academy.

The composition practicum is an ideal location in which to help beginning scholars make reflective connections between their teaching, research, and service activities. As professional scholars, they will be called on to construct a professional persona that demonstrates a coherent "intellectual quest," as well as to defend their activities as professional work to policymakers—showing how all of their activities intellectually overlap and intersect with one another. By starting the process of assessing and reflecting on all components of their scholarly life early, in the TA practicum, new scholars will have their scholarly persona prepared for their future professional steps beyond the practicum.

Works Cited

Boyer, Ernest L. *Scholarship Reconsidered: Priorities of the Professoriate*. Princeton, NJ: Carnegie Foundation for the Advancement of Teaching, 1990.

Crow, Michael. "Four Guiding Principles Drive Crow's Vision for ASU." *ASU Insight* 13 Sept. 2002: 1, 6.

Glassick, Charles E, Mary Taylor Huber, and Gene I. Maeroff. *Scholarship Assessed: Evaluation of the Professoriate*. San Francisco: Jossey-Bass, 1997.

Lynton, Ernest A. *Making the Case for Professional Service*. Washington, DC: American Association for Higher Education, Forum on Faculty Roles and Rewards, 1995.

McNabb, Richard. "Making the Gesture: Graduate Student Submissions and the Expectations of Journal Referees." *Composition Studies* 29.1 (2001): 9–26.

Roen, Duane, Veronica Pantoja, Lauren Yena, Susan K. Miller, and Eric Waggoner, eds. *Strategies for Teaching First-Year Composition*. Urbana, IL: NCTE, 2002.

Schön, Donald A. *Educating the Reflective Practitioner: Toward a New Design for Teaching and Learning in the Professions*. San Francisco: Jossey-Bass, 1987.

Shulman, Lee. "From Minsk to Pinsk: Why a Scholarship of Teaching and Learning?" *The Journal of Scholarship of Teaching and Learning (JoSoTL)* 1.1 (2000): 48–53. 22 Aug. 2003 <http://www.iusb.edu/~josotl/Vol1No1/shulman.pdf>.

CHAPTER FIVE

Plug and Play: Technology and Mentoring Teachers of Writing

SAMANTHA BLACKMON AND SHIRLEY K. ROSE
Purdue University

I n this chapter, we discuss the ways in which the development of our technology integration mentoring for instructors in our first-year writing program has exposed, intensified, or revived underlying and persistent issues and concerns in our mentoring program more generally. For many years, the Department of English at Purdue University has offered a nationally recognized and admired mentoring program for new teaching assistants in its introductory writing program. The design and evolution of this mentoring program has been described elsewhere (Weiser), so we describe the program only briefly in this chapter.

We do provide here a more detailed history of our mentoring program for instructors teaching with computers, a program that has evolved from informal support for a few self-selected instructors beginning in the early 1990s to a formal required mentoring program for all new instructors in the fall of 2003. The evolution of this mentoring program has paralleled the increasing integration of digital composing into the first-year writing curriculum. Beginning in fall 2003, all sections of our new four-credit first-year composition course meet in a computer classroom once a week.

The focus of this chapter is a discussion of the ways in which the new challenges of technology mentoring have raised old concerns that have never been satisfactorily resolved for our mentoring program in general. These older concerns reemerge with a new intensity as we design, develop, and deliver our "tech mentoring" program. In addition, these problems are exacerbated by a comparative lack of pedagogical scholarship and research on preparing composition teachers to integrate technology into their teaching modes and curricular approaches. Most of our incoming TAs are members of a generation that has had little formal experience with learning to use new computer technologies. They want computers to be a "plug and play" element of their classrooms and long for "techie angels" on their shoulders to solve problems and answer questions when and if—and *only* if—they arise. No legitimate formal mentoring program, focused on pedagogy and scholarship, can successfully meet either of these needs. We know this. But there is so much we don't yet know about how writers learn to use new digital composing technologies effectively and critically. Scholarship and research on preparing composition teachers to integrate digital composing technologies into their teaching modes and curricular approaches are only very recent developments in the centuries-long tradition of pedagogical inquiry.

This chapter examines the possible movement from the practicum to the *praxicum* (the practical application of a course of study that is informed by theory) in the context of an exploration of the need for a theoretical component for technology mentoring. We hope this exploration will help us move beyond the idea that anyone can teach writing without training and theoretical grounding and the notion that anyone who knows how to teach writing and how to use a computer can teach writing in the computer-mediated classroom. In the process, we examine how the field of computers and writing (C&W) differs from traditional rhetoric and composition (R&C) rather than being simply another technological plug-in that upgrades rhetoric and composition to a new "cutting edge" version of a preexisting set of knowledges.

A Brief History of Mentoring for FYC Instructors at Purdue University

The English department at Purdue has provided formal mentoring for graduate teaching assistants since at least as early as the 1960s (see Weiser for a more detailed sketch of the history of the mentoring program). Though the design of the mentoring program has evolved over the years, one feature has remained constant: teaching assistants are mentored during their first year of teaching in any of the department's instructional programs. Graduate teaching assistantships are awarded to students in all of the graduate programs offered by the department: literature, linguistics, creative writing, theory and cultural studies, and rhetoric and composition. Except for those courses exclusively for students in the department's undergraduate majors, TAs teach introductory courses in all areas of the department's undergraduate curriculum: literature, creative writing, linguistics, professional writing, English as a Second Language, and first-year composition (FYC).[1] When TAs teach a course for the first time in any of these programs, they receive formal mentoring. Given the staffing needs of our FYC program (around 6,000 students in academic year 2003–04), it's necessary for as many TAs as possible to be qualified and available to teach in the program. Therefore, in their first year as graduate teaching assistants in the department, TAs teach in the first-year composition program, and their first year of mentoring focuses on teaching composition.

For their mentoring in teaching FYC, graduate teaching assistants are assigned to "mentoring groups" made up of a mentor and six to nine first-year TAs (the size of the group depends on the number of new TAs and the number of available qualified mentors). With the exception of the rhetoric and composition graduate students, who are all assigned to the same group, new TAs are assigned to mentor groups based on their teaching experience, academic backgrounds,[2] or teaching interests[3] rather than on the areas of emphasis for their own graduate study.

TAs who are being mentored enroll in English 505A and 505B, Approaches to Teaching College English: Teaching Introductory Composition, a two-semester sequence that extends from the fall through the spring semesters of their first year of teaching in the department. Initially, English 505A and 505B were one-credit courses designed as practica; typically, the mentoring groups met for seventy-five minutes each week at a mutually convenient time arranged by group members and mentors. In 1998, 505A and 505B became three-credit courses in recognition that the mentoring was involving increasingly more attention to and explicit discussion of theory, which often required the mentees to complete extensive outside reading and writing assignments; at about that same time, the course began to be regularly scheduled for two seventy-five-minute meetings a week, with all mentoring groups meeting at the same time, though in separate sections.

Over the years, mentors have been drawn primarily from the full-time faculty. Before the department offered a graduate program in rhetoric and composition, the mentors were faculty from a variety of areas in English studies. After the establishment of the PhD program in rhetoric and composition in 1981 and the subsequent increase over time in the number of R&C specialists among the department faculty, however, mentoring assignments[4] were given almost exclusively to R&C faculty. In the last few years, some mentoring positions in the department's undergraduate writing programs (first-year composition, ESL writing, professional writing) have been filled by advanced PhD students (ABDs) in rhetoric and composition when faculty were unavailable due to leaves, retirements, or assignment to required graduate courses.[5]

Other details about the design and history of the mentoring program will emerge in the following discussion, but this brief history describes two interdependent developments: an increasing emphasis on composition theory in the mentoring course and an evolution in the definition of mentor qualifications from general teaching expertise to increased disciplinary specialization. TAs teaching in FYC, regardless of their own area of graduate studies, are mentored by teachers with long-term professional interests and commitments and highly developed disciplinary expertise in composition and rhetoric. Though these developments are, without reservation, ones we have worked for and welcomed, they have not occurred without conflict, as the following section briefly explains.

Old Problems

It is difficult to convey to new GTAs the importance of the formal course in which the mentoring is provided when the course credit does not count toward graduate degree requirement and students are graded on a "Satisfactory/Unsatisfactory" basis. The department faculty as a whole holds the mentoring program in high regard and recognizes the important contribution it makes to our graduate students' professional development and preparation for academic careers. Yet most faculty do not consider learning to teach an essential element of study for an advanced degree in English, and they are reluctant to allow credit for the course to fulfill degree requirements. When graduate students have to set priorities, earning high grades in courses that count toward completion of their degrees will usually take precedence over earning a "satisfactory" mark in a course that does not.

Though the 505A & B mentoring course has been theoretically grounded and had a strong explicit theoretical component for many years now, it was offered under the rubric of a one-credit "practicum" until relatively recently. As a result, perceptions of the course as practice oriented persist in the department's cultural memory. Add to this the department faculty's awareness that graduate teaching assistants need practical guidance in their teaching, and it's easy enough to understand why they would expect the mentoring course to provide it.

The diversity of quality and extent of previous teaching preparation and experience among teaching assistants who are participating in the mentoring program always presents challenges to those designing and teaching the mentoring courses. Usually it is impossible to assign mentoring group membership on the basis of previous teaching experience alone, and as a result a group may include both an MA student who has never taught before and has had no previous formal preparation for teaching and a PhD student who has two or more years of experience and as much as a year of formal course work in teaching composition. Both need mentoring in teaching introductory composition at Purdue, but their needs are not the same.

Designing and teaching the mentoring course is also made problematic by the diversity of the long-term professional, disciplinary, and intellectual interests in composition pedagogies among teaching assistants in the mentoring program. Only roughly one in five TAs is a student in the graduate rhetoric and composition program; for the remainder, learning composition theory is often not compatible with their strongest intellectual interests and does not self-evidently contribute to their development of disciplinary expertise. Many of the TAs do not expect to teach composition again once they graduate, so they do not see their work in the composition program as a contribution to their long-term professional development. Though their expectations may not in fact be met if and when they do become full-fledged career academics, their expectations are confirmed for the time being by their observations that full-time faculty in the department teach composition only rarely if ever.

A Detailed History of Mentoring FYC Instructors Teaching with Computers

In 1991 the department began offering a few sections of FYC in computer-equipped classrooms taught by experienced instructors who made a special request that their classes be taught in this environment. By 1996, enough students and instructors were requesting "C" sections of our FYC courses to justify offering mentoring in teaching FYC with computers, and the department offered English 505I, Approaches to Teaching College English: Teaching Composition with Computers. From this time until the 2003–04 academic year, continuing TAs who taught in computer-equipped classrooms were required to participate in a semester of mentoring that addressed the theoretical and practical issues of integrating technology into teaching writing. The mentors who taught 505I were all advanced PhD students in rhetoric and composition with experience, expertise, and long-term professional interest in the study of computers and composition. The TAs who elected to enroll in 505I for mentoring in teaching with computers came from all of the graduate programs in the department.

For the first time, in 1998, in addition to 505I for continuing TAs, we offered a first-year composition mentoring (505A and 505B) group with a teaching-with-computers focus for new TAs who indicated an interest in teaching in computer-equipped classrooms. These sections of 505A and 505B have been taught either by advanced graduate students or by a faculty member specializing in computers and composition.

As a result of this development of experience, expertise, and theoretical interests in teaching composition with computers in the first-year composition program, by 1999, when we began to plan for a major curricular revision in the FYC program, the new design called for all sections of FYC to meet once a week in computer-equipped classrooms. Furthermore, the "Goals, Means, and Outcomes" statement developed for the new FYC course explicitly identified helping students to "develop effective and efficient processes for writing by providing practice with planning, drafting, revising, and editing their writing in multiple genres using a variety of media" as a course goal; "[c]ompletion of textual interpretation and production assignments in a variety of genres and a variety of media, including print, computer-mediated, and mass media" and "[w]eekly in-class instruction in using computers to compose" as shared means; and knowing "how to use commonplace software to create visuals that effectively make or support arguments" as a shared outcome for all sections of the course.

In the spring of 2003, in anticipation of implementing the new first-year composition curriculum in the fall 2003 semester, we offered supplemental technology workshops for all first-year composition instructors. Though this mentoring program was formal, it was not required and it was not offered under an "English 505" rubric. Now, mentoring for our first-year teaching assistants in fall 2003 (the time at which we write) consists of 505A and 505B supplemented by weekly technology workshops that are currently being led by PhD candidates who have identified C&W as an area of specialization.[6] Participation in these workshops is required, except on the rare occasions when 505A and B mentors reserve this time slot for their own use due to their group's special needs.

As this history suggests, we have at least two significant narratives of the development of computers in composition within our program: (1) the narrative of our FYC and R&C graduate program's contributions to developing computers and composition theory and practice as a discipline, which constructs C&W as an area of special expertise; and (2) the narrative of increasingly wider and deeper practice of teaching with computers required across the program, which constructs the integration of digital composing technologies into teaching composition as something anyone can learn to do because everyone must learn to do it. It is difficult to maintain the integrity of C&W as an area of special disciplinary expertise and simultaneously support adoption of digital composing technologies by nonexperts without seeming to advocate a "banking" model of education for computer literacy instruction. Likewise, it's difficult to require a large group of instructors with diverse experience, expertise, and interests to learn to integrate digital composing technologies into their teaching without seeming to be failing to acknowledge that C&W (like R&C itself) is an area of specialty that must be studied and researched in order to be done effectively.

We now find ourselves at a critical juncture in defining (at least contingently) both the purpose of the formal program of mentoring in teaching with computers and our expectations for teaching with computers by a very large (140 instructors) and diverse group of teachers. For the time being, we have developed a statement of technology goals for the academic year that distinguishes between

- ◆ Practices we will provide formal instruction in and require of all instructors
- ◆ Practices we encourage and provide instruction in but do not require for all instructors
- ◆ Practices we will provide programmatic support for without providing formal instruction

Simply put, the purpose of the technology mentoring is to help program instructors meet the program's goals for technology integration. But, of course, it's not that simple. The process of developing the specific design and content of the technology mentoring and of coordinating that mentoring with the existing FYC mentoring program has forced us first to articulate and then to choose among three competing models for integrating new technologies into teaching composition:

Model 1: an informed, theorized, and clearly articulated technology mentoring curriculum for composition instructors underlies and determines the integration of new composing technologies in the composition curriculum these instructors teach.

Model 2: an informed, theorized, and clearly articulated composition curriculum that integrates new composing technologies underlies and determines the technology mentoring curriculum for the instructors who teach that composition curriculum.

Model 3: the technology mentoring curriculum and the first-year composition curriculum are interdependent, reciprocally determined, and constrained by material, ideological, and political elements of the local institutional culture.

In the process of identifying these initial goals for integrating technology, developing this contingent definition of the purpose of the technology mentoring for program instructors, and articulating and choosing between these models for integrating technology into teaching composition, we have been forced to acknowledge old problems in our mentoring program that have not yet been resolved, though we may, in some cases, have found ways to ignore them. In the following section, we describe some of the circumstances that have exposed again for us the potential for conflict between three important goals for the program in introductory composition at Purdue:

1. To provide a coherent composition curriculum for our first-year students

2. To provide theoretically sound preparation to teach for graduate students who are pursuing a variety of professional goals

3. To provide a locus and site for research and innovation in teaching composition for faculty and graduate students with a long-term disciplinary and professional commitment to the field of rhetoric and composition studies

New Challenges

Conveying the importance of formal mentoring for our graduate teaching assistants continues to be a daunting task on many levels, despite our long history of developing the mentoring program and the involvement of a large number of faculty in the effort. Some teachers still don't recognize the importance of the traditional mentoring, reasoning that everyone in the program can write and therefore should be able to "teach writing." In a similar line of thinking, teaching writing with technology (or computer-mediated composition [CMC]) is seen as something that writing teachers don't need to be mentored in because they already write using technology (such as word processors), and for that reason they are capable of teaching others to write using these technologies.

The perception that any writer can teach writing (and subsequently teach writing with computers) is widely held across the university and is apparent in the level of technological support for development and training that computers and writing programs receive from the university. While formulating support programs for our TAs who were to be teaching English 106, we were approached by Instructional Computing Services (ICS) about helping with technology integration. ICS agreed to do a series of weekly hands-on workshops that followed the pedagogically and theoretically based workshops designed and conducted by C&W faculty and graduate students. Planning for and conducting these workshops led to disagreements over pedagogical practices and which software applications should be used in the computerized writing classroom. These disagreements, along with some apparent confusion about the scheduling of these workshops,[7] led us to refashion the organized ICS workshops into open office hours for the instructional staff in Introductory Composition at Purdue (ICaP).

This lack of understanding on the parts of ICS and non–rhetoric and composition instructional staff demonstrates the lack of understanding and/or acknowledgment of the body of theory that we, as computers and writing teachers, use in the computerized writing classroom. It is this lack that leads to the assumption that anyone who knows how to write and use computers can dictate best pedagogical practices for writing teachers. In the case of ICS departments on campuses, this assumption, coupled with the fact that they are positioned as the resident "experts" (and don't seem eager to share that title), leads to a struggle over the domain of technology.

Similar issues of expertise and responsibility are present in the mentoring program within the English department. In the same way that IT professionals on campus are reevaluating their responsibilities, so are technology mentors in ICaP. The integration of technology into the writing curriculum has us questioning the necessary qualifications of future mentors. Currently, mentoring is done jointly by faculty members and graduate students, with mentoring in the integration of technology in the classroom being done by a faculty member who specializes in computers and writing and graduate students who have a focus in digital rhetorics. We are currently formulating future designs for the mentoring program. With a limited number of faculty members who specialize in computers and writing, future iterations of the mentoring program will have to take one of two forms. The first would continue to separate "traditional" composition mentoring from computers and writing mentoring and continue to utilize graduate students for the technology mentoring. The second would merge the traditional and the technology praxica, which would require using only mentors well versed in both traditional composition pedagogy and C&W pedagogy and also require a heavier reliance on graduate teaching assistants to run the praxica. While this would be a great opportunity for the graduate student mentors in terms of professionalization, it would be a great burden in terms of responsibility and could also raise questions of expertise and the status of the mentoring program as a whole because of the lack of professorial participation in the program.

While dealing with the perceptions and arguments of ICS and instructional staff members about the lack of necessity for technology mentoring, and mentoring in general, we are also faced with justifying the need for separate technology mentoring for the new and continuing instructional staff who must be mentored. While there are several different groups of people who must be mentored to teach writing (MA and PhD R&C students, lecturers, and graduate students in other programs in the English department and other departments and programs), they tend to react to the mentoring in different ways for different reasons.

As might be expected, students at different stages of their graduate school careers and in different disciplines react differently to the mentoring program here at Purdue. Students who have never taught before often are more receptive to the mentoring process because they are unsure of themselves as teachers and they want to know the theory behind what they are doing in the classroom. Typically, the younger students in this group who are familiar with computers are most interested in learning how to effectively integrate this technology into their teaching. There seems to be a direct correlation between a lack of familiarity with computers and a lack of interest in learning to teach with technology.

When graduate students are coming to traditional R&C theory and C&W theory for the first time simultaneously, they tend to see the two bodies of theory as being in conversation with each other rather than being two different and divergent bodies of theory they are being asked to learn. Many advanced rhetoric and composition students, regardless of whether they have taught before, seem to be less receptive to technology mentoring specifically because most of them already have some basic knowledge of traditional R&C theory. In these cases, the students see technology mentoring, and the theory that accompanies it, as being an additional burden. Unless they have identified an interest in digital rhetoric as a secondary area of study for their graduate work, they may see technology mentoring as a mandated (but not necessary) evil that must be tolerated at best if they wish to teach composition in our department.

Separate from these aforementioned students are a few who are teaching FYC only because it is a requirement if they are to teach courses in their discipline in the future. For them, R&C theory in general, and C&W theory in particular, is seen as being useless. Some of them do not see themselves ever teaching FYC again and have no real interest in doing any more than is necessary to demonstrate that they will be able to effectively teach other non-composition courses in subsequent years.[8]

New Challenges and Old Problems

As the preceding section demonstrates, these new challenges bear a striking resemblance to the old problems:

1. It is difficult to convey the importance of formal mentoring for effective integration of technology into teaching and learning composition to instructors who have developed many of their own computing skills and abilities informally.

2. It is difficult to persuade participants in technology mentoring to explore the theoretical issues surrounding the integration of

technology into their teaching of composition when they have not yet mastered the "nuts and bolts" of the technology.

3. It is difficult to meet the needs of technology mentoring participants who have a wide developmental range of computing skills and experience.

4. It is difficult to tailor theoretical discussions of the pedagogical implications of new technologies to fit the diverse intellectual and professional interests of participants, to demonstrate that learning to teach with technology can be valuable to GTAs in programs other than R&C.

Table 5.1 details the resemblances between the old and the new challenges. We haven't solved the old problems yet, but these new challenges have given us an opportunity to approach those problems again with some fresh insights. We are learning to put our focus on our inquiry; that is, to view the practicum as a praxicum—a site for research.

The praxicum as a site for research has already begun to present us with rich opportunities. The students in Samantha's English 605: Computers in Language and Rhetoric course decided to take on social action projects as their group midterm project. Based on the challenges that they see currently being faced by the program in Introductory Composition at Purdue in terms of mentoring, classroom space, and the rumor of the requirement of standardized course management software, the students chose to do proj-

TABLE 5.1 Resemblances between Old Problems and New Challenges

Old Problems: Attitudes toward Composition Mentoring	New Challenges: Attitudes toward Technology Mentoring
I can write, therefore I can teach writing.	I can use technology, therefore I can teach the use of technology.
I need practical advice on teaching, not theory.	I need lessons in the technology, not theory.
I already know this/This is too much too fast.	I already know how to do this/This is too much too fast.
I don't plan to teach writing long term.	I won't use these technologies if I teach other courses.

ects that could effect change within the program. These projects included a usability study of WebCT course management software, a grant proposal for computer classroom spaces that are more conducive to learning in humanities classrooms rather than simply being computer labs, a proposal for connecting work done in online writing labs to work done in computerized writing classrooms, and a project that looked at the ethics and possibilities of online documentation for scholarly and pedagogical purposes. As the focus of this graduate course is traditionally more theoretical than pedagogical, it seems to be no small coincidence that during this period of transition from the old first-year composition sequence to the new FYC course all of the group projects from this semester were pedagogically centered. In this case, the idea of the praxicum has extended itself beyond first-year composition and graduate teaching assistant mentoring and into the scholarship of the broader graduate student population.

As we give ourselves—program directors, mentors, and instructors—the freedom to try new approaches and judge for ourselves how well they work, we also take on the responsibility of accounting for these trials to one another and to our colleagues at other institutions who may recognize their own problems in this description of ours. This chapter is a contribution to that accounting. While we recognize that we do have an established mentoring program in place, we also recognize that as our understanding develops and as technology evolves, our mentoring program will evolve as well.

Notes

1. TAs may also receive teaching assignments as tutors in the Purdue Writing Lab.

2. For several years, for example, we have grouped international TAs together.

3. Some groups, for instance, have focused on feminist pedagogies or cultural studies pedagogies.

4. Since the mentoring program is offered through a formal course, an assignment to mentor is equivalent to any other course assignment.

5. For the current academic year, for example, three of five mentors for 505A and B are advanced graduate students. Next year, we anticipate that all but one of the mentors will be tenured or tenure-track rhetoric and composition faculty.

6. Students in the PhD program in rhetoric and composition at Purdue who select "digital rhetorics" as a secondary area of study complete four courses related to this emphasis.

7. The missed workshops seem to have been caused by the recent reorganization of the information technology departments. In 2001 the Purdue University Computing Center (PUCC) was reorganized to better serve the computing needs of the university instructional staff and student population. The reorganization of PUCC resulted in the formation of ICS, which serves instructional faculty; Instructional Technology at Purdue (ITaP), which deals primarily with hardware and software issues; and the Digital Learning Collaboratory (DLC), which primarily provides high-end computer equipment and training for students. With the reformation of technological services here at Purdue, there seems to be some confusion about which department handles what, because of the overlap of duties and because many of the employees are still becoming accustomed to their new responsibilities.

8. Here we do not mean to suggest that these things are true of all graduate students in the specified categories, but rather to generalize about the attitudes we have observed in our experience of mentoring incoming graduate teaching assistants at Purdue. On the contrary, we have met and mentored many TAs in a variety of disciplines (literature, R&C, C&W, and education) who were committed to being the best FYC teachers they could be.

Work Cited

Weiser, Irwin. "When Teaching Assistants Teach Teaching Assistants to Teach: A Historical View of a Teacher Preparation Program." *Preparing College Teachers of Writing: Histories, Theories, Programs, Practices.* Ed. Betty P. Pytlik and Sarah Liggett. New York: Oxford UP, 2002. 40–49.

CHAPTER SIX

Unraveling Generative Tensions in the Composition Practicum

KELLY BELANGER
Virginia Polytechnic Institute and State University

SIBYLLE GRUBER
Northern Arizona University

Unlike a typical graduate seminar, the composition practicum functions within a larger ecology of writing program concerns that call for the instructor's attention, particularly when that instructor is also the writing program administrator.[1] During conversations in the spring of 2003,[2] we reflected on teaching the composition practicum and on our roles as administrators, teachers, and researchers. While we identified shared concerns, we were also aware that we faced vastly different dilemmas emerging from localized stories about the writing programs at Northern Arizona University (NAU) and University of Wyoming (UW).[3] For Kelly, tensions emerged from teaching the composition methods course while building UW's writing program within a literary studies–focused English department. The department's ongoing but fitful process of professionalizing the WPA position initially placed the WPA–practicum instructor in the contradictory position of building and promoting a new program (with all the concomitant messiness) while exposing GTAs to a range of other theoretical and practical possibilities that call into question aspects of the developing program. Sibylle, too, serves as both WPA and practicum instructor, but in contrast to Kelly's situation, she rotates with writing studies colleagues as director of an established university writing program in a department with a successful graduate program in rhetoric. In her first years as WPA and practicum instructor, her major tensions emerged from conflicts between theories of composition and literacy studies and the practices of administering a large writing program with a standardized curriculum. Considered together, our experiences teaching the composition practicum represent a range of dilemmas common to WPAs working within English departments. In this chapter, we address the many and often competing challenges that we have experienced as composition practicum teachers, drawing on our localized experiences as tenured WPAs to consider the practicum as a generative organizational site where tensions in a writing program can be foregrounded, examined, and transformed into opportunities for insight and curricular improvement.

Initially, Kelly conducted case study research in Sibylle's practicum course to look closely at students' perspectives on the usefulness of the practicum for teaching English 105, NAU's first-year writing course. She found that GTAs at NAU shared many of the same concerns with their UW counterparts. In both programs, GTAs were deeply committed to being effective teachers, yet many seemed unprepared to wallow in the complexities and choices presented by a range of pedagogical theories. When dealing with the daily stresses and practical concerns inherent in a "new on new" situation, where new graduate teachers are teaching new college students, many of them were simply not ready to embrace added cognitive dissonance related to their teaching. Repeatedly, GTAs described negotiating among often competing identities and allegiances: in addition to their personal lives, they are simultaneously graduate students becoming initiated into disciplinary values of their chosen areas of English studies, teachers with their own (often tacit) pedagogical philosophies, and employees who work within a larger programmatic context.

Kelly's findings started a conversation about GTA's positions and our own positions within and outside our institutions, our conflicting identities as practitioners and theoreticians, and our fear of suffering permanently from split personality syndrome if we continued to serve as writing program administrators for much longer. We realized that we occupied a position similar to that of our new GTAs, one in which the many expectations that others have of us, and the expectations that we have of ourselves, can put a strain on our professional lives as administrators, teachers, researchers, and students. These expectations profoundly influence how we organize, conduct, and talk about the practicum course; they also affect how GTAs respond to the course and manage their own multiple expectations.

Structures and Contexts for Composition Practica

As Catherine G. Latterell's survey research has shown, the composition practicum takes different forms depending on the context—variously delivered as a course, proseminar, colloquia, series of workshops, or some combination of these formats. At NAU, the writing program administrator teaches English 601: Practicum, a three-hour graded graduate seminar that is intended to train close to forty graduate assistants to teach a one-semester introductory composition course and to tutor in the university writing center. The actual training begins during a two-week orientation session before fall classes start in which GTAs are introduced to the approaches to the composition course, the specific reading and writing assignments, and the incorporation of technological literacy into the course. During the first semester of teaching, every GTA is required to take English 601, which, in addition to training them for the daily aspects of teaching composition, introduces GTAs to various methodological and pedagogical theories and practices that are used to teach writing in an academic setting. The course, taught by the WPA, is designed to help GTAs develop a conceptual framework that allows them to formulate their own philosophy of teaching and to guide their students through the writing process. The course description specifically points to four goals:

- ◆ We will learn about and apply key concepts and philosophies for teaching writing.
- ◆ We will learn about and apply the writing process.
- ◆ We will learn about and apply response and evaluation criteria.
- ◆ We will learn about current issues in writing pedagogy, institutional politics, and identity politics.

These goals show the intended theoretical and practical nature of the course, encouraging GTAs to apply the theoretical principles acquired by reading composition scholars' explorations of writing instruction.

In UW's smaller program, the WPA prepares approximately eight to ten GTAs a year. The GTA education requirements consist of two parts, the first part a one-credit, pass/fail practicum (English 5900) that begins during a weeklong summer colloquium in which students are introduced to a common course syllabus, textbooks, lesson planning, portfolio group grading, and a range of teaching strategies to facilitate common activities such as peer review and one-to-one conferencing. During this time, GTAs also practice teaching sample lessons and receive feedback from the group, which includes several of the second-year GTAs (who are often employed to work on the course curriculum with the WPA in the summer), four faculty mentors who meet with first- and second-year GTAs in groups of four or five throughout the year in an extension of the summer colloquium, and the WPA, who leads monthly grade-norming sessions throughout the year and facilitates the group grading of portfolios. The second of the GTA requirements is a graded, four-credit graduate seminar typically taught by the WPA called the Practical Teaching of English (English 5010). Kelly's fall 2003 course description lists the course's purposes as follows:

> Participants in this seminar will examine connections (and disconnections) between classroom teaching practices and key theories of composition pedagogy, rhetoric, and literacy studies. Goals of the course include these:
>
> ◆ learning practical teaching strategies applicable to teaching English 1010, UW's university-wide first-year composition course
>
> ◆ connecting classroom practices to research and theory
>
> ◆ examining a range of approaches to teaching first-year college writing
>
> ◆ understanding how theoretical currents in composition studies inform the way the program at UW operates
>
> ◆ developing your own philosophy of teaching writing

These goals mirror the major concerns of the NAU practicum/methods course, except that the NAU seminar is also responsible for providing the practical guidance that GTAs at Wyoming typically obtain from the summer colloquium and their weekly English 5900 mentor groups. In effect, then, the GTA course requirements at each of our institutions blend what Latterell's overview of GTA education categorizes as practica, defined as immediate practical support during the first semester of teaching, and teaching methods courses, which present pedagogically focused theory, "immerse GTAs in the language and methods of a program's writing pedagogy," model practices GTAs might use in their own classes, and "imbue GTAs with practical teaching strategies, pedagogical texts, and most of all, a language for talking about teaching from a number of perspectives" (144–46).

Most important, in different ways, both of our programs are or have been what Jeanne Gunner calls "WPA-centric," with the WPA primarily responsible for both the first-year curriculum and the practicum or methods course. Of course, there are some real advantages to this format—the WPA is well informed about the goals and contexts for the first-year curriculum in ways another faculty member might not be. But the complicatedness of the WPA position has been an ongoing concern for both of us: the position requires presenting different sides of ourselves to GTAs, students, colleagues, and administrators, and at local and national conferences. The result can be a persistent sense of conflictedness—being administrators on the one hand with practical concerns foremost in our minds, and theoreticians and researchers on the other hand who might not always agree with the pragmatic solutions we have implemented for the "good" of the program and the institution.

Having experienced the tensions inherent in the dual role of WPA and practicum director, we agree with Gunner's argument that "WPA-centric programs" run the risk of "dispensing authority in a top-heavy fashion, no matter how collaborative or student-centered we seek to make our teaching or administrative styles" (13). As administrators, we want GTAs to follow specific guidelines and to adopt some of the philosophies, methodologies, and theories considered essential for providing a large number of undergraduates with the basic tools for writing in an academic setting. As instructors of the GTA practicum, however, we would like the GTAs to consider a variety of theories and methodologies that would strengthen their skills as teachers of introductory composition. We encourage them to think critically about their own practices and, implicitly, about the practices used in the writing program. As long as we hold the WPA position, however, pragmatics require us to admit that we want GTAs to stay within a specified framework, and that the theories they encounter should only be used if the newly acquired knowledge fits that framework. Do we want them to tell us that they consider our very well-thought-out plan (from the WPA's perspective) in need of an overhaul? In a sense, we are putting GTAs in a no-win situation: we want them to teach what we have established as important, we want them to teach the material using a specific lens, but then we also tell them that we want to make sure—to a limited extent—that the practicum or methods course moves them beyond the framework that we consider suited for the program.

Sometimes initial responses from GTAs and other writing program stakeholders—such as colleagues, department chairs, deans, university presidents, parents, community members—to decisions made by a WPA or practicum instructor may not take into account the multiple discourses that construct the composition practicum. Figure 6.1 illustrates how writing programs are influenced by (and in turn influence) a wide range of sometimes overlapping, sometimes incompatible discourses. Broad influences include disciplinary conversations about composition and rhetorical theory and the growing movement to legitimize writing program administration in U.S. colleges and universities. Just as important are local contexts, needs, and constraints such as diversity or homogeneity of student and GTA populations, GTA selection processes, departmental and institutional committee decisions, or a new English department MFA program.

As a result of these influences, program ideologies often represent compromises forged in efforts to synthesize our own perspectives as WPAs with the ideologies set forth by national political/educational trends (such as the recent and growing focus on assessment), the state or local community with its regional values, and our institutions' upper administrators and trustees (which include

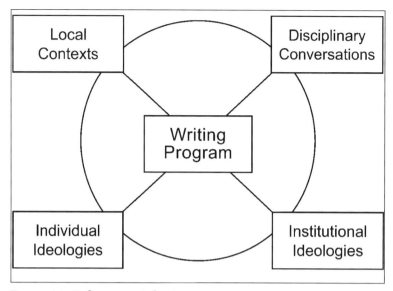

FIGURE **6.1.** *Influences on/of writing programs*

agendas for premier undergraduate and graduate institutions, residential campuses, writing across the curriculum, learning communities, learner-centered education, etc.).

As current and former WPAs, we realize that our concern for coherence and consistency in the first-year writing program tends to subdue or silence other equally compelling discourses despite our intent to provide multiple models of teaching first-year composition in the practicum or methods course. Some disciplinary conversations on composition practica may be subdued because the values they imply or promote just don't fit within practical constraints, the local institutional context, our own areas of interest, or the program's ideology. At the same time, some disciplinary conversations are so foundational to the teaching of writing that their influence on most composition practica seems necessary and inevitable.[4] The sections that follow describe our attempts—working within a developing writing program (UW) and within an established one (NAU), respectively—to understand and address the challenges inherent in teaching a course at the nexus of so many competing concerns.

Tensions in the UW Practicum

As the only tenure-track rhetoric and composition faculty member during her first years at UW, Kelly had to consider how her approach to writing program administration and teaching the practicum course might fit within and/or challenge the expectations of the department and university culture. She was hired as a tenured associate professor to coordinate the composition program with scholarly interests including literacy and basic writing pedagogy, critical pedagogy, collaborative learning, professional communication, and writing program development. The existing program consisted of the required graduate methods seminar and a practicum course taught by the coordinator and four faculty mentors. With strong support from the English department, the dean of the College of Arts and Sciences, and Academic Affairs, she was also charged with developing a minor in writing and applying for internal grants to create computer-supported writing classrooms. Because the university had mainstreamed most of the students who might have been identified (or identified themselves) as basic writers, she also sought ways to better support students who struggled to succeed in first-year writing course.

When Kelly began at UW as practicum instructor and WPA, the first-year writing program had been without a rhetoric and composition faculty member for several years, had no common curriculum or assignments, and was guided by an outcomes statement with a current traditional slant, something that Kelly sought to enlist faculty and GTAs in revising to reflect national discourses on outcomes for first-year writing courses ("WPA Outcomes Statement"). Faculty associated with the program had also reached a consensus that, as the only first-year writing course and as the foundation for the university's WAC program, the writing curriculum should emphasize argument writing, with little emphasis on writing from personal experience or literary analysis (the focus of a sophomore-level writing-intensive course called Introduction to Literature). Given this consensus, it seemed appropriate to develop a rhetorically based approach in revising the curriculum and working toward a common syllabus, which many of the GTAs themselves requested. Even though Kelly's own most recent scholarly and program development work focused on critical pedagogies, she determined that creating a new curriculum at UW based on, say, a Freirean model, seemed an impractical and ill-advised approach considering a department culture that expects more traditional approaches to teaching, combined with the inexperience of most of the GTAs, many of whom were concerned about establishing some degree of authority and control in the classroom where they already sometimes felt like "imposters." At the same time, it seemed possible and important to engage GTAs and interested faculty in developing and assessing the curriculum and to encourage them to voice opinions about the GTA program and the new assignment sequences.

Working together each year, a group of interested GTAs and faculty developed a rhetorically based process pedagogy and a common syllabus, and for several years created custom readers based on GTA preferences for readings and themes. These changes, the increased time commitment required for collaborative decision making, and the promise of new computer classrooms for integrating technological literacies into first-year writing courses were welcomed by many of the GTAs and faculty. At the same time, to some faculty mentors and GTAs who expected or were used to a more loosely organized system (one that gave them more freedom to use a wider variety of assignments and pedagogies), the changes seemed restrictive, unfamiliar, and perhaps unnecessarily complicated. Kelly's insistence that she and the mentors teach at least one first-year writing course a year following the common syllabus also made greater demands on the faculty mentors, who received a course release for their mentoring work but missed the freedom of the previously more ad hoc approach to mentoring.

During the initial years when these changes took place, Kelly considered the composition methods practicum as a rare and valued site in which to discuss pedagogical and composing theories with GTAs, the only group (aside from a few lecturers) who regularly teach the English department's first-year writing course. During her first year at UW, a honeymoon period when the GTAs and faculty seemed grateful for renewed attention to the writing program, a nascent teaching community began to form. But in subsequent years, a different mix of GTAs, some of whom had been undergraduates in UW's literary studies major, mirrored some department members' skepticism of composition and rhetoric

studies as a field. Some of these GTAs also had difficulty embracing pedagogies grounded in active learning, having been apt students of some of the department's accomplished lecturers.

The initially warm sense of community seemed in danger of
slipping away as GTAs' and faculty mentors' understandable anxieties in the face of program changes grew. Without a cohesive
team of faculty who understood and wholeheartedly supported
the new curriculum and pedagogies, the composition methods
course became an increasingly charged site. Kelly began to experience an increased sense of role conflict, pulled in different directions as the administrator who needed to "sell" GTAs on a new
curriculum not initially well understood by colleagues outside her
field, while as the practicum instructor she wanted to encourage a
more theoretically based critical examination of the methods she
was promoting. She found herself in the delicate position of
encouraging critique of a newly designed program that was still
little understood in the department and university, a program she
had developed as a WPA with little institutionally conferred
power and no departmental colleagues in composition studies.

Another layer of tension emerged from the structure of the
GTA development program. As WPA, Kelly had designed the new
curriculum collaboratively with GTAs and lecturers and taught the
methods course, but it was the tenured faculty and extended-term
lecturers serving as mentors (who seemed conflicted between a
genuine desire to be collegially supportive and their skepticism
about some of the changes) who were responsible for guiding
GTAs in their day-to-day teaching practices. The different ideologies of the faculty involved in GTA mentoring could not help but
be communicated to the GTAs, and mixed messages no doubt contributed to making the methods course an increasingly charged site
for the WPA as teacher.

Adding to the situation's complexities was the fact that the
composition and rhetoric track is underdeveloped in the UW graduate program, and despite the weight placed on the methods
course institutionally (as a graded, four-credit course), GTAs at
UW sometimes entered the course feeling resentful about having to
"use up" one of their graduate courses on a composition studies
course when their main focus was literature or creative writing. At

worst, they saw the course as a requirement to get out of the way, at best a place where they might be able to get some teaching tips or a chance to talk over what was happening in the first-year course they were teaching. As a result, one additional challenge the practicum seminar posed for an instructor in a traditional English department was confronting the frustration of some GTAs when faced with significant, challenging reading and writing assignments grounded in an unfamiliar field of study often devalued in part because of its association with pedagogy. At the same time, Kelly felt torn between at least two possible teacher identities that seemed particularly distinct in a practicum seminar where students weren't necessarily seeking or expecting intellectual challenges or a serious time investment in reading and writing. One identity was that of supportive mentor, similar to the role of other faculty members who worked with the GTAs in the one-credit, nongraded part of the TA program. This position was inherently difficult to assume in a graded course, yet making the course pass/fail would threaten the status of the only graduate course the department offers. To move toward the position of mentor would compromise a second identity position—that of a seminar instructor responsible for assessing graduate-level work that addresses theoretical and pedagogical questions in composition studies and employs basic research methods and genres used in composition and rhetoric. This position could be most feasibly assumed in a department with a strong culture of research and professional development for all writing faculty, a culture UW is still working to develop. Unless they could be reconciled, these different perceptions of the course and the instructor's role threatened to set the stage for increased conflict and dissatisfaction with the methods course and the writing program.

Resituating the Practicum at UW

To address, or diffuse, the growing tensions rooted in different ideologies and changes in the first-year writing curriculum, Kelly worked with the English department chair and the College of Arts and Sciences dean to make programmatic changes that, in effect, began decentering the WPA position. This decentering process coincided with efforts already in motion by key department members and the chair to enhance the professional status of the academic lecturers teaching in the writing program (e.g., improving pay for temporary lecturers and converting temporary positions to extended-term positions). When Kelly decided to resolve the growing role conflict she felt by stepping aside from teaching the methods course, the door was opened for a decentered model of program administration to emerge. Further opportunities for other writing program faculty to participate in program administration resulted when she requested to change her position to half time and share the WPA responsibilities with Carolyn Young, an extended-term professional lecturer and GTA mentor.

As a result of these changes, the methods course was taught for the next two years by the UW Writing Center director, who is not a member of the English department. During this time, Kelly assisted in directing the Writing Center and pursued her goal of developing a learning community for conditionally admitted students, many of them "basic writers." Drawing on her WAC expertise, Writing Center director Jane Nelson was able to build on a WAC perspective that had been well received when Kelly used John Bean's *Engaging Ideas* in previous methods courses. Jane's outside perspective on rhetoric as an area of study and her distance from the first-year writing curriculum worked in some ways to her advantage. She shared some of the students' skepticism about the value of studying rhetorical theory or principles (presented through Crowley and Hawhee's *Ancient Rhetorics for Contemporary Students*) and gave students another audience for concerns they wanted to voice about the common syllabus or their teaching responsibilities. Meanwhile, she could offer an insider's–outsider's perspective to Kelly as WPA that was helpful in assessing and continuing to improve the program.

A key contribution Jane made to the practicum grew out of her WAC perspective. She designed an assignment that allowed students to explore connections between composition pedagogies and complementary approaches used in teaching literature, creative writing, or courses in other disciplines. For this assignment, students become an "expert" on one of the pedagogies introduced in Tate, Rupiper, and Schick's *A Guide to Composition Pedago-*

gies. They interview any faculty member on campus about his or her use of, for example, a feminist or cultural studies pedagogy. At the same time, they explore applications of that pedagogy in composition studies through outside readings suggested in Tate, Rupiper, and Schick. This assignment acknowledges the value GTAs often place on their favorite literature professors' expertise and teaching abilities while encouraging them to examine critically applications of these pedagogies in the context of teaching composition.

In a subsequent change for fall 2003, Carolyn Young stepped into the WPA role and, in a move to further professionalize the composition coordinator position, the department chair instituted a policy that allocated an additional course release to the position, clarified the authority it carries, stipulated the term of service, and spelled out the means by which the coordinator would be evaluated and would in turn evaluate the mentors. Meanwhile, Kelly resumed responsibility for teaching the methods course, keeping assignments and readings that had worked well in the past while adopting and adapting some of the assignments Jane had designed. In revising the course, she kept in mind GTA comments about what they most want out of the methods course: assessment of teaching strengths and weaknesses; strategies for building on teaching strengths; opportunities to explore whether teaching is a viable career option for them; guidelines for explaining strategies of rhetoric; ideas for working with unmotivated students; and connections between the methods class and the first-year writing class.

In response to these needs and desires, along with adopting a version of the pedagogies assignment, Kelly revised the course to appeal to the GTAs' desire for practical matters by employing a "just in time" approach that connects urgent, practical teaching concerns with composition research and rhetorical theory that is accessible to nonspecialist audiences. On Mondays, the first hour of class focuses on practical concerns prompted by readings from *Engaging Ideas* (Bean), *Ancient Rhetorics for Contemporary Students* (Crowley and Hawhee), or GTAs' immediate classroom concerns (which they share with Kelly in essays reflecting on the weeks' work submitted each Friday). The second hour overlaps with the practicum and is devoted to grade-norming sessions led by the composition coordinator or to small-group meetings led by faculty mentors. Kelly, along with any graduate students in the methods course who are not GTAs, attends the whole-group meetings and rotates among the small groups. On Wednesdays, the GTAs lead the class in examining composition pedagogies presented in Tate, Rupiper, and Schick based on readings, class observations, and interviews with faculty. This format allows for a focus on GTAs' immediate exigencies—how to introduce a concept in class next week—while motivating them to wrestle with more theoretically oriented texts because they have control over the text selection process. Through teaching and learning in parallel, GTAs begin to view the first-year writing course as a kind of laboratory for applying and questioning the best practices and theories introduced in the graduate methods course.

Equally key to the process of resituating the practicum at UW has been a new tenure-track hire in rhetoric and composition who is serving as a GTA mentor. In effect, a new, more cohesive team of WPAs has been assembled within the department: a group of mentors, a WPA, and a methods instructor with a closely shared set of disciplinary ideologies. Several of the second-year GTAs, too, sometimes function as part of this team, alternately advocating program policies as they mentor first-year GTAs and agitating for change or reconsideration when they think the program is heading off track or a decision is being made without sufficient GTA input (second-year GTAs have considerably more freedom to design their own assignments and select course texts). One suggestion that two second-year GTAs made was to establish more specific guidelines for discussing student work in norming sessions to ensure a tone of respect for the writers and their texts, making certain we spent as much time describing strengths as we did weaknesses. Another GTA suggested that when the Writing Center director teaches the practicum, she attend the summer colloquium or teach the first-year writing course so that she can more closely connect with their experiences. The GTAs seem to recognize the importance of connections between the key faculty and administrators of the GTA development and writing programs.

The new format, which links the practicum and methods courses and situates them within a distributed model of program leadership, promises greater efficiency while exposing GTAs to a wider range of perspectives on teaching writing than they encountered in previous, more WPA-centric models. Even so, no format will completely subdue the tensions inherent in a program involving multiple courses and the appropriately divergent perspectives of faculty and GTAs. A colleague pointed out that despite changes that move away from the WPA-centric model, the faculty mentors remain in the position of "listening to GTAs challenge the curriculum/program and facing the conflict between upholding principles upon which the program is based or encouraging spirited inquiry into those principles and the practices born thereof" (Michael Knievel, personal communication). A similar dilemma exists for the practicum instructor who is not the composition coordinator: she or he too needs to balance support for the program with encouragement of inquiry and exploration. The Writing Center director hinted at her own sense of conflict a number of times when she expressed her concern that she might somehow be "undermining" the program in the practicum course. But rather than viewing these tensions as a problem to be solved, they can be seen as an impetus for creative curricular and administrative innovations within a democratized administrative model. They also remind everyone involved in a distributed model of program administration how much depends on the continued communication and goodwill of everyone involved. An ongoing challenge is to take concerns and questions of GTAs seriously while recognizing that their issues sometimes emerge from genuine insights or concerns, and other times they emerge from inexperience, lack of knowledge about factors affecting the WPA's decisions, or frustration, anger, and anxiety in response to the unexpectedly hard work of teaching first-year writing. As of this writing, the new format appears to be a successful step in the continued development of a collaborative, democratic, and broadly professionalized model of writing program administration and GTA development.

Conflicting Perspectives at NAU

Although she stepped into a more established writing program when she took on the position of director of the University Writing

Program at NAU, Sibylle realized when talking with Kelly that we face similar shifts in identity when working with GTAs. She also realized that her own ideologies sometimes are in conflict with her role as WPA and instructor of the practicum course. Very much like Kelly, her role as the instructor of the practicum course is only one of many roles, augmented by her research interests (literacy, computers and writing, cultural rhetoric, feminist studies, and interdisciplinary approaches to writing), by her other teaching responsibilities, and by her responsibilities as the WPA to the department and the institution. Also, the practicum course is not the only venue where GTAs and instructor meet. Sibylle, similar to writing program administrators at UW and elsewhere, also mentors the GTAs, visits their classrooms, and provides suggestions for how GTAs can improve classroom interactions in their respective sections of English 105, might apply different delivery methods, and can work with resistant students. And she encourages each GTA on days when teaching seems an insurmountable obstacle on the way to success as a graduate student. These roles are often carried over to the practicum course and for the most part complement practicum interactions, but they sometimes make it more difficult to focus on the more theoretical and therefore "abstract" texts used in the practicum.

GTAs, who are required to take the practicum course during their first semester of teaching English 105, are encouraged to apply their extensive reading from T. R. Johnson and Shirley Morahan's collection, *Teaching Composition: Background Readings*, to their teaching practices. They are introduced to key concepts and philosophies for reflective practice, thinking about the writing process, responding to and evaluating student writing, as well as understanding the influences of institutional politics (Johnson and Morahan v–xii). Additionally, the course serves as a forum in which to discuss lesson plans, problematic classroom situations, and technological challenges, as well as to exchange success stories. Theory and practice, in effect, should be perfectly aligned. As it turns out, however, the discourses of theory and of practice often compete with each other, with practice most often subsuming the language, values, and perspectives of theory. Furthermore, the conflicts between theory and practice are reinforced by Sibylle's own conflicting notions of how theory can and sometimes needs to give way to the practical concerns of the instructors and the institution.

What becomes problematic for Sibylle, and what carries over to the practicum course as well, are her own ideological perspectives on teaching writing and teaching writing with technology, and the institutional constraints on realizing these ideologies. A firm believer in the diverse needs of a diverse student body and, subsequently, the need for providing a multitude of approaches to teaching writing, Sibylle is aware of the problems a standardized curriculum can create. Based on institutional requirements to show similar course outcomes, however, the department and institution have strongly encouraged and supported the standardization of the first-year writing curriculum. Although GTAs, especially in their second year, can make changes to the standard syllabus, the tight structure (specified number of assignments, required reader, required handbook) has often limited the GTAs' ability to experiment with their pedagogical approaches, text choices, or assignments—experimentation that Sibylle sees as essential for establishing a productive teaching and learning environment.

Similar ideological perspectives on technological literacy create a split between Sibylle's theoretical approach to computer technologies in the classroom and her support as the WPA of standardized technological literacy modules in the first-year writing curriculum. The institutional context requires students to be proficient in specific functional computer skills by the end of their undergraduate college career. Based on the large numbers of first-year students moving through the writing program, the institution considered it only logical to ask the department and the WPA to integrate the majority of the required skills into the first-year writing program. During the first year of implementing these skills, Sibylle and the GTAs created a variety of modules that would be part of a writing curriculum and also provide students with introductions to functional technology skills. Although Sibylle is very conscious that gender, socioeconomic status, racial and cultural backgrounds, and age influence approaches to and the need for technology, the modules used in the writing program assumed a specific audience with specific material needs. Certainly, as the

WPA Sibylle hoped to expand the functional technological skills to critical skills by incorporating modules on Web analysis, cultural representations online, or rhetorical tools for evaluating online sources. During the first year of implementation, this was especially difficult because, for students and for GTAs, the functional overwhelmed the critical. GTAs specifically focused on teaching word processing, PowerPoint, sending attachments, and other functional skills because they were not comfortable—and did not have the extensive and in-depth training—to approach technology from a more critical perspective.

What this shows is that WPA concerns are based not only on the GTAs' focus on the practical but also on the conflicting and conflicted roles of the writing program director. In her role as administrator, Sibylle knows that GTAs need to follow specific guidelines and to adopt the philosophies, methodologies, and theories considered essential for providing a large number of undergraduates with the basic tools for writing in an academic setting. In her role as the instructor of the GTA practicum and as a researcher actively engaged in exploring new ways to approach the teaching of writing, she wants the GTAs to consider a variety of theories and methodologies that would strengthen their skills as teachers of introductory composition. Because of her own conflicted perspective on standardized composition curricula, she would also like GTAs to question the institutionalization of writing programs, but knows that the integrity of the program and its success rely on a cohesive curriculum that has taken many years to establish, refine, and institute on a large scale. In a sense, Sibylle's various roles and her conflicted perspectives on the ideological foundations of the writing program can limit the explorations and conversations that take place in the practicum.

Finding a Middle Ground: Structure, Freedom, and Technology

One lesson Sibylle learned early on in her career as a WPA was that she needed to work closely with the GTAs—more so than with the institution as a whole—to create a curriculum that would satisfy the structure of the program but also allow participants the freedom to choose and change within that structure. The GTA practicum was especially useful in slowly working toward a curricular—not necessarily programmatic—compromise. In the spring 2003 GTA practicum at NAU, the initial reading students were asked to complete was George Hillocks's "Some Basics for Thinking about Teaching Writing." Hillocks calls for reflective practice and discusses how such practice will encourage continuous research and "generate important ideas for theory" (9). He provides readers with a six-phase model for improving their teaching, a model that is intended to encourage constant growth and change. Hillocks points out clearly that "every teacher has a set of theories that provide a coherent view of the field and means of approaching the task of teaching" (5). Furthermore, the theories used by teachers "will necessarily be the basis for the content and organization of students' experiences in any program intended for helping people learn to write" (7). The GTAs focused less on Hillocks's emphasis on the interconnections of theory, practice, and research, but they considered the article useful because of its focus on the reflective process in the teaching of writing.

What struck students as an important statement in the article was Hillocks's mention that "only the failure to try assures failure" (16). The class fervently agreed with this statement, and the discussion leaders for this session provided their colleagues with a number of reflective process ideas to improve their teaching practices. They encouraged everybody to keep a teaching journal, to try different teaching methods that would incorporate different learning styles, and to learn students' likes and dislikes and incorporate them into lessons. They also pointed out that it would be beneficial to get feedback from students and to provide ongoing assessment of how students are doing in the class. They explained that we all need to assess what our teaching theory is and that we can always change our theory. As the teacher of the practicum, Sibylle was concerned that GTAs put too much focus on the practical without paying attention to the theoretical context of such practice. She could also, however, see the reflections that students engaged in as the basis for theory, whether GTAs used this terminology or whether they focused more on what they could relate to more closely based on their experiences in the classroom.

Similarly instructive for helping GTAs find their own pedagogical and methodological strengths was David Bartholomae's article "Inventing the University." GTAs at NAU considered this reading very useful to their experiences in the classroom. The discussion leaders especially pointed out the first paragraph in the chapter:

> Every time a student sits down to write for us, he has to invent the university for the occasion—invent the university, that is, or a branch of it, like history or anthropology or economics or English. The student has to learn to speak our language, to speak as we do, to try on the peculiar ways of knowing, selecting, evaluating, reporting, concluding, and arguing that define the discourse of our community. (274).

Bartholomae comments that the primary role of writing instruction is to critically evaluate the commonplaces of academic writing so that it is no longer a foreign language to students. During the discussions of this piece, GTAs related many stories of their own students to the rest of the class, and they pointed out the many difficulties students had in their writing for academic purposes. What the article unfortunately did not address to the satisfaction of the GTAs was the very hands-on questions of "so what do we do with our students who are trying to invent the university?" They wanted to have quick fixes for students' problems, but fortunately they realized in the course of the conversation that, although there are some underlying similarities between the students described by Bartholomae and their own students, they needed to pay close attention to the context in which they were teaching, and they also needed to realize that there were no simple solutions to a very complex problem. At a basic level, GTAs suggested that as instructors they needed to determine the conventions of the academic community, and to introduce students to terminology that seems quite clear to us, such as *think, argue, describe,* or *define*. These were initial steps that GTAs took to move beyond "telling stories" about their students and the problems these students seem to have with academic discourse. Furthermore, GTAs started to realize that academic discourse is specialized and needs to be taught explicitly. Students saw "Inventing the University," like the Hillocks article, as a starting point for exploring their approach to their students' writing. They also suggested alternative readings and assignments to make sure that their students would receive the best learning experiences in their respective sections of English 105.

Based on readings such as those by Hillocks and Bartholomae, GTAs realized that student needs, as well as their own needs, required them to think critically about how they positioned themselves within a standardized curriculum. Despite using a required reader, following an assignment sequence, and applying rhetorical tools to the texts they were teaching, they had freedom within this structure to apply their own pedagogies, methodologies, and theories to teaching first-year composition. The reader, for example, could be supplemented with electronic reserves; the assignments could be innovative and could, for example, include a rhetorical analysis of an article, a Web site, a poem, a music video, or a current event. The process approach to writing could be taught by applying Elbow's theories, clustering exercises, peer-editing exercises, or instructor conferences. What Sibylle came to realize, and what the GTAs taught her, was that structure did not need to overpower a vast array of pedagogical approaches, and that theory could become an integral part of the practicum, even though GTAs and instructor might not have the same definition of successful integration of theory into practice. Sibylle also realized that her ideological concerns about the discord between theory–practice and administrative requirements were alleviated once GTAs were provided with opportunities to adapt the curriculum to their own needs and strengths.

One aspect of the writing program that caused much concern was the integration of the technological literacy modules into the first-year composition curriculum. Because of the university's new emphasis on having students show their mastery of functional technological literacy skills, and because of Sibylle's conviction that students needed to become critical readers of technological literacy, Sibylle was extremely concerned about the focus on the functional, a focus that she hoped to change over the course of the academic year. Having GTAs read Charles Moran's "Computers and the Writing Classroom: A Look to the Future" and Dean Rehberger's "Living Texts on the Web" provided an initial stepping stone for GTAs to think about their use of computer technology in the classroom and the implications of such use for themselves and their students. To provide GTAs with experiences similar to those of their students, the discussion of Moran's and Rehberger's pieces was conducted in an online forum similar to those used by composition students. GTAs experienced the initial chaotic nature of reading and of writing their own comments while others added to the discussion. GTAs posted comments that showed their ambivalence and also their belief in the benefits of using online technologies. As one GTA pointed out, "online discussions are a bit more difficult to manage. My teacher-voice is just one more green block, not the all-eyes-on-me voice I use in the classroom." Another one wrote, "I have found online discussions a great way to get the quiet students involved—especially if it's an out-of-lab synchronous discussion where they can't see each other." Other discussions in this online forum addressed the best ways of integrating technology into a writing curriculum, the usefulness of teaching students technology skills, and the need to focus more closely on the connections between teaching critical thinking, reading, and writing skills and teaching computers skills.

This discussion during the practicum started to address one of Sibylle's concerns as a researcher—how can we institute technological literacy (and what does it mean) and also meet the needs of the diverse student population at NAU and the needs of the university administration? GTAs, based on this discussion and on their teaching experiences, advocated a change from the functional to the critical—making sure that all modules incorporated critical technological literacy skills. Although Sibylle is still conflicted about a wholesale integration of technological literacy into a mandatory first-year writing course, she is encouraged by the GTAs' renewed interest in emphasizing the critical before the functional, in effect using the functional only as a starting point for exploring the complexities of new technologies. In addition, the writing program's continued assessment of student perceptions of the technological literacy modules, continuous feedback from GTAs, and continuous revisions of the existing modules should ensure improvements in the existing approach to technological literacy. And, based on the assessment of students' functional skills at the beginning and the end of their composition course, Sibylle can show the university administration that students' functional skill levels have significantly improved over the course of the semester while also knowing that instructors shifted their focus to critical technological skills.

The practicum course has helped Sibylle reach compromises between her own ideological convictions, the needs of the GTAs, and the needs of the writing program. Working closely with GTAs from many backgrounds has convinced Sibylle that no program will be able to implement a standard curriculum without also allowing for and encouraging individual GTA ideologies, pedagogies, methodologies, and theories, in effect changing the curriculum, the readings, assignment sequences, and computer modules. As a WPA and as a teacher of the practicum, Sibylle realized to her relief that she could only guide her instructors to follow the outline of a complicated and intricate enterprise—teaching the tools of rhetoric to a campuswide array of first-year students.

Conclusion

As these descriptions of tensions centered in the practicum course demonstrate, we are both seeking a happy middle ground for our programs, ourselves, the GTAs, and our institutions. For a developing program, the route to that middle ground may begin in finding the most appropriate structure for coordinating key elements of the GTA program. When a structure suitable to a local context is in place, we can contemplate additional questions: How, as WPAs and as instructors, do we want to see ourselves, the GTAs, and our writing program colleagues? Do we encourage the GTAs to teach according to our own goals and objectives for the program even though we see these goals as tentative and as a multidirectional compromise, or do we really want them to question the program we have built and act outside of its parameters and guidance—which is inevitable if we encourage critical approaches to a variety of theories and methodologies? Can we tell them that their newly acquired knowledge is important, and their intentions to apply new theories and methodologies are invaluable, but that they don't know the context in which the program exists, the president's goals for educating citizens of the twenty-first century, or the provost's interest in technology or environmental issues or multicultural programs? If we had answers to these questions, we would also have been able to answer our questions about our positions, our concern about the compromises we make, and our doubts about the integrity of the programs in their current forms. In other words, we would be able to find perfect solutions for the sometimes conflicting approaches mandated by local contexts, disciplinary conversations, and ideological restraints.

Some, or even most, of the professional identity issues surrounding the writing program and the composition practicum may be unavoidable because the practicum is likely to remain a site frequently charged with a complex agenda. And as long as graduate assistantships fund the teaching of first-year writing courses, GTAs will continue to function simultaneously as students and as employees. Even so, the practicum course would benefit from changes that can and must occur in how writing program administrative work is perceived and carried out.

One key to addressing these concerns is continued support for a broader understanding of how program administration can be deeply informed by disciplinary, scholarly knowledge and also add to that knowledge. Admittedly, writing program administrative work is not inherently or automatically intellectual work—it can be all too easy to succumb to the way we are constructed by others and find ourselves, for instance, teaching the practicum purely as a service course for the English department. But when programs and courses become a laboratory for applying and questioning theories and best practices of the field, the intellectual work of writing program teaching and administration comes to the foreground. This kind of critical engagement with pedagogy and curricula is essential if we want to move the GTA practicum out of its frequent position as a service course and instead firmly establish it as a seminar integral to developing scholar-teachers in English studies.

A second step we can take that would affect how our writing program work is carried out and perceived is for WPAs and practicum instructors to acknowledge—to ourselves, to the GTAs, and to faculty colleagues in our departments and across the university—that any existing writing program is often an amalgamation of many compromises. Foregrounding for ourselves and for other stakeholders in the writing program the various, often competing influences on practica formats and pedagogies would lay programmatic and curricular decisions open for an informed examination and understanding of the complexities involved. Making these influences visible might also help the multiple stakeholders in the work of the practicum understand and support our choices as instructors. As WPAs, we have to make sure that our visions and best intentions for creating a program also address the constraints imposed by local and national contexts (administrators, university requirements for general education or liberal studies, students' backgrounds, GTA hiring processes, changing approaches to writing instruction, state and federal mandates, etc.). We also, however, need to make sure that we don't allow these constraints to force us into becoming stagnant, but that we instead point out the changing nature of any situation as well as the inevitable exigence addressed by Lloyd Bitzer in his 1968 article "The Rhetorical Situation": "Any exigence is an imperfection marked by urgency; it is a defect, an obstacle, something waiting to be done, a thing which is other than it should be" (6). We need to learn to acknowledge these exigencies, and we need to be willing to continuously work and rework the writing programs we administer so that we can easily admit that no program can be perfect, that change is inevitable and necessary, and that continued discussions and negotiations about the program— with GTAs, students, colleagues at our institutions and nationally, and administrators—provide a stimulating environment. Writing programs, then, can be seen not as pathologically "imperfect" based on the many constraints we learn to live with, but as works in progress that will continue to evolve in their local and national contexts.

Finally, we suggest that faculty move into administrative work or practicum teaching after intense periods of writing and research in order to spark new ways of incorporating theory and practice into the GTA practicum. Such a move may be difficult in departments with few rhetoric and composition faculty (or few interested in administrative work). It may require consciously reshaping the way we perceive our jobs and present our professional selves to others, emphasizing different parts of our professional identities at different points in our careers. Making these changes possible may need to be a condition of employment in departments without standing rotation policies for WPA-related teaching and administrative assignments. Such changes, though, are in the best interest of everyone affected by the WPA's work. Stepping in and out of administrative work, including the teaching of the composition practicum, helps decenter the WPA, allowing him or her to avoid the burnout and entrenchment that many long-term WPAs experience and that can have a negative effect on everyone's morale.

With several faculty contributing their own approaches to teaching the practicum, the course is more likely to be intellectually inspiring, enhancing our own and the GTAs' teaching experiences by grounding them in essential theories of rhetoric, composition, and literacy studies. Equally important, moving out of administrative work allows us to avoid being too closely tied to programs of our own design; therefore, we are better positioned to view the practicum as a site that can provoke new scholarly inquiry. We can take time to analyze what we've learned through teaching the practicum, where questions and discussion likely served to highlight comfortably smooth intersections of practice and theory and to uncover knurly contradictions of theory and practice. These discussions can reveal our own contradictions as writing program administrators and as teachers of the practicum. And with some distance from the program, instead of seeing these contradictions as a threat to established practice, a WPA can more readily use the likely inconsistencies in theory and practice as an impetus for examining and reenvisioning practicum curricula, first-year writing course curricula, and theories of composition. Best of all, in achieving this dialectic between researching and teaching, administering and reflecting, we can model for GTAs what may be the most important outcome of a composition practicum—how to be engaged, reflective teachers in our own classrooms.

Notes

1. Charges directly tied to the practicum might include mentoring new teachers through their first semester of college composition teaching,

introducing graduate students to the field of composition studies, and encouraging in GTAs a critical stance on theory and pedagogy while requesting their compliance with an established and, ideally, coherent program. At the same time, the practicum instructor might be responsible for creating and coordinating a writing program that responds to local, institutional, and national concerns; communicating the goals, methods, and effectiveness of the program to colleagues and administrators in the department, university, and state; advocating for non-tenure-track writing colleagues; and perhaps most important for one's own career, keeping up a research agenda while immersed in the daily demands of a writing program.

2. Kelly spent the spring 2003 semester in Flagstaff observing NAU classes, conducting research, and preparing for the fall 2003 term at UW.

3. Since this chapter was written, Kelly accepted a position at Virginia Polytechnic Institute and State University.

4. For example, GTAs at NAU and UW are being prepared to teach basic rhetorical tools that students can ideally apply throughout their academic career. Our respective approaches to GTA education share these goals with many other programs: to guide GTAs as they practice a rhetorically focused, process-based writing pedagogy; integrate technological literacy; follow general tenets of social constructivism and active learning; coach first-year composition students in self-reflective, analytical, and argumentative writing strategies; understand the complexity of their dual position as both students and teachers; and adapt their teaching as appropriate to the needs of a diverse and complex student body engaged in a sometimes difficult transition from high school to college.

Works Cited

Bartholomae, David. "Inventing the University." 1985. *Perspectives on Literacy*. Ed. Eugene R. Kintgen, Barry M. Kroll, and Mike Rose. Carbondale: Southern Illinois UP, 1988. 273–85.

Bean, John C. *Engaging Ideas: The Professor's Guide to Integrating Writing, Critical Thinking, and Active Learning in the Classroom*. San Francisco: Jossey-Bass, 1996.

Bitzer, Lloyd F. "The Rhetorical Situation." *Philosophy and Rhetoric* 1.1 (1968): 1–14.

Crowley, Sharon, and Debra Hawhee. *Ancient Rhetorics for Contemporary Students*. 2nd ed. Boston: Allyn and Bacon, 1999.

Elbow, Peter. *Writing without Teachers*. New York: Oxford UP, 1973.

Freire, Paulo. 1970. *Pedagogy of the Oppressed*. New York: Seabury.

Gunner, Jeanne. "Decentering the WPA." *WPA: Writing Program Administration* 18 (Fall/Winter 1994): 8–15.

Hillocks, George. "Some Basics for Thinking about Teaching Writing." *Teaching Composition: Background Readings*. Ed. T. R. Johnson and Shirley Morahan. Boston: Bedford/St. Martin's, 2002. 2–18.

Johnson, T. R., and Shirley Morahan, eds. *Teaching Composition: Background Readings*. Boston: Bedford/St. Martin's, 2002.

Latterell, Catherine G. "Training the Workforce: Overview of GTA Education Curricula." *The Allyn & Bacon Sourcebook for Writing Program Administrators*. Ed. Irene Ward and William J. Carpenter. New York: Longman, 2002. 139–55.

Moran, Charles. "Computers and the Writing Classroom: A Look to the Future." *Teaching Composition: Background Readings*. Ed. T. R. Johnson and Shirley Morahan. Boston: Bedford/St. Martin's, 2002. 271–89.

Rehberger, Dean. "Living Texts on the Web: A Return to the Rhetorical Arts of Annotation and Commonplace." *Weaving a Virtual Web: Practical Approaches to New Information Technologies*. Ed. Sibylle Gruber. Urbana, IL: National Council of Teachers of English, 2000. 193–206.

Tate, Gary, Amy Rupiper, and Kurt Schick. *A Guide to Composition Pedagogies*. New York: Oxford UP, 2001.

"WPA Outcomes Statement for First-Year Composition." *WPA: Writing Program Administration* 23.1–2 (Fall/Winter 1999): 59–66.

CHAPTER SEVEN

The Benefits and Challenges of Including Undergraduates in the Composition Practicum

JONATHAN BUSH, GEORGINA HILL, AND JEANNE LaHAIE
Western Michigan University

B ecause of historical and institutional factors beyond our control at Western Michigan University, our introductory composition program employs upper-level undergraduates in English education to teach sections of basic writing. While these undergraduates are supported by means of intensive mentoring, the simple fact remains that these undergraduate students are the instructors of record in their basic writing courses, teaching other undergraduates. Despite all the inherent complexities of this unique and complicated situation, the program works with surprising efficacy. Students show satisfaction with the classes; we have seen a strong rate of success from former basic writing students as they take regular introductory composition courses; and there are benefits to our program's other teaching assistants, as well as the strong professional development opportunity offered to these undergraduate instructors.

Mentoring the English 100 instructors runs simultaneously with our graduate mentoring for English 105, the required first-year writing course. Dual practica are held during the fall semester—one for undergraduates who teach basic writing and the other for first-year graduate instructors—as well as a combined one-week presemester preparatory seminar. During this time, a teaching community develops that affects and directs the professional development of both groups in positive ways. While we are still concerned about the situation of having some of the youngest, most inexperienced members of our profession teaching basic writing, we have been intrigued by the success of our undergraduate teaching assistants and the positive effects their experiences have had on their development and the development of our graduate students. Our English education faculty continually point to the practicum and its ability to guide young teachers as they work within a close mentoring group as one of their most effective means of teacher development.

Likewise, student evaluations and student achievement show that, despite their inexperience, our undergraduate teaching assistants are performing admirably in the classroom. Students generally describe their undergraduate instructors as being knowledgeable, enthusiastic, and interesting. And, more telling, these students commonly leave the course feeling better prepared for the rigors of college writing. A typical comment from a recent exit survey concludes, "This was the best class I've taken at WMU. I've learned so much. I wish [she] could teach my next writing class."

The three of us authoring this chapter represent different aspects of this program. Georgina is the director of composition, whose role includes the mentoring of all composition instructors—adjunct, graduate, and undergraduate. Jeanne is a recent MA graduate of Western Michigan who mentored the undergraduate English 100 instructors during the 2002–03 academic year. Jonathan is a member of the English education faculty whose Teaching Writing in the Secondary School course is an application prerequisite for the English 100 instructor positions.

When we began to consider sharing this situation with an outside audience, our first concern was to represent our belief that our situation is problematic. We are by no means endorsing this system for other programs. From each of our perspectives, we see both complications and positives of this unique situation. Separately, based on our different roles and relationships with the program, we see different advantages and disadvantages to the program. Jonathan, for example, is enthusiastic about the experiences it gives his English education students in a supportive environment before they begin their student teaching, whereas Georgina, often beset by stressed and nervous phone calls from instructors of all levels, often questions her choices for teaching appointments. Jeanne has seen, close up, both the difficulties and the triumphs of our basic writing teachers and their students. She comes with a guarded perspective that tells her that the program can work, but it also sets up instructors and mentors for difficult situations that require constant effort and reflection. Despite our different perspectives, we agree that our story is one with implications for other composition program directors, English educators, and composition mentors in other first-year composition programs. We hope that our story can provide support and guidance for administrators who are thinking about bringing undergraduates into a professional development community and making use of their talents in college composition settings.

We focus our discussion on the following questions:

◆ What are the institutional traits that have helped this program succeed?

◆ How can we best support undergraduate instructors in a composition professional development and teaching program? And what activities need to be duplicated in order for other institutions to support these novice composition instructors?

◆ What are the challenges and rewards of including undergraduates in composition professional development programs?

And ultimately,

◆ What implications does our story have for other graduate-centered composition mentoring programs?

What Contributes to the Program's Success: Institutional Factors

We want to begin by describing the ways that we feel advantaged. We realize that this program may not work in all places, and we want to forefront the factors that we believe help this seemingly disastrous situation work. We see three key institutional elements that assist this success. The first of these is the presence of a large and well-developed secondary English education program. This not only leads to teaching candidates who are well prepared and strongly professionalized but also gives us a large number of qualified candidates from whom we choose only the most outstanding applicants. Another element is the type of preparation these novice teachers receive. The writing methods course they take is rigorous and focused on teaching, as well as theoretically compatible with the composition program's approach to English 100. Thus not only are we able to choose the "cream of the crop" among this pool, but the pool itself is quite large and knowledgeable about the issues that lead to successful teaching.

The characteristics of the students who are placed in English 100 are also important to the program's success. Most of these students have adequate language skills but for various reasons have not had sufficient writing instruction and practice to adequately support college-level writing. Our university is self-described as being "moderately selective," and the students we accept on a conditional basis may need some remediation, but they are not as challenging as many others typically characterized as basic writers. Thus, while the novice teacher still faces challenges in working with these students, they are not in the same range as those described by Mina Shaughnessy and other basic writing theorists.

English Education Program and Preparation in Composition Studies

Western Michigan University is home to an extremely large and well-developed secondary English education program. As of the 2002–03 school year, over 500 full-time students were majors enrolled in the program leading to certification in English language arts. An equal number are registered as minors, which also leads to teaching certification and intensive core course work in composition pedagogy. This allows us to be quite selective in the application process for undergraduate teaching positions, both in the prerequisites for applying and during an interview process.

While many of our graduate students define themselves as writers or scholars first, with little identity based on teaching, our undergraduate instructors see themselves first and foremost as teachers, with career goals within pedagogy. Also, while most of our graduate teaching assistants are just beginning their course work and are apt to feel pressure to stay afloat in their new academic contexts, our undergraduates are approaching the end of their studies and are often simply completing ancillary course work in a minor or neglected general education areas while awaiting a student teaching placement. Because of these factors, the undergraduate instructors are in a strong position to make their composition teaching their top priority.

WMU's English education program makes a great effort to ensure that composition is a key component of teacher preparation. All potential English 100 instructors have successfully completed a writing pedagogy course that focuses on theoretical and practical elements of teaching writing. In an exit survey, our fall 2002 instructors pointed to their prepreparation as one of the most important elements that led to their success. Stated one, "Before I began, I thought I was prepared for this. After a few weeks, I knew that I was prepared. By the end, I was simply thankful that I was prepared." Another considers, "I believe that one of the most contributing [factors] was that I already knew about writing. I wasn't just one step ahead of my students. I had a plan and an idea of what I wanted to do. I think a lot of this has to do with 479" (the writing pedagogy course).

An important element of this preparation and the ways it leads to the success of these novice teachers is the similar approach taken by the instructors in the English education program and the administrators in the composition program. There is a clear theoretical and pedagogical correlation within and between the programs. This is a key factor that helps the novice instructors make the transition from students to teachers. They immediately see connections between their English education writing preparation and the course they are tasked with teaching—assignments, processes, response and evaluation philosophies and systems are all similar to the ones discussed and practiced in their methods course. As one instructor later stated, "I always saw connections to the [issues] we discussed in class. I felt like I was in a 'lab,' testing out things we [had] talked about."

English 100 Student Characteristics

We must also admit that perhaps the most important element in this success is the student population. Shaughnessy's description of basic writers as "strangers in academia, unacquainted with the rules and rituals of college life, unprepared for the sorts of tasks their teachers were about to assign them"(3), does not often apply to the majority of students at our school and in our English 100 program. In a typical class of eighteen students there might be one for whom English is a second language and two or three students with learning disabilities ranging from dyslexia to ADHD. While these problems might seem too much for the average undergraduate teacher, even ones as gifted and motivated as ours, in reality they rarely cause much difficulty. The university offers an ESL program for those who need it, so most of those students who opt for Basic Writing have lived in the United States for a significant amount of time. One typical student was from India and came to this country when he was twelve years old. By the time he entered this class six years later, he was highly proficient in the language and only occasionally struggled with choosing words and phrases. He sometimes wrote, for example, "I was filled with joy" instead of "I was happy." His errors were relatively innocuous and were easily recognized by his peers who helped him revise his work. Likewise, the students with learning disabilities present few challenges for the new instructors because most have already developed useful learning strategies. Most of them need extra time to work and extra help recognizing mistakes; our curriculum naturally allows for both without making the writer stand apart as being different.

For the most part, our basic writers come from middle-class families where Standard or nearly Standard English is the norm; nearly all have at least one parent who went to college, and most are capable of doing college-level writing. This, of course, begs the question of why we place them in a remedial class at all. When Jeanne polled her students last year, they overwhelmingly cited the fact that they simply didn't work up to their abilities in high school and were subsequently behind. Some said they didn't like English, some didn't like the teacher, and others blamed the school system, but they all admitted to a certain lack of effort on their part. For students who simply need to catch up, the enthusiasm and creativity of our undergraduate instructors is invaluable, and the vast majority of our basic writers go on to succeed in the first-year course.

What Must Be Done to Support Undergraduate Instructors?

Despite some inherent advantages available to our program, we believe that much of our success comes from how our program prepares and supports our undergraduate instructors immediately before and during their English 100 teaching experiences. In the following sections, we list and explain activities we see to be essential to an undergraduate composition instructor's success. This list, based on many years of making a difficult situation work, may be a useful tool for other composition administrators who include undergraduates in teaching roles.

Careful Selection of Instructors

A careful and rigorous selection process is an extremely important element of our program's success. Without high-quality under-graduate instructors, other programmatic features designed to support and develop these teachers would be ineffective. We publicize opportunities widely within the English education program and then select only the top candidates who apply. This process is, in some ways, even more rigorous than that used to select graduate teaching assistants who teach other composition sections, since the criteria are developed solely around teaching rather than around teaching balanced with potential for literary scholarship or creative writing ability.

To be eligible, we require the following minimum qualifications:

- Successful completion of English 479: Teaching Writing in the Secondary School and most of their education courses
- Strong recommendations from English education faculty, with particular emphasis on composition
- A minimal overall GPA of 3.15 (out of 4.0)
- A portfolio of writings (with particular attention to academic writing) and materials relating to the teaching of writing
- A maximum course load of twelve credit hours during their teaching semester
- Willingness and ability to have no other job

We look for those individuals who have demonstrated a strong commitment to *teaching* English and who understand the importance of integrating pedagogy with content knowledge. GPA gives us one measure of their knowledge base, and perhaps more important, it frequently is an indicator of good student behaviors, behaviors necessary for teaching success. We also look carefully at the applicants' writing samples of typical academic papers. Besides their academic performance, the other major variable is time. Since these individuals are typically high achievers, they usually have unrealistic ideas of the time and energy teaching will require. Built into the recruiting process are restrictions on both the number of credits students can take and additional work for pay. Applicants must agree not to engage in any other work assignment without Georgina's permission. Students unwilling or financially unable to agree to these conditions are not hired. (Currently our 100 instructors are paid $2,200 for teaching this four-credit course.)

Careful Selection of Mentors

Graduate student mentors are selected on more intangible qualities. They have demonstrated a fascination with teaching composition, have developed a strong teacher persona, and have good insights into solving teacher–student conflicts. These mentors have taught both the general first-year comp course and the basic writing course. Their graduate assistantship includes teaching one section of basic writing and then working with the undergraduate instructors during the fall semester. (A typical teaching assistant would teach two sections of English 105.) The mentors have taken Methods in Teaching College Composition during their first semester, and they have taken an additional course in composition theory.

Ideally we have two graduate mentors—one new and one returning—so that an experienced mentor is always on staff. One mentor to no more than seven or eight instructors works well.

Close Discussions with English Education Faculty about Skills and Expectations

With the close connections and faculty crossover between composition faculty and English education faculty, it has not been difficult to ensure a strong understanding of the skills and expectations we desire in English 100 instructors. In particular, we have relied on English education faculty to inform the composition program about modifications to the writing methods curriculum, and we have created an active dialogue to ensure that skills, theories, and practices discussed in this course are theoretically compatible with English 100 teaching expectations. Jonathan also hosts a session in his composition methods classes wherein current and past undergraduate instructors come to describe their experiences to potential future instructors. This interchange has resulted in a large group of enthusiastic and well-informed potential candidates for English 100 teaching positions.

Inclusion in Preteaching Workshops

The undergraduate instructors, along with the graduate instructors for English 105, are required to attend a workshop on teaching college writing the week before fall term begins. During this event, we review objectives for the two courses, expectations for instructors, and then a variety of classroom techniques. All instructors meet for general presentations on topics such as strategies for responding to student writing; they then divide into small groups to work on application. Much of the time, the English 100 instructors work together on problems specific to a basic writing classroom. Their graduate mentors oversee these groups and lead the wrap-up discussions so that the applications stay specific to teaching basic writing.

Required Weekly Practica

Along with the workshop, the instructors are required to attend an hour-and-a-half weekly practicum meeting led by the graduate mentor. These meetings clarify upcoming lessons and address current problems. Frequently instructors share lessons that worked well in their classrooms and analyze those that went awry. Mentors set the agenda for half of the time, presenting and discussing particular issues or methods. The other forty-five minutes is given over to general discussion of how things are going. Instructors are quick to use this time to address problems in their classroom, seeking advice both from their peers and from the mentor.

Development of a Structured Role for Undergraduate Instructors

Mentoring for undergraduate instructors focuses first on implementing specific plans and assignments developed by the mentor. The first paper assignment is already developed; the first two weeks of materials are closely scripted, with minor room for individualized planning. With each subsequent paper assignment, more planning responsibility is allotted to the undergraduate instructors. In the final paper cycle, instructors are given rhetorical goals for the assignment and then asked to design their own project, with close advice and mentoring. Thus the practicum sessions in the early part of the semester are focused more on issues of teaching presence and day-to-day administrative support, with room at later sessions to support the instructors' small steps into curriculum design.

Regular Reflective Writing Assignments

As with most mentoring, one of our goals for undergraduate instructors is to have them not only be successful teachers but also know how and why their classroom lessons do or don't work. We do this by requiring weekly reflective writing assignments. Instructors submit outlines of their lessons, supporting classroom materials, and a summary of how they felt the lessons went and why.

This writing serves two purposes. First, it emphasizes the importance of being a reflective, thoughtful instructor. More important, from the perspectives of our roles as mentors and administrators, these short pieces provide early indications of problems and issues that require intervention and counseling.

Attention to the Development of Community and Collaboration

The ability to develop a sense of community and collaboration is perhaps the one trait that we see as most essential for undergraduate instructors. Our undergraduate instructors thrive on this sense of community. (One recent group of instructors took to calling themselves "the Pack" and often socialized together in much the same ways that early-career public school teachers tend to do.)

These instructors draw strength from their collective knowledge, skills, and abilities. The structure of the practicum encourages collaborative problem solving on all issues, from classroom management to planning. The end result has been a community of teachers who typically work to solve one another's problems and assist in developing the teaching skills of all members. This community provides an opportunity for these teachers to rehearse and articulate their ideas on teaching, writing, and other professional issues.

Overcoming Challenges

While our program has been largely successful, we continue to face many challenges and have been effective in meeting them to different degrees. Certain factors are simply beyond our control, so we seek to mitigate them as much as possible. We have found that the following elements are those that seem to constantly confront us and require continuous monitoring and intervention.

Integrating the Two Groups

In an ideal situation, graduate teaching assistants and undergraduate basic writing instructors would interact freely, and each group would benefit from the other; however, there are several reasons why this is not easy to accomplish. The new graduate instructors are at the beginning of the next phase of their academic careers. They are often unsure of themselves as teachers but fairly confident about their place in the English department. In contrast, the undergraduates are readying themselves to leave school, and they identify themselves as students rather than as faculty. Both groups work hard to balance their studies with the demands of teaching, leaving them unwilling to take on the added burden of fostering relationships that will likely be temporary.

There are also more pragmatic reasons why the two groups don't interact more; these reasons are easier to identify but no less difficult to overcome. Beginning with the weeklong orientation, graduate and undergraduate students are largely separated because they have different needs. The sections that are exclusively for the graduate students focus on pedagogical practices such as higher-order verses lower-order concerns, lesson planning, and the entire process method. The undergraduates review the same topics, but since these subjects are already familiar to them, discussions are directed at the ways these practices play out in the classroom. Both groups of instructors have specific needs that the orientation session addresses, but they also have some of the same concerns, and we work to integrate the groups whenever possible. The instructors as a whole, for example, tend to be very young, in many cases only a few years older than the students they will be teaching. We generally offer some instruction on how to maintain classroom authority; these talks are directed to both groups. We also serve lunch to both groups at the same time, allowing for some social interaction.

Once the orientation is over, new instructors attend a weekly practicum. The graduate practicum is a credit-bearing class, held on Friday mornings because there are no other English classes that day. Students graduating from the College of Education generally have more credit hours than they need, so their practicum does not earn them credit. Many of the undergraduate instructors are finishing up classes in other departments, so the weekly meeting has to be arranged around individual schedules. Integrating the instructors into a single practicum is neither feasible nor desirable, so the two groups are further segregated.

Integrating the graduate and undergraduate instructors is a challenge we continue to face, and we have to ask ourselves how we can balance the possible benefits of interaction with the difficulty of making that interaction possible. We also realize that even if we could effectively mingle the two groups, we might not get the results we hope for.

Getting the Graduate Students to Learn from the Undergraduate Students

Like most graduate students, ours come into the program feeling somewhat unsure about and unprepared in pedagogy. They quickly identify those returning instructors who are willing to unofficially mentor and guide them, and, combined with Georgina's teaching and ready advice, these new instructors mature into capable instructors over the course of a semester or two. The key is that they are always looking to those who have been where they have been and done what they have done. With very few exceptions, none of them has ever taken a basic writing class, and while they may idly wonder what the other instructors are doing, they rarely make a real connection between the two classes or recognize the abilities that basic writing instructors bring with them. Also, a certain amount of relief comes with the realization that there are instructors with even less institutional status and inherent authority to teach at the university level than they have. Combined, these factors often inhibit an exchange of ideas between undergraduate and graduate.

Closely connected to the issue of graduates' unwillingness to learn from undergraduates is the complication of the undergraduates' lack of comfort in a graduate setting. Although often little more than a diploma and an acceptance into the graduate program separates the two groups in terms of academic preparation, the distance seems much greater. The undergraduates are likely to see themselves as less mature and less able without realizing that their English education training gives them an advantage many graduate TAs don't have.

Sharing Resources

Undergraduates and graduate students share many resources, and while some of the sharing has been beneficial, some has been detrimental to students. One of the most obvious problems is the lack of space. Most composition instructors, along with a few doctoral students, have office space on a small portion of the eighth floor in an already overburdened building. Fifty-five instructors share nine offices. Graduate students are crowded into small offices while the undergraduates take up residence in a single room originally designed as a reception area. In some ways, this communal space is advantageous. Basic writing instructors use it as a place to gather between classes, both the ones they are taking and those they teach. It promotes a strong sense of community and allows the instructors to share ideas, materials, and encouragement. When instructors need to meet with students during office hours or for conferences, however, they rarely have free space in which to do so. This necessitates the use of other areas on campus that may not be sufficient in terms of privacy or convenience.

Space is not the only challenging resource. While graduate teaching assistants generally lean toward others teaching English 105 (first-year composition) for teaching materials, the undergraduates quite willingly borrow activities and ideas for paper assignments from instructors of either 100 or 105. Most of our basic writers go on to take English 105, so borrowed activities from this course become problematic when students begin to feel as if the second class is simply a rehash of the first. Last year we tackled this problem by printing up a booklet of activities exclusively for basic writing instructors. We have had to be even more diligent about shared paper assignments. Assignments for the introductory composition course are more rhetorically complex and thus not appropriate for the basic writing curriculum. Furthermore, students resent repeating a writing task they have already done. We have been able to avoid this problem by giving the basic writing instructors the first paper assignment and requiring them to turn in copies of subsequent assignments before they present them to the class. Anyone contemplating a program similar to ours should be aware that these problems, while fairly simple to avoid, could have a negative impact on the composition program as a whole.

Lack of Continuity

The last challenge we face is perhaps the most difficult: lack of continuity. Our basic writing instructors most often come to us the semester before they do their student teaching. Once that student teaching is finished, they graduate and begin looking for a job. Last year several instructors expressed an interest in returning to teach the basic writing class, but they were ultimately unable to do so because of their full-time jobs teaching at the secondary school level. This unfortunately leaves us in the position of beginning each fall semester with an inexperienced group of instructors.

We have been able to moderate this problem in several ways. The first, and most important, is the use of graduate mentors who have already taught the basic writing course. These people work closely with the new instructors through the practicum, teaching journals, and direct observation, ensuring that any difficulties are dealt with in a timely and effective manner. Another way we have been able to provide some continuity is through the use of part-time faculty. Jeanne returned this fall to teach two sections of basic writing, and another former graduate mentor taught one section. Previous graduate mentors are encouraged to participate in the orientation session, and they make themselves available to incoming instructors.

With the amount of training and mentoring the basic writing instructors receive throughout their semester of teaching, we would certainly prefer to have them teach more than one semester; however, that has rarely been possible.

Benefits

Despite the challenges, we believe there are some important benefits to including undergraduates in teaching roles within our program. In particular, we see benefits for our undergraduate instructors and the students they teach. We also see some benefits for our graduate students. All of these combined lead to a net benefit for our entire composition program.

How Undergrad Instructors Benefit

Clearly, those who benefit most from this experience are the undergraduate instructors themselves. A Kalamazoo area school principal recently told Jonathan that he interviewed and subsequently hired one of our former students primarily because of the English 100 experience she was able to claim on her résumé.

The opportunity these novice teachers get to practice their craft in a relatively low-risk environment with a close support network is one that many other preservice secondary teachers can only envy from a distance. We often hear from other former undergraduates in the English education program during their internship/student teaching. They compare their struggles to those of the students who taught English 100 and lament their own lack of practical experience and knowledge compared to their contemporaries'.

In retrospect, the undergraduate instructors also see the experience as an important professional opportunity. Stated one recent instructor, "Now that I'm interning, and by myself mostly, I draw on the experiences I had last year. The crises I would have had, I had last year, and I had the "pack" to help me out. If it happened this year, I would be lost."

How the English 100 Students Benefit

We also believe that students who take classes with our undergraduate instructors benefit. We want to emphasize one key point: for whatever reasons, both institutional and programmatic, our undergraduate instructors do an excellent job. The results as evidenced by their students are clear: a strong success rate in our first-year composition course, positive course evaluations, and informal comments from other introductory instructors about the surprising quality of writing coming from former English 100 students.

These basic writers come into contact with enthusiastic teachers who are committed and excited about teaching. After years of training, thought, and preparation, our undergraduate instructors get a chance to "try out" all their ideas and develop relationships with students. As a result, they tend to get excited about "good" work and provide positive feedback. They are encouraging and nurturing, with a vested interest in helping students to succeed. This is particularly important for the student population that is usually placed in English 100—those who were habitually forgotten or ignored (many times due to their own apathy) during their high school education.

English 100 students are almost uniformly positive about their experiences with their instructors. Typical comments include these from the fall of 2002:

> "I learned so much about writing. I thought I knew how to write before I got here. Now I really know. I feel ready for college."

"This was the only class where I felt like I was important. I knew [she] knew when I missed class."

"This is the BEST instructor. I wish I could have him next semester."

How Graduate Students Benefit

As we discussed in the Overcoming Challenges section, this is an area we are still struggling to develop. Many of our graduate students distance themselves from the undergraduate instructors, isolating themselves from the potential benefits to be gained from the intense pedagogical preparation of the undergraduate instructors. We see so many connections between the two groups that could benefit both—the pedagogical knowledge of many of the undergraduates and their commitment to teaching could offer alternative narratives about the professional roles of our graduate students. Likewise, the greater maturity often seen in our graduate students could help temper some of our undergraduates' overenthusiasm.

This is not to say that some graduate students do not benefit in important ways by interacting with the undergraduate instructors. This benefit is most strongly apparent in the opportunities for leadership and professional development provided by supervisory roles as mentors for these instructors. Jeanne is an excellent example of the result of this professional opportunity. After an outstanding teaching experience as a graduate instructor, she used her time as a mentor for the undergraduate instructors as an opportunity to develop her professional knowledge in composition and to position herself for a doctoral program in composition studies and English education. The mentor who followed Jeanne into the same role (and served as the incoming "co-mentor" during her tenure) is using the opportunity in much the same manner, developing his professional portfolio for future graduate experiences.

How the Program Benefits

In short, we believe that our composition program, despite the challenges, has received a net benefit from the presence of these novice instructors. In addition to the specific benefits already discussed, we see institutional benefits for the program as well. This is particularly relevant to our program's institutional status. At Western Michigan, the English department tends to place its priorities in other areas, leaving composition to run with minimal institutional support. Georgina *is* the composition program—mentor, administrator, graduate professor. She holds a primarily administrative position; there are no other tenure-track composition positions in the department. The English 100 program provides important professional connections between Georgina and the composition program and her natural colleagues in pedagogy within English education, and specifically with writing teacher education and the local Writing Project site.

Conclusion: It's Not Perfect, but We'll Keep It . . .

When Georgina was recently asked (in a roundabout way) what she thought of "farming out" English 100 to a local community college rather than using the undergraduate instructors, her answer was an emphatic "No!" Despite the liabilities of undergraduate instructors, their service provides more control over the appropriateness and quality of the basic writing curriculum, allowing us to build continuity from English 100 to 105. Basic writing students enrolled in the area community colleges have different literacy needs from those of our students. Also, it is likely the community college would hire contract instructors to teach these courses, with limited resources for training and mentoring, and the community does not have a ready pool of experienced basic writing instructors. Since hiring undergraduates remains the cheapest way to teach these courses, administration opted to continue this practice, for the time being.

As with many other institutions hitting rocky financial times, our administration is again looking at remedial courses as a place to trim expenses. It is likely we will be put in the position of arguing that our basic writing program best serves our secondary education program—that it provides a unique professionalization opportunity for our best majors—in order to justify providing these struggling writers with an opportunity to develop their abilities. If given a choice between farming out or maintaining the program, we would choose to continue to teach this course with the assistance of undergraduate instructors, select them carefully, nurture and mentor them, and serve our students while giving upcoming middle school and high school teachers an important professional development experience. It's not perfect, but we'll keep it . . . for now.

Work Cited

Shaughnessy, Mina P. *Errors and Expectations: A Guide for the Teacher of Basic Writing*. New York: Oxford UP, 1977.

CHAPTER EIGHT

Chickens, Eggs, and the Composition Practicum

ANNE TRUBEK
Oberlin College

Why It Is Impossible to Teach This Course

The comment I receive most often from students about the syllabus for Teaching and Tutoring Writing Across the Curriculum, the undergraduate composition practicum I teach, is "maybe we should have read 'x' sooner." Funny thing is, "x" varies widely; sometimes it's Mary Louise Pratt's "Arts of the Contact Zone," sometimes it's Lisa Delpit's "The Silenced Dialogue," sometimes it's a tip sheet on how to set an agenda for a tutoring session.

Teaching a composition practicum, particularly one for undergraduates, requires innumerable steps backward, and each time I prepare a new version of the syllabus, I agonize over what to assign first. I consider the divergent suggestions made by previous students, and I struggle with my own set of "maybe we should read 'x' sooner" questions. To discuss the strategies for initiating a tutoring session, for example, I need to explain that tutoring goes beyond editing and proofreading. To explain what tutoring does mean, I need to introduce them to the field of rhetoric and composition. To avoid dogmatism, I need to introduce them to the many debates within the field. To help them understand these debates, I need to provide them background in the history of rhetoric and composition. To do that, I need to situate the field within the history of its relationship to English. . . . I never reach the starting line.

It's no wonder that students often suggest another order for the readings. How I order the readings says as much about what

I value and privilege as any discussion I might lead about those readings. A syllabus is a blueprint, a rhetorical form that embodies theoretical precepts.

As I prepare the syllabus each semester, I run up against three interrelated problems: (1) How do I simultaneously train peer tutors and introduce undergraduate students to the field of composition studies? (Summarized by the question "What do I assign first?) (2) How do I organize the course so as not to continue a common, dissonant approach to the composition practicum? The comp practicum, as I understand it from experience, readings, Web searches, and other sources, is usually a traditional seminar focused on discussion of academic essays that transmit the conventional wisdom of writing center practices. The course is often hierarchically structured and requires students to produce a conventional, academic final paper proving their grasp of the material. The students are expected, however, to demonstrate in said essay their understanding of process-based principles. They are trained, or instructed, to become convention-questioning, nondirective, discovery-eliciting pedagogues. (3) How do I teach heuristic methods heuristically?

This chapter narrates attempts I've made to solve these problems in various iterations of the tutor training course I teach. At some point in this chapter, I conclude that the composition practicum should not include composition theory. This leads me to troubling conjectures about the field: the project of composition studies is impossible, because it is undergirded by composition theory, much of which claims that writing can't be taught. Composition studies is disseminated primarily through the practicum. The conflict between composition theory and the aims of the practicum makes teaching others composition studies well-nigh impossible if one accepts a theory position, which means the field of composition studies cannot be self-sustaining. Such slippery slope logic tempts me to throw up my hands in despair, write a memo to my dean telling him I believe Oberlin's rhetoric and composition program should wither away, and look for a new line of work.

Writing an essay about pedagogy, however, affords me a realm of action substantively different than does teaching a tutor training course. The twain can never exactly meet. Therefore, I can come to conclusions here without being beholden to future tutors when I next sit down to prepare a syllabus. The syllabus, however, lies between the abstraction of theory (and scholarly essays) and practice (teaching tutors, tutors tutoring). And that is the cause of my chicken/egg dilemma.

Why I Teach It: Rhetoric and Composition at Oberlin College

I work in very different institutional circumstances from those of most contributors to this volume, and of most in the field of rhetoric and composition. These differences make my concerns somewhat ancillary to the field and afford me a perspective from which to contribute another, hopefully instructive, point of view.

Oberlin College has no composition course requirement. Students must demonstrate writing proficiency in order to graduate. Writing proficiency can be earned one of two ways: by receiving a 710 or above on the SAT II or by completing writing intensive or writing proficiency courses in two different departments. Writing intensive courses are those that require at least fifteen pages of writing and include some instruction in writing; proficiency courses require fifteen pages of writing.

I teach within a freestanding rhetoric and composition program. The program consists of three FTEs (full-time equivalents). Our mission is to support the college's writing proficiency requirement. Every year, we offer basic writing, first-year writing, advanced composition, and the practicum, Rhetoric 481, Teaching and Tutoring Writing Across the Curriculum (hereafter referred to as RHET 481). We do not offer a major, but a handful of students declare a minor in rhetoric and composition each year. All faculty within the program are tenured or tenure track.

RHET 481 is open to any junior or senior who writes well. Students must apply to take the course, and the application process consists of a writing sample and a paragraph describing why the student wants to enroll. Usually, two-thirds of the students are English majors. In fall 2003, fourteen students enrolled. One was a biology major, six were English majors, three were religion majors, one was a politics major, one was a creative writing major, one was a Spanish major, and one was an environmental studies major. The course is cross-listed in the English department and counts as a 300-level course for English majors.

While students are enrolled in the three-credit RHET 481, they must work in Oberlin's Writing Associates Program, thus ensuring the practicum component of the course. Currently, there are four separate options for employment within the program: working at the drop-in writing center, assisting professors teaching a writing intensive course, working in the community-based writing program, or serving as a discipline-specific writing associate.[1] Writing associates are paid well. In any given semester, there are twenty-five to forty writing associates in the program.

Faculty interested in having a writing associate send the program coordinator a note to that effect, and potential students are then put in touch with those faculty members. An average of sixteen writing associates assist courses each semester. The drop-in writing center is open in the evenings and weekend afternoons.

While my institution affords me the institutional prestige so many rightfully demand of their own—including tenure and the opportunity to teach a three-credit practicum—a familiar status differential remains because our program is perceived to be a lamentable locus of service to many faculty, administrators, and students. If only high schools would better prepare their students for college-level writing, the misguided logic goes, we wouldn't need to have this program or teach these courses. The infrastructure, however, makes these unfortunate perceptions annoying but not systemically troublesome. Many who desire the opportunity to construct a three-credit syllabus for a practicum from a space of relative institutional security would be so lucky to have the luxury to critique their own syllabus, as I will now do. The syllabus is available in the appendix at the end of this chapter.

Why I Bang My Head against the Wall

Before each semester starts, I know what I will encounter on the first day of class: a roomful of eager, earnest students nervous about the prospect of helping peers with their writing. They may be about to meet with members of a first-year seminar, or they may be about to staff the writing center, waiting for that first tutee to open the door and ask for help.

The easiest way to allay their anxieties, of course, is to tell them what to do. I have done this by assigning them articles on process-based pedagogy that provide helpful techniques: don't hold a pen, ask heuristic questions, focus on ideas. When I do this, the anxiety level in the classroom drops noticeably. I can see them go through stages of relief: this might be fun, this might be intellectually challenging, thank god I don't have to fake my knowledge of grammar anymore. Here is a typical response, written for the second day of class, after the student completed the introductory set of readings:

> Upon reading Stephen North's "The Idea of a Writing Center" and "Revisiting 'The Idea of a Writing Center,'" I must admit that I am guilty of believing a number of the misconceptions about writing centers he is so forcefully trying to uproot within these essays. My previous dealings with the writing center are of the type North dislikes: they were merely visits to polish final papers, perhaps gain a new perspective on my topic or to catch spelling and grammatical errors that had gone by unnoticed. (And to boot, I have only ever been twice, despite the large number of my papers that no doubt would have benefited from a second opinion.) I believed that is what the writing center was there for. . . . North's point regarding experimentation with methods struck me and altered the view I had of this course. I expected there to be a template by which we run a series of steps carried out with every student that came to the writing center. But molding the approach to each individual that comes in, catering to where they are at that point and finding the right way to work with that person seems much more practical and efficient. North emphasizes the importance of meeting someone where they are in their compositional process and finding what works. I expect to learn to think on my feet and to be creative with the suggestions I make to others.[2]

This student has unconsciously absorbed a basic contradiction inherent in process pedagogy: she has applied North to her own nascent pedagogy and concluded she should "mold her approach" to each individual student and not use a "template." Of course, that guideline, which soothes the student's anxiety, is itself a template of sorts.[3] She has also conveniently failed to account for the opposing viewpoints expressed in Berlin's Marxian "Rhetoric and Ideology in the Writing Class," the third reading assigned that day. Her response, as are many students' to these three readings, is built on neglect of a less user-friendly, more complicated article.

When I provide tutors with techniques for how to tutor, I am transmitting methods derived from a specific, historically based theory about the writing process. There is no "right" way, of course, to tutor, only different choices. But process-based pedagogy has a stranglehold of sorts in the field when it comes to *techniques* for one-on-one writing instruction. My students must do something when they meet that first tutee, and I feel compelled to give them some tips. So I tell them that telling, or directive methods, may be unnecessary, even damaging. I do this so they will feel more equipped to tutor, but as I do I hear myself getting caught in a contradiction I keep trying to escape: "When you tutor, *I am telling you* don't tell students what to do *even though that's exactly what I, your teacher, am doing right now*."

I cannot practice what I preach, and I don't preach what I practice. Over the years, I have grown increasingly disillusioned with the gospels of process-based tutoring techniques. I have rethought these precepts based on pedagogical experiences and study of composition theory. I don't know when or how exactly these changes in my pedagogy occurred; it would impossible to prune genealogical branches to answer a which-came-first question. But my students and I differ in that they lack the luxury of reflection.

So how should I train tutors if I lack full faith in the almost exclusively process-based techniques available to novice tutors? How do I allow my students to decide for themselves whether they must learn on the job? I've attempted to address these problems by borrowing a page from Gerald Graff's book and "teach the conflicts." Thus, in fall 2003, the first readings I assigned were, as noted earlier, Berlin's "Rhetoric and Ideology in the Writing Class" and North's "The Idea of a Writing Center" and "Revisiting 'The Idea of a Writing Center.'" The second set of readings consisted of Harris's "Talking in the Middle," Bruffee's "Peer Tutoring and the 'Conversation of Mankind,'" Gillespie and Lerner's "The Tutoring Process," and Brooks's "Minimalist Tutoring: Making the Student Do All the Work." I asked students to complete the readings in the order they were listed, so they would read, say, critiques of Murray after having read Murray. This is the simple move of laying bare ideology so as to prompt reflection.

While the syllabus itself offers no clear "answer" to how to tutor, I still need to decide how to organize the class time during class itself. Heuristic methods are expressions of underlying theoretical precepts. And constant questioning leads me to feel that I must hold back knowledge, often to ridiculous ends (feeling abashed, for example, if I tell tutors how I would have handled a given scenario, even if they directly ask me for input). I hear the frustration this method causes tutors when they ask me questions such as "Why can't I just tell them that's how I would do it? Why does it have to be some sort of guessing game?"

Meanwhile, while teaching first-year composition, I have slowly shed my hesitancy about offering models and explaining grammatical rules, two no-nos of process pedagogy. I've overcome my fear of telling, and I'm teaching better as a result. My first-year students have responded gratefully. After explaining to an introductory composition class what made one sample essay better than another, one student told me: "Often it's like there's this mystery behind the process; now it doesn't seem so mysterious to me." I've found that teaching grammatical rules does in fact help students' grammar when it is done in context and at a point when students are seeking information. As Lisa Delpit has so convincingly argued, holding back the codes of power only works for those who already know them.

But, to go back to the first week of RHET 481, how do I teach these initiates? They should be free to choose a process-based peer tutoring pedagogy should they so desire. They needn't arrive at the same conclusions I have: after all, if they all did, I would have failed as a teacher. How then should I lead them through the material? Should I ask them questions, thus modeling and underwriting one approach, leaving me feeling as if I'm acting in bad faith? Or should I tell them what works for me, the rules for semicolons, and other "directive" approaches?

In fall 2003, I decided to mix it up all the time and in the process created collective anxiety. One student explained that he had chosen to assign Nancy Welch's "Playing with Reality: Writing Centers after the Mirror Stage" for his teaching session because "one thing I like about this article is that it seems to encourage the neurosis that we all seem to have developed by taking your class." In our first mock tutoring session, I played the role of tutor for the first time; in the past, I had two students do it, so as not to overly direct or influence them. I asked students to write discussion questions for the class in advance so that my questions wouldn't dictate the tenor of discussion too much. Despite my convoluted attempts to redress the problem of training-without-indoctrinating, halfway through the semester, with tutoring experience and more contradictory, taking-opposite-sides readings under their belts, students were saying things like this: "Despite what you've taught us is the best way to tutor, professors think we should be teaching grammar." "Even though we're told not to tell students anything, sometimes I say something like 'Professor X likes papers that do this or that' and then I feel really guilty." It seemed the tutors were chronically feeling guilty for one thing or another, and they were streaming into my office for one-on-one conferences in which they asked me for pedagogical penance: "Is it okay that I told an ESL student that her verb tenses were wrong?" "Is it okay that I told a tutee that I disagreed with this thesis?" It bothered me that somehow I was making students feel bad about what they were doing. Not only was it troubling pedagogically, but also I wondered if I had inadvertently perpetuated a moralistic strain in rhetoric and composition, related to our service ethos and our sometimes overblown self-described roles as saviors of the academic downtrodden.

Disturbed by the neuroses and secret confessionals, I asked my RHET 481 students (with whom I had not yet shed my fear of "telling") the following question: "Why is it that, even though I have endeavored to introduce you to varying pedagogies and theories, told you I aimed to introduce you to the debates within the field, and assigned you many readings that argue against nondirective approaches to tutoring, you assume there is one way you are supposed to tutor, and that way is based on process pedagogy?" One student offered this explanation: "When you're new to a field and starting to tutor for the first time, you are going to hold on to things that tell you it's okay if you don't have expert knowledge." The others concurred. In other words, a nondirective, nondisciplinary method that argues that knowledge of grammatical rules is unnecessary is simply going to be more appealing to novices. (Perhaps, if this student is right, rhetoric and composition would have as much status in academia as physics if we had founded our discipline on the precept that only very technical, specialized training would do?)

At the end of the semester, I asked the students to read the abstract for this essay and offer comments. In the abstract, I discuss my decision to assign both theoretical and practical articles. One student asked which of the articles they had read were theoretical and which were practical. I went through the syllabus and, wincing, listed those that I felt fell into each camp. Two students said that, while they had liked reading the theoretical articles, they didn't think those articles had "changed the way we tutored." I asked them how, then, they came to tutor the way they do, and they said, "It was the readings we did early on, you know, the ones about not holding a pen, asking questions, etc. You're always most influenced by what you read first." We then looked back at the syllabus and saw the early readings, Grimm and Delpit alongside Harris and Sommers. To be fair, some students said that they were constantly questioning how they tutored. "Every time I sit down with a student," one said, "I think about the last five articles I read and all the various different things I should be thinking about." To my satisfaction, one student said, "Right now, I think we all tutor quite differently. A few weeks ago, I don't think that was true."

In my aim to be as nondoctrinaire as possible, and to encourage self-reflection on practice generated by divergent theoretical positions (as well as experience), I have had some success. Nonetheless, I'm haunted by the finality of early readings built on the intentional forgetting of complexity. Accessible, tip-friendly readings inevitably create a template. I'm haunted as well by what a former student said to me, the semester after she took the practicum, of her current tutoring job: "It's not like last semester. I don't think about it so much. I just do it."

I Think I Think Too Much

When I started teaching RHET 481, I wanted to assert the rigor and difficulty of the course. I wanted to do this because, as a new junior faculty member, I wanted my colleagues to take me seriously. I wanted faculty and students to perceive the work I do as just as important and serious as the work being done in politics, history, and even, perhaps especially, other English classes. In addition to vanity, I did it because I believe theory to be crucial to reflective practice. What I didn't consider is whether theory need be assigned to undergraduate tutors-in-training. I require theory to create a responsible syllabus, and good tutors should work from a theoretically informed position. But I needn't include theoretical articles on the syllabus to accomplish those goals.

So I began to consider how else to approach the syllabus. Because I no longer wanted to "hold back knowledge," I culled practical articles to assign those I felt would offer the best nuts-and-bolts tips. I integrated methods from my introductory courses that focus on production rather than consumption of texts. I assigned, for example, weekly projects. Previously, the course was structured more like a traditional graduate seminar, with presentations, midterm, and final papers. Now students would need to write every week. I assigned topics that required them to synthesize readings with tutoring experiences but to do so by writing in the modes discussed: revise an essay using a handbook during "grammar week," construct an argument during "rhetoric" week, write internal and terminal comments on an essay during "responding to student writing" week. I altered the longer assignments so they more clearly emphasized the practicum nature of the course; rather than ask students to write an academic essay, I asked them to add a resource to the Writing Associates Program. Examples of such projects include guides for professors working with tutors, Web sites on working with ESL students, and proposals for online tutoring.

No longer do I feel that, although the focus in composition is on production rather than consumption, the practicum still focuses on consumption. Still, I'm frustrated by the readings: the practical articles still assume an unexamined process-based pedagogy; the theoretical articles still seem largely beside the point. I vowed I would no longer assign "tertiary theory"—articles that draw on other theories that are applied to composition studies, which I then translate to an audience of undergraduates—and would instead assign "primary" texts: Aristotle, Burke, Freire. But I could never pull the trigger.

Not until I began outlining all these various changes, responses, and frustrations did I realized that the answer was not more theory, but less. I've been going about it wrong all along. The best way to train peer tutors is to put them through the same paces I put my other students through, to actually teach by doing rather than telling them to teach by doing. And so the next time I teach the course, I will supply a bibliography comprising the theoretical texts assigned in past semesters. But I won't make students read them. Instead, I will require them to write, write often and imaginatively, revise their work, edit, and proofread. I will teach them the rules of grammar. I will ask them to model and imitate other writers. I will ask them to review one another's work. And then they can decide—without my convoluted moves to tell them without telling them—how to tutor their peers.

Conclusion: Why the Conclusion of This Article Will Not "Apply" to Teaching

I came to the conclusion to purge theory from my syllabus through practice, the practice of teaching a tutor training course. No one taught me how to teach a composition practicum, and I came to this decision through the process of reflection on practice, a habit of abstract theorizing integral to my pedagogical method. The syllabus is the text through which I manifest conclusions arrived at through practice and reflection. If composition studies could be metaphorized through an academic genre, it would be the syllabus. Not the classroom, not the graduation requirement, not the scholarly article. The syllabus.

I could suggest we suspend theory until after students have had tutoring experiences. But, for me, this would be an act of bad faith. It would solve the problem of what to assign first by, metaphorically, not assigning anything, but with the promise that next semester answers would be revealed. Holding back theory until after students have practiced doesn't solve my problem. Nor would the opposite solution I've toyed with, allowing students to tutor only after they have completed the training course. Abstract knowledge does not transmute into know-how. If there were an answer to the chicken/egg dilemma, we wouldn't still be wrestling with it.

Next time I teach RHET 481, I'll assign this essay first. And I will keep teaching the same way because in the world of the practicum, you've got to have chickens and eggs together. We'll probably create more collective neuroses, and students will complain about my assigning this text first, and I will have nagging doubts about my pedagogical choices. Still, I will not eliminate the tension from my syllabus that has led me to make the arguments I have in this essay. I value the composition practicum because it viscerally proves the claim that you cannot "apply" theory without rendering it untheoretical. I value scholarship because it releases us from the burden of application. I can preach what I cannot practice. Here, on this page, it's chickens all the way down.

Appendix

Teaching and Tutoring Writing Across the Disciplines

Fall 2003
Rhetoric and Composition 481/English 399
Anne Trubek

Course Objectives and Procedures

This course combines two ways of knowing, the practical ("how") and the theoretical ("what"). It aims to help you learn how to tutor writing, including pedagogies, techniques, protocols, and strategies that help students not only write better papers but also become better writers. It also aims to provide you with a theoretical understanding of what writing is, what writers and readers are, how we compose, how we revise, what institutions of higher learning assume or desire writing to be, and what we mean by "Rhetoric and Composition." If all goes well, these two ways of knowing will test each other: your tutoring experiences may lead you to revise your theoretical views and vice versa.

Practical and theoretical knowledge aren't easily segregated, and the most successful tutoring often involves a merger of the two. The course is designed with the goal of complicating any easy taxonomies between theory and practice and between differing theories and practices. In the course, we will mimic the kinds of shifting skills and points of views required of good tutoring. For example, many of the readings explicitly contradict each other, presenting you with opposing views to sift through. The readings are rhetorically vastly varied: some of them consist of short tips for tutoring, some are theoretical essays written by and for professors of Composition, some are experimental style exercises.

Not only do theory and practice blur while tutoring but so too do the boundaries between reading and writing. As tutors, you will read student writing, tutees will be writing in response to readings, you may write on student essays, etc. The course tries to emulate this element of tutoring by breaking down traditional boundaries between the "writing" and "reading" required in an academic course. You will be asked to write frequently, informally, and experimentally in response to readings; you will be asked to read the writings of your classmates as part of the course's "texts," and some classes will be set aside to write about readings in the form of in-class workshops.

Finally, tutoring writing is as much about speaking as about reading and writing, as most tutoring situations involve talking to each other. Therefore, I have built a significant oral component into the course, and in our discussions and presentations you should reflect upon orality—not only your oral skills but also how orality differs (or doesn't) from writing as a mode of communication.

The result of all this mixing and blurring of boundaries is a course that requires you to navigate between many different ways of knowing, reading, writing, speaking, tutoring. You may, at times, be confused and frustrated. One week you may understand that the best way to tutor is by adhering to dogma x; the next you may read an article convincing you of the political backwardness of dogma x and the true path offered by dogma y. If the course objectives are met, though, you will learn how to be flexible and willing to rethink, revise, and retheorize what you're learning and practicing as you are learning and practicing it. You'll be doing all this while on the job—working with student writers. It may be daunting and intimidating, but it will also—hopefully—be exhilarating and rewarding, both for you (as tutor and student) and for the students you tutor.

Course Requirements

Write: You will complete a short project, whether informal essay, copyediting, observation of a tutoring session, etc., every week. Projects are meant to help you think through issues addressed in readings, discussions, and tutoring. The most successful projects will integrate practical experience with theoretical issues, referencing both particular tutoring situations and readings for that week. Projects must be posted to Blackboard by 9:35 on Thursdays. You will hand in all your projects twice during the semester for holistic grades. *Projects 1–6 20%; projects 7–9: 20%*

Ask Good Questions: Good tutors (and teachers) ask good questions. And asking good questions is an art—it's called heuristics. Heuristic questions guide learners, who adopt the role of discoverers. These questions will ideally elicit desire in learners to invent or construct knowledge for themselves, rather than be told answers. To practice this demanding art, I ask you to ask questions. The readings for each class session have been selected to highlight debates, and often present divergent views of an issue. Once during the semester, you will submit three questions about these readings for discussion. These questions should help prompt the class to consider readings more closely, consider connections between readings, and consider our own positions on debated issues. You will initiate class discussion, using the questions as the basis for your response. Questions will be evaluated on their ability to produce better understanding and new ways of thinking about readings (and not simply controversy or confessions). Questions must be posted to Blackboard at least two days before the readings will be discussed. *10%*

Contribute a Resource: During the semester, you will encounter tutoring issues, be they grammatical, cultural, rhetorical, or organizational, that may cause you to seek out further resources for assistance. Undoubtedly, other tutors will run across the same issues during their work. To help us all in the Peer Tutoring Program have more resources ready at hand for addressing these issues, I ask you to contribute one resource to the program on one issue. The resource could be a handout, an addition to our webpage, or a reading to be assigned in subsequent sections of 481, with accompanying rationale. These can be turned in at any point during the semester, but all must be completed by November 13. *10%*

Teach: You will be asked to teach part of one class session at the end of the semester. You will need to plan the session (what readings to assign, what to ask your classmates to discuss, do, etc.). The best classes will be neither "nuts and bolts" explanations of a writing issue nor abstract explanations of a theoretical concept. Instead, they will demonstrate both know-how *and* know-what. Class sessions will be assessed based upon organization, demonstrated understanding of relevant scholarly and practical issues, advance preparation, careful consideration of audience, ability to lead others in a classroom setting, and creativity. *30%*

State Your Purpose: Many professors and educators are being encouraged to write statements of teaching that explain the reasons behind the choices they make as teachers—why they construct their syllabi as they do, why they assign what they do, why they say what they do. These statements are included in job applications, grant proposals, etc. At the end of the semester, you will write your own such statement of yourself as a peer tutor. (You may find it will come in handy for your own applications down the road. . . .) Statements should be 2–3 pages long. Successful statements will be well-written, concise, thoughtful, original explanations of your views, values, and practices. *10%*

Tutor: You must tutor for at least 6 hours a week at the Peer Tutoring Center, assist a writing intensive course, or participate in the Community-Based Writing Program. Please spend some time on our website at **http://www.oberlin.edu/ptp.**

483: Tutoring Lab. You must attend every meeting of 483. All tutors working in the Peer Tutoring Program, including those who have already taken 481, will meet 4–6 times during the semester to discuss assignments and schedules, tutoring successes and mishaps, readings, and suggestions for improving the program. As this is a required staff development meeting, you will be paid for your time: each meeting is equivalent to one hour of tutoring.

Course Texts

Available at Mindfair Bookstore:

Villanueva, ed. *Cross-Talk in Comp Theory*, Second Edition
Williams, *Style: Ten Lessons in Clarity and Grace*, Seventh Edition

Also required, but not purchased for you:

Any recent handbook (easily found used)

Syllabus

CT = *Cross-Talk in Comp Theory*
eres = Electronic Reserve (password: RHET481)

Week 1   Introduction: Why We're Here

Sept. 2   Introductions

Sept. 4   Discussion of Readings

> Berlin, "Rhetoric and Ideology in the Writing Class" (CT)
> North, "The Idea of a Writing Center" (handout)
> North, "Revisiting 'The Idea of a Writing Center'" (handout)

Project 1: After completing the readings, write an informal essay on your preconceptions about Oberlin's Peer Tutoring Program—what led you to apply? What do you think tutoring will entail? Have the readings altered your assumptions?

Week 2 Theories and Practices of Peer Tutoring: What to Do and Why Not to Do It

Sept. 9 Discussion of Readings

> Harris, "Talking in the Middle" (eres)
>
> Bruffee, "Peer Tutoring and the 'Conversation of Mankind'" (handout)
>
> Gillepsie and Lerner, "The Tutoring Process" (eres)
>
> Brooks, "Minimalist Tutoring: Making the Student Do All the Work" (handout)

Sept. 11 Discussion of Readings

> Grimm, "Toward a Fair Writing Center Practice" (eres)
>
> Shamoon and Burns, "A Critique of Pure Tutoring" (handout)
>
> Clark and Healy, "Are Writing Centers Ethical?" (handout)
>
> Trimbur, "Peer Tutoring: A Contradiction in Terms?" (handout)
>
> *Mock Tutoring Part One*
>
> *Project 2: Be tutored by someone in the class or an experienced tutor. Take notes on your experience. Write up your notes, incorporating readings from this week.*

Week 3 The Writing Process and the Post-Process Critique

Sept. 16 Discussion of Readings

> Murray, "Teach Writing as a Process Not Product"(CT)
>
> Sommers, "Revision Strategies of Student Writers and Experienced Adult Writers" (CT)
>
> Breuch, "Post-Process 'Pedagogy': A Philosophical Exercise" (CT)
>
> Delpit, "The Silenced Dialogue: Power and Pedagogy in Educating Other People's Children" (CT) [available only in CT First Edition]

Sept. 18 *Mock Tutoring Part Two*

> *Project 3: Observe two tutoring sessions by two different tutors and take notes. Write up notes, incorporating readings where appropriate.*

Week 4 Responding to Student Writing—Some Advice and a Cautionary Tale

Sept. 23 Discussion of Readings

> Sommers, "Responding to Student Writing" (eres)
>
> Straub, "Responding—Really Responding—to Other Students' Writing" (eres)
>
> Brodkey, "On the Subjects of Class and Gender in 'The Literacy Letters'" (CT)

Sept. 25 In-Class Workshop on Responses

> *Project 4: Write internal and terminal comments on a draft by a classmate.*

Week 5 Style—There Is No Error There

Oct. 30 Williams, *Style* (read Lesson 10, "The Ethics of Prose," first)

Oct. 2 Style Workshop

> *Project 5: After reading Williams, revise anything you've recently written, whether an essay for another class,* Review *article, job application material, project for this class, etc. Post reflection to Blackboard, integrating readings where appropriate.*

Week 6 ESL and What We Do When We "want to work on grammar"

Oct. 7 Discussion of Readings

> Hartwell, "Grammar, Grammars, and the Teaching of Grammar" (CT)
>
> Young, "Can You Proofread This?" (eres)
>
> Harris, "Tutoring ESL Students" (eres)
>
> Gillespie and Lerner, "Working with ESL Students" (eres)

Oct. 9 ESL and Grammar Workshop

*Project 6: Working with the Bedford handbook, copyedit any-
thing you've recently written, whether an essay for another
class,* Review *article, job application material, project for this
class, etc. Post reflection to Blackboard, integrating readings
where appropriate.*

Hand in Projects 1–6

Week 7 What Should We Do with Those Computers?

Oct. 14 Discussion of Readings

> Anson, "Distant Voices: Teaching and Writing in a Culture
> of Technology" (CT)
>
> Hobson, "Straddling the Virtual Fence" (handout)
>
> Coogan, "Towards a Rhetoric of Online Tutoring" (hand-
> out)

Oct. 16 Mid-Term Reflections/Evaluations

FALL BREAK [Week 8]

Week 9 What Is Rhetoric Anyway?

Oct. 28 Discussion of Readings

> Kinneavy, "The Basic Aims of Discourse" (CT)
>
> Berlin, "Contemporary Composition: The Major Pedagog-
> ical Theories" (CT)
>
> Corbett and Connors, Introduction to *Classical Rhetoric
> for the Modern Student*, pp. 15–27 (handout)

Oct. 30 Argumentation Workshop

> *Project 7: An argument that persuades the Peer Tutoring Pro-
> gram to change a current practice.*

Week 10 What Is/Should Be Academic Discourse?

Nov. 4   Discussion of Readings

> Royster, "When the First Voice You Hear Is Not Your
> Own" (CT)
>
> Bartholomae, "Inventing the University" (CT)

Miller, "The Arts of Complicity: Pragmatism and the Culture of Schooling" (CT)

Nov. 6   Pratt, "Arts of the Contact Zone" (eres)

Hairston, "Diversity, Ideology, and Teaching Writing" (CT)

Project 8: Inventing Oberlin: A topic of your choosing in a discourse of your own.

Week 11 Inside and Outside the Academy: Service Learning, Basic Writing, Disciplinarity

Nov. 11 Discussion of Readings

Shaughnessy, "Diving In: An Introduction to Basic Writing" (CT)
Bizzell, "William Perry and Liberal Education" (CT)
Cushman, "The Public Intellectual, Service Learning, and Activist Research" (CT)

Nov. 13 Discussion of Readings

McLeod, "The Pedagogy of Writing Across the Curriculum" (eres)
Kiedaisch and Dinitz, "Look Back and Say 'So What'": The Limitations of the Generalist Tutor" (handout)

Project 9: An extended reflection upon one relevant tutoring experience, integrating the appropriate readings.

Hand in Projects 7–9.

Resources Due

Weeks 12–14 Student-Led Class Sessions

Dec. 13 *Statement of Purpose Due*

Notes

1. The community-based writing program, founded in spring 2003, matches tutors with English courses at Oberlin High School and a GED

preparation course for adult learners at a county vocational school. The discipline-specific tutors have expert knowledge of the material of the course, are mentored by their professors in their field, and are asked to do work beyond writing tutoring.

2. Post to course Blackboard Web site, September 2003.

3. That her prior experience at the writing center showed no evidence of such training, though all writing center tutors have been through the tutor training course, is evidence of problems in process pedagogy that lie outside the scope of this essay.

Works Cited

Anson, Chris M.. "Distant Voices: Teaching and Writing in a Culture of Technology." *Cross-Talk in Comp Theory: A Reader*. 2nd ed. Ed. Victor Villanueva. Urbana, IL: National Council of Teachers of English, 2003. 797–818.

Bartholomae, David. "Inventing the University." *Cross-Talk in Comp Theory: A Reader*. 2nd ed. Ed. Victor Villanueva. Urbana, IL: National Council of Teachers of English, 2003. 623–53.

Berlin, James. "Contemporary Composition: The Major Pedagogical Theories." *Cross-Talk in Comp Theory: A Reader*. 2nd ed. Ed. Victor Villanueva. Urbana, IL: National Council of Teachers of English, 2003. 255–70.

Berlin, James. "Rhetoric and Ideology in the Writing Class." *Cross-Talk in Comp Theory: A Reader*. 2nd ed. Ed. Victor Villanueva. Urbana, IL: National Council of Teachers of English, 2003. 717–37.

Bizzell, Patricia. "William Perry and Liberal Education." *Cross-Talk in Comp Theory: A Reader*. 2nd ed. Ed. Victor Villanueva. Urbana, IL: National Council of Teachers of English, 2003. 319–28.

Breuch, Lee-Ann M. Kastman. "Post-Process 'Pedagogy': A Philosophical Exercise." *Cross-Talk in Comp Theory: A Reader*. 2nd ed. Ed. Victor Villnueva. Urbana, IL: National Council of Teachers of English, 2003. 97–125.

Brodky, Linda. "On the Subjects of Class and Gender in 'The Literacy Letters.'" *Cross-Talk in Comp Theory: A Reader*. 2nd ed. Ed. Victor Villnueva. Urbana, IL: National Council of Teachers of English, 2003. 677–96.

Brooks, Jeff. "Minimalist Tutoring: Making the Student Do All the Work." *Writing Lab Newsletter* 15.6 (1991): 1–4.

Bruffee, Kenneth A. "Peer Tutoring and the 'Conversation of Mankind.'" *Writing Centers: Theory and Administration.* Ed. Gary A. Olson. Urbana, IL: National Council of Teachers of English, 1984. 3–15.

Clark, Irene L., and Dave Healy. "Are Writing Centers Ethical?" *Writing Program Administration* 20.1-2 (1996): 32–48.

Coogan, David. "Towards a Rhetoric of On-line Tutoring." Annual Convention of the Conference on College Composition and Communication. Nashville Convention Center. 17 Mar. 1994. (ERIC Doc. Reprod. Service No. ED370102)

Corbett, Edward P. J., and Robert J. Connors. Introduction. *Classical Rhetoric for the Modern Student.* 4th ed. New York: Oxford UP, 1999. 1–24.

Cushman, Ellen. "The Public Intellectual, Service Learning, and Activist Research." *Cross-Talk in Comp Theory: A Reader.* 2nd ed. Ed. Victor Villnueva. Urbana, IL: National Council of Teachers of English, 2003. 819–28.

Delpit, Lisa D. "The Silenced Dialogue: Power and Pedagogy in Educating Other People's Children." *Cross-Talk in Comp Theory: A Reader.* Ed. Victor Villanueva, Jr. Urbana, IL: National Council of Teachers of English, 1997. 565–88.

Gillespie, Paula, and Neal Lerner. *The Allyn and Bacon Guide to Peer Tutoring.* Boston: Allyn and Bacon, 2000.

Graff, Gerald. *Beyond the Culture Wars: How Teaching the Conflicts Can Revitalize American Education.* New York: Norton, 1992.

Grimm, Nancy Maloney. "Toward a Fair Writing Center Practice." *Good Intentions: Writing Center Work for Postmodern Times.* Portsmouth, NH: Boynton/Cook, Heinemann, 1999.

Hairston, Maxine. "Diversity, Ideology, and Teaching Writing." *Cross-Talk in Comp Theory: A Reader.* 2nd ed. Ed. Victor Villanueva. Urbana, IL: National Council of Teachers of English, 2003. 697–713.

Harris, Muriel. "Talking in the Middle: Why Writers Need Writing Tutors." *College English* 57.1 (1995): 27–42.

Harris, Muriel, and Tony Silva. "Tutoring ESL Students: Issues and Options." *College Composition and Communication* 44.4 (1993): 525–37.

Hartwell, Patrick. "Grammar, Grammars, and the Teaching of Grammar." *Cross-Talk in Comp Theory: A Reader*. 2nd ed. Ed. Victor Villanueva. Urbana, IL: National Council of Teachers of English, 2003. 205–33.

Hobson, Eric H. "Introduction: Straddling the Virtual Fence." *Wiring the Writing Center*. Ed. Eric H. Hobson. Logan: Utah State UP, 1998. xi–xxvi.

Kiedaisch, Jean, and Sue Dinitz. "Look Back and Say 'So What': The Limitations of the Generalist Tutor." *Writing Center Journal* 14.1 (1993): 63–75.

Kinneavy, James L. "The Basic Aims of Discourse." *Cross-Talk in Comp Theory: A Reader*. 2nd ed. Ed. Victor Villanueva. Urbana, IL: National Council of Teachers of English, 2003. 129–39.

McLeod, Susan. "The Pedagogy of Writing Across the Curriculum." *A Guide to Composition Pedagogies*. Ed. Gary Tate, Amy Rupiper, and Kurt Schick. New York: Oxford UP, 2001. 149–64.

Miller, Richard E. "The Arts of Complicity: Pragmatism and the Culture of Schooling." *Cross-Talk in Comp Theory: A Reader*. 2nd ed. Ed. Victor Villanueva. Urbana, IL: National Council of Teachers of English, 2003. 655–75.

Murray, Donald M. "Teach Writing as a Process Not Product." *Cross-Talk in Comp Theory: A Reader*. 2nd ed. Ed. Victor Villanueva. Urbana, IL: National Council of Teachers of English, 2003. 3–6.

North, Stephen M. "The Idea of a Writing Center." *College English* 46.5 (1984): 433–46.

———. "Revisiting 'The Idea of a Writing Center.'" *Writing Center Journal* 15.1 (1994): 7–20.

Olson, Gary A. "Toward a Post-Process Composition: Abandoning the Rhetoric of Assertion." *Post-Process Theory: New Directions for Composition Research*. Ed. Thomas Kent. Carbondale: Southern Illinois UP, 1999. 7–15.

Pratt, Mary Louise. "Arts of the Contact Zone." *Profession 91*. New York: Modern Language Association, 1991. 33–40.

Royster, Jacqueline Jones. "When the First Voice You Hear Is Not Your Own." *Cross-Talk in Comp Theory: A Reader*. 2nd ed. Ed. Victor Villnueva. Urbana, IL: National Council of Teachers of English, 2003. 611–22.

Shamoon, Linda K., and Deborah H. Burns. "A Critique of Pure Tutoring." *Writing Center Journal* 15.2 (1995): 134–52.

Shaughnessy, Mina P. "Diving In: An Introduction to Basic Writing." *Cross-Talk in Comp Theory: A Reader.* 2nd ed. Ed. Victor Villnueva. Urbana, IL: National Council of Teachers of English, 2003. 311–17.

Sommers, Nancy. "Responding to Student Writing." *College Composition and Communication* 32.2 (1982): 148–56.

———. "Revision Strategies of Student Writers and Experienced Adult Writers." *Cross-Talk in Comp Theory: A Reader.* 2nd ed. Ed. Victor Villnueva. Urbana, IL: National Council of Teachers of English, 2003. 43–54.

Straub, Richard. "Responding—Really Responding to Other Students' Writing." *The Subject Is Writing: Essays by Teachers and Students.* 3rd ed. Ed. Wendy Bishop. Portsmouth, NH: Boynton/Cook, Heinemann, 2003. 162–72.

Trimbur, John. "Peer Tutoring: A Contradiction in Terms?" *Writing Center Journal* 7.2 (1987): 21–29.

Villanueva, Victor, ed. *Cross-Talk in Comp Theory: A Reader.* 2nd ed. Urbana, IL: National Council of Teachers of English, 2003.

Welch, Nancy. "Playing with Reality: Writing Centers after the Mirror Stage." *College Composition and Communication* 51.1 (1999): 51–69.

Williams, Joseph M. *Style: Ten Lessons in Clarity and Grace.* 7th ed. New York: Longman, 2003.

Young, Beth Rapp. "Can You Proofread This?" *A Tutor's Guide: Helping Writers One to One.* Ed. Ben Rafoth. Portsmouth, NH: Boynton/Cook, Heinemann, 2000. 111–26.

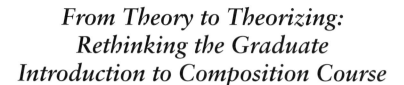

CHAPTER NINE

From Theory to Theorizing: Rethinking the Graduate Introduction to Composition Course

ANTHONY J. MICHEL

California State University, Fresno

In the fall of 2002, I enthusiastically prepared and taught the Composition Theory and Practice course, which is the writing pedagogy course required of all teaching assistants at California State University, Fresno. The course, which for the purposes of clarity I will refer to as the practicum, was designed to encourage an awareness of the theoretical assumptions about writing and writing instruction that students already held, introduce a wide range of theoretical arguments, and encourage students to apply their more developed theoretical understandings to practical situations. Through a strategic sequence of texts and assignments, I fully intended for the course to inspire students to develop theoretically informed writing pedagogies and, in the process, help them make practical sense of potentially abstract and complicated theories.

The semester work culminated in the Assignment Sequence, a pedagogical project in which students applied their understanding of composition theory to specific teaching strategies. When I picked up the papers, the results were not quite what I had expected. Some students wrote innovative papers that reflected a genuine engagement with theory as a means to rethink their assumptions about language and literacy. A number of the other papers, however, evinced perfunctory applications of theory, with limited or undeveloped discussions of the student's theoretical assumptions. And a few of the students used the Assignment Sequence as a way to express a rather strong resistance to composition theory, like the student whose paper was titled, "All I Ever Needed to Know I Learned in the Third Century B.C.E.: A Call for Rhetorical Pedagogy in the College Classroom."

Why, despite the emphasis on theory in the class, had a number of student projects reflected a striking lack of engagement with it? Why were the connections between theory and practice often undeveloped? Such problems are, I suspect, common given the complex and unique location of the practicum as a course that introduces both theory and composition to students who may have limited exposure to and interest in either. Despite the increasing scholarly emphasis on pedagogical approaches to theory, less emphasis has been given to experiences and insights that come out of classroom attempts to teach theory in the practicum. This paper draws on one such experience with the practicum to identify often overlooked factors that limit productive student engagement with composition theory, and offers some strategic approaches to teaching a more productive practicum.

Critical to this effort is my attempt to employ "theorizing" as a central concept in the class. Patricia Bizzell and Sid Dobrin refer to theorizing as an active process that is distinguished from the broader notion of Theory with a capital T. Bizzell usefully clarifies this distinction, stating that "'Theory' tends to be thought of as something static, like a table of laws." On the other hand, "theorizing" can be better thought of as a process or an activity in which one is "thinking about what one is doing—reflecting on practice" (Bizzell 2–3). Theorizing challenges the more problematic tendencies of Theory, which students are likely to draw on to explain, rather than to think through, their assumptions. In contrast to such "law-like" prescriptions, theorizing presents "rules of thumb, which will not dictate practice, but . . . may guide it" (Bizzell 3).

Although I have found theorizing a useful concept, the argument I make in this chapter stems from an attempt to rethink the course based on my misapplication of the concept. Drawing on lessons learned from the fall 2002 practicum, I argue that we should encourage students to make the critical move from the *acquisition* of theoretical knowledge to *theorizing* as a critical, self-reflexive process. To encourage this shift, we must identify and address student resistance to theory and develop alternative pedagogical strategies that facilitate productive classroom practices of theorizing.

Part I of this chapter, Theorizing the Practicum—A Course Overview, establishes the framework for this argument by providing a detailed overview of my initial attempt to theorize the practicum. Part II, Challenges to Theorizing in Institutional Contexts, focuses on problems and lessons learned from teaching theorizing in the practicum. Finally, in Part III, A Revised Practicum—Theorizing in Institutional Contexts, I rethink the practicum to encourage theorizing. Before I address the specific problems and strategies appropriate to the course, it will be useful to clarify the institutional context that plays such an important role in the configuration of the class and, ultimately, in the student's perceptions of composition theory.

The Graduate Introduction to Composition Course at Fresno State

Reception to theory in the graduate course is influenced by a series of local, institutional conditions. Each year at California State University, Fresno, the English department hires approximately twenty-five graduate assistants who, along with a few part-time instructors, teach all sections of English One, the school's one semester first-year writing requirement. In addition, another ten graduate assistants are hired to teach sections of English 1L, a one-hour lab required of students who score below a specific mark on the university's English placement test. All of the graduate instructors must take the practicum during or immediately subsequent to the semester in which they are teaching.

As an institution that offers terminal master's degrees, most of our new instructors have little or no prior teaching experience. In addition, there are no minimum criteria for hiring the teaching assistants besides their status as graduate students. At the end of each semester, we look at the needs for the upcoming semester, interview new candidates, and fill the positions. In most cases, our needs are such that we hire everybody we interview and hope for the best.

The situation is further complicated by a historical lack of attention to composition studies. The practicum itself was established along with a master's degree in composition in 1991, and, for five years prior to our hiring a compositionist, it was taught by literature faculty. From 1996 to 2002, the year I was hired, the English department had hired two compositionists who taught the course. By the time I was hired, both of my predecessors had left, and the lack of continuity in the program had given composition studies a low profile among new graduate students.

As a result, most of the students in the practicum are unfamiliar with composition studies when they enter the class. They often resent having to take a course that, although it counts as an elective toward their degree, they view as a digression from their more important focus. Of the twenty students in the practicum in the fall of 2002, eight were in the creative writing program, ten were pursuing their degrees in literature, and one student was studying linguistics. Only one student came to the class with an interest and background in composition studies.

Although these students were unfamiliar with the scholarship of composition studies, many had been around long enough to perceive a departmental culture that often positioned composition studies in opposition to the interests and assumptions that guided the study of literature and creative writing. Many had heard that the two compositionists who preceded me had struggled in their attempts to influence perceptions about composition studies, and they gauged my status as the only compositionist of twenty-eight English department faculty as indication of its lack of seriousness.

Despite these challenges, inexperienced teachers instruct much better than we have a right to expect or deserve, and we should continue to develop approaches to the course that help them theorize their classroom practices. To do so means that we attend to the significant administrative and pedagogical challenges the course introduces. At Fresno State, the department has made significant strides, in terms of hiring practices and departmental policies, toward giving composition a more prominent place in the department. But despite these efforts, the practicum will continue to function, as it does at most institutions, as a contact zone through which questions about theory, writing, and the writer are contested in terms that are often determined by local, institutional politics. To make these courses productive spaces for theorizing different pedagogical approaches and assumptions, it will be important to address the limitations in the ways both the course and the students construct theory. This analysis of the fall 2002 practicum takes as its starting point a limited attempt to develop a pedagogical approach to theorizing in the practicum.

Part I: Theorizing the Practicum— A Course Overview

As I prepared for the practicum, I developed a syllabus that sought to emphasize the dialectical relationship between theory and practice that I then conceived of as theorizing. The course syllabus stated that the class was designed to "engage students in extensive, close readings in major trends and current debates in composition theory *as a means to* articulate and rethink pedagogical assumptions," including the "nitty-gritty, day-to-day practices we will bring into the classroom." The primary goals of the course, then, were first to introduce students to various theories in composition studies and then to encourage students to critically integrate their theoretical knowledge with their practices.

To achieve these goals, I divided the course into three sections: (1) a two-week introduction-to-course framework developed around key theoretical concepts of literacy, rhetoric, and pedagogy, (2) a seven-week immersion in theory, and (3) a concluding seven weeks in which students applied theoretical understandings to their own pedagogy, culminating in the Assignment Sequence. This format reflected an overall concern for exposing students to a large body of theory framed as tools from which to interrogate pedagogical assumptions.

For the first section, on theory applied to practice, we read Mike Rose's *Lives on the Boundary*. Because Rose relates his experiences as both student and teacher to the broader social questions of literacy and the purpose of education, particularly in writing courses, this text provides an excellent model of theorizing. Drawing on Rose and discussions of literacy and rhetoric in the works of Paulo Freire, E. D. Hirsch, and James Berlin, students wrote their own literacy autobiographies—a common exercise in composition that encourages students to consider how much of what we assume about pedagogy comes from our experiences with reading and writing.

The second section of the course concentrated on immersing students in a body of theory that, I thought, would provide conceptual tools as a foundation for later application. For this seven-week period, students engaged in close readings of seminal essays in composition, most of which came from Victor Villanueva's anthology *Cross-Talk in Comp Theory: A Reader*. Reading and responding to theorists from Donald Murray to Maxine Hairston, I hoped, would not only familiarize students with key theories in the field, but it would also encourage them to rethink the assumptions they expressed in their literacy autobiographies.

In the final, third section of the practicum, students applied the theoretical knowledge they had accumulated throughout the semester by developing a five-week Assignment Sequence for first-year composition. Tate, Rupiper, and Schick's *A Guide to Composition Pedagogies* provided specific pedagogical readings to help students develop a statement of rationale to support their efforts. This structure, which separated readings in composition theory from application, was guided by the assumption that theoretical knowledge is necessary for developing informed classroom practices. Bizzell describes this relationship between theory and practice with reference to an anecdote from Freire's *Pedagogy of the City* in which a group of literacy instructors in Brazil required exposure to "theoretical knowledge" to move beyond an impasse about a pedagogical problem. Bizzell explains that the introduction of theory helped the instructors consider alternative solutions to those provided by their immediate contexts. Therefore, Bizzell suggests, theoretical knowledge helps us move past individualized assumptions about the problem (4). The analysis of my class that follows points to a critical distinction between Freire's conception of theorizing, where theoretical knowledge is a means to addressing a specific pedagogical problem, and a curriculum in which theoretical knowledge too often becomes separated from considerations of the practical.

After collecting the final Assignment Sequences, I realized that I had misperceived the students' willingness to apply theoretical insights to their pedagogical practices. Several of the students seemed to ignore or diminish the importance of the large body of theory we had read and written about. In fact, some students designed curricula that, it seems, they would have created at the beginning of the semester. This final writing assignment suggests that when the relationship between theoretical knowledge and theorizing is not carefully articulated, there is a distinct danger that our practices can contribute to, rather than complicate, student resistance to composition.

Part II: Challenges to Theorizing in Institutional Contexts

Perhaps the most challenging aspect of teaching theory is to make it comprehensible to students who often feel that it is too abstract to be applicable to their teaching. While I have tended, in other theoretically oriented courses, to see some degree of success by strategically immersing students in theory prior to practical application, the unique institutional location of the practicum often shapes students' preconceptions about theory in ways that complicate this approach. As the course developed, students adopted some specific and problematic assumptions about theory that are directly related to the unique institutional location of the class.

As is often the case in many universities, students with graduate assistantships to teach first-year composition must enroll in the practicum. Although the practicum is a credit-bearing course, it is often viewed as an unnecessary digression from the student's major. Students who perceive of the course in terms of a service function often expect the course to be exclusively concerned with "training" students in the practical "nuts and bolts" information they will need to know to teach first-year composition. Students often expect that the practicum will focus on concrete skills necessary for composition teaching such as syllabus writing, classroom management, and grading.

It is important to consider that the reception of the theory–practice relationship is negotiated in a context where many students may, for institutional reasons, be predisposed to resist conceptions of theory that are not closely associated with classroom practices. Reflecting on these complicated classroom dynamics has caused me to rethink my earlier question. Instead of asking why, despite the heavy emphasis on theory, students had separated it from practice, it may be more useful to address the possibility that, in the complex context of the practicum, this separation was a direct result of too much emphasis on theory early in the class with too little attention to how it was perceived and understood by students. To develop pedagogical approaches to theorizing the practicum that may better account for student resistance, it is useful to first identify some of the ways that students construct theory in the practicum.

In the fall 2002 practicum, the gap between the theoretical and the practical material in the course contributed to the assumption that theory and practice do not meaningfully affect each other and that certain types of theoretical writing (i.e., abstract) have little bearing on classroom practices. In the "immersion in theory" part of the course, students read a number of essays that presented major debates and theoretical assumptions in the field of composition studies. The emphasis on building theoretical knowledge involved having students read specific texts related to theoretical debates regarding process writing, collaborative learning, cognitivism, and academic discourse.

Students were often able to critique and engage the theoretical readings as conceptual exercises for which they were well prepared, based on their experiences with literary criticism. In other words, students were proficient at summarizing, analyzing, and critiquing theoretical arguments. Often graduate seminars become settings for highly skilled critiques and problem producing in relation to the text at hand. But this ability to enter *into* the theoretical conversations in a field—the theoretical knowledge—did not mean that students would be able to translate it into their own experiences. Instead, the students often felt removed from the conceptual loop that would enable them to rethink pedagogical assumptions based on theoretical insights.

One unique set of student responses to course readings provided an unexpected indication that if theoretical knowledge is too removed from the practical, the practical might actually preempt any engagement with theory. In this instance, students wrote illustrative responses to two essays related to cognitivism: Andrea Lundsford's "Cognitive Development and the Basic Writer" and

Ann E. Berthoff's "Is Teaching Still Possible? Writing, Meaning, and Higher Order Reasoning." In contrast to previous exercises in which students had written sophisticated responses to theoretical arguments, students almost unanimously focused their responses on the practical exercises embedded in Lundsford's piece. They praised Lundsford's essay as both "clear" and "useful," adding that they could see themselves incorporating such exercises in their own classes.

One explanation for the unusually enthusiastic preference for Lundsford's essay is that students were beginning to see theory and practice as distinctly separate conceptual activities. By the middle of the semester, the emphasis on theoretical knowledge had removed students so far from its relationship to the practical that it was difficult for them to see a meaningful relationship between Lundsford's practical exercises and the theoretical arguments that framed them in her essay. Moreover, I suspect that students preferred Lundsford's essay because the piece helped quell some of the anxieties surrounding teaching that students felt. Compared to Lundsford's practical emphasis, Berthoff's more abstract and indeterminate discussion of how meaning is made seemed too removed for students who were not used to making the more difficult moves necessary for theorizing. Because the students had not practiced applying theory to read the practices in Lundsford's piece, they did not connect the two. What can happen in the practicum, then, is that students who learn about the theories and engage in some understanding of them will nonetheless struggle to connect these ideas to their actual curriculum.

Student alienation from theory and theorizing in the fall 2002 practicum, then, was partly an effect of the separation implied in a course framework that followed a progression from an "immersion in theory" in the first half of the course toward a more thorough consideration of its "application" in the second half. While there were a few concrete applications, by this point in the semester the gap between theoretical knowledge and its application had widened.

In some cases, students made sense of a theory by selecting one that served to validate, not interrogate, their own position. This conceptual move was particularly common in the literacy autobiography, which marked the students' first attempts to connect their experiences to theory. Students often wrote insightful essays about how certain teachers or experiences at home shaped their appreciation for the study of language. Instead of using theory to rethink their assumptions, however, students often chose theories that reflected and validated their positive experiences in literacy. For instance, one student arrived in the class describing himself as a "die-hard romantic poet" who wanted to use poetry as a way to express his true and authentic voice or self. Therefore, when he encountered expressivism, he saw it as an appealing theory because it confirmed his own preconceived notions. In another instance, a former honors student whose high school and college experiences emphasized grammar and structure was particularly receptive to objectivist and current traditional schools. This is a common experience in the practicum where, in my experience, creative writing students often view language as a medium for accessing inner truths and literature majors have internalized the notion that language is to be decoded for the truths embedded in the text. Theory in these formulations served primarily as self-validation rather than as a means to scrutinize, disrupt, or adapt prior notions. Critical inquiry, based on theorizing, becomes particularly difficult when students view theory as an affront to their understanding of their course of study.

It could be argued that these responses are understandable coming from students who encounter theory for the first time and that, with time and further study, these teachers will develop more nuanced and theoretically informed understandings of their teaching practices. Given the lack of attention to pedagogy in other areas of English studies, however, and the historic tendency to reproduce rather than to challenge existing pedagogical models, I am not optimistic that teachers, who are not encouraged to theorize now, will develop an interest in doing so later. If teachers do not learn to interrogate their own perspectives in courses like the practicum, they will most likely reproduce and internalize the idea that that which "worked for me" is the best method for teaching. The result is often a pedagogy that privileges an instructor's experiences rather than one that is responsive to the multiple, dynamic concerns of the students in the composition classroom.

The tendency to reproduce familiar models was particularly apparent in the part of the final Assignment Sequence that called for students to discuss the relationship between the function of the course, their conceptions of rhetoric, and the pedagogical exercises they advocated. Students were to draw on theories in order to revisit and rearticulate previous assumptions for their broader composition student audiences. Because they often assumed that what worked best for them would work best in their own classes, students often failed to consider important distinctions between themselves and their students. One student, for example, expressed an allegiance to humanist ideals about what literature could do for all of humanity. By the end of the semester, despite his exposure to a series of theoretical arguments that might have encouraged him to clarify his position or complicate his thinking, his Assignment Sequence stated that reading "fine literature" such as Hemingway and the book of Ecclesiastes would help his students develop into better people. This student's graduate work had focused specifically on Hemingway, and it was clear that he assumed his students would necessarily share the effect the texts had on him. The problem with this assumption was that it rested on the notion of universal value associated with canonical writers. What was lacking was any attempt to articulate how his approach to these readings might have helped students, many of whom may not have shared his appreciation for "fine literature." Such universal and universalizing models are particularly suspect at an institution like California State University, Fresno, where many of the students are first-generation, non-native English speakers who may have alternative ideas about what constitutes value in writing.

This student's lack of engagement with theory can also be understood as a form of resistance. Like some of the other students in the class, he expressed a concern that theory does a sort of violence to writing instruction. Pedagogy, this student suggested in his Assignment Sequence, is a "complex and beautiful act that cannot be defined in the terms we've been using." As a result, he resisted what he perceived as the call to "align" himself with one theory and instead drew on a mixture of strategies and assumptions to support a humanist pedagogical project.

As I have suggested, in the practicum there were several situations such as this one in which students felt pressed, and reasonably resisted a call, to "align" themselves with a specific theoretical approach. One unproductive effect of this resistance was for students to dismiss all theory and theorizing activities out of hand and to then figure out how to do the necessary work in a way that suggested enough engagement with theory to pass the class. This is a tendency that presents a significant challenge to those of us who would like to encourage reflective instruction.

Part III: A Revised Practicum—
Theorizing in Institutional Contexts

One of the central contentions of this essay is that instructors who seek to incorporate theory into the practicum need to address student perceptions about theory, assumptions that are often determined by a number of institutional factors. A more theoretically informed practicum requires that we teach students to *theorize*— not to continue to see theory and practice as essentially different practices with different objectives. Ultimately, a critical aspect of encouraging students to theorize their own practices lies in encouraging the students' abilities to self-critique their theoretical assumptions. This focus has influenced my rethinking of the way theory is employed in the major course assignments and day-to-day classroom activities. In my own attempts to rethink the practicum, I have developed practices that encourage students to interrogate the often-obscured conceptions of theory that circulate in the academy.

As I have suggested, in the earlier practicum's literacy autobiographies and Assignment Sequence, students often used theory to validate preexisting assumptions, or they viewed it as a fixed body of knowledge with little or no relevance to their applied practices. The fact that the course structure separated the immersion into theory from its practical application encouraged these uses, particularly for students who had a limited investment in the course. Missing in this course configuration were serious revisions that would have encouraged students to rethink (theorize) their earlier assumptions. For this reason, I restructured the course around a series of revisions of the major class assignments. In essence, these documents shift from expressions of theoretical identity or position at a specific moment to sites of constant renegotiation. Ultimately, students produce these documents in an end-of-the-semester portfolio that is supplemented with a reflection on their developing processes.

This shift in structure also requires an ongoing engagement with theory that, in contrast to the earlier practicum, does not construct theory as a separate body of knowledge. The current version of the course introduces a comparable series of theoretical essays, but this scholarship is framed in relation to specific pedagogical problems. Reading assignments and writing assignments are developed to constantly integrate theory and practice in concert with day-to-day practices. In my construction of the 2002 version of the practicum, I devoted a good deal of attention—in the construction of the syllabus, in the development of the course curriculum, and in the day-to-day teaching of the class—to encouraging students to theorize their practices. What I did not do was introduce students to the various constructions of theory that might inhibit their efforts to do so.

In rethinking the class, I have addressed the question of theory head on and encouraged interrogations of its various constructions in much the same way that we discuss various conceptions of rhetoric and literacy. In doing so, I have employed the earlier-mentioned student perceptions of theory as subjects of classroom discussion. The course begins, for example, with a discussion of the various conceptions of theory with which students are familiar. Last year this discussion was facilitated by the circulation, by one of my colleagues in creative writing, of the recent *New York Times* article "The Latest Theory Is That Theory Doesn't Matter" (Eakin), which quotes Stanley Fish among others in suggesting that there is no practical usefulness for theory. Failing to address the many alternative arguments to Fish or, for that matter, what the commentators meant by the term *theory*, this article contributed to problematic characterizations of theory as "grand narrative" and a separate body of knowledge. In the context of the practicum, however, the article became the vehicle through which we discussed multiple conceptions of theory and theorizing. In addition, I introduced narratives that significantly complicate the "theory is dead" argument, including works by Robert Scholes, James Berlin, and Sid Dobrin. The primary focus of much of this work is encapsulated in Bizzell's advice that while we ought to "reject ill-applied or jargon-filled theories," this "does not mean that all forms of theory must be rejected" (2). Early in the semester, moreover, students are introduced to the central problematic expressed by Bizzell that, I tell the students, will guide our discussions of theory:

> "Theory" tends to be thought of as something static, like a table of laws; "theory" is better thought of as a process or an activity—"theorizing" or "theory talk." Theorizing does not claim to generate laws or predict instances with invariant rigidity; indeed, it presents itself as provisional. (2)

In addition to foregrounding the various constructions of theory, I have also introduced common perceptions about theory that have come out of the class itself. I am careful to suggest that these ideas are understandable *as a place to start*, and that it will be one of the projects of the class to probe the assumptions that guide various constructions of theory, including the too-easy dismissals.

To better facilitate critical engagement with theories, I have employed a variation of John Trimbur's notion of a dissensus-based community. In "Consensus and Difference in Collaborative Learning," a critique of the repression of difference in Kenneth Bruffee's notion of consensus-based communities, Trimbur argues that dissensus-based learning

> poses consensus not as the goal of conversation but rather as a critical measure to help students identify the structures of power that inhibit communication among readers (and between teachers and students) by authorizing certain styles of reading while excluding others. . . . [Students] learn why readers disagree about what counts as a reading, where the differences they experience as readers come from, and how we might usefully bring these differences into relation to each other. (453)

Trimbur's example invokes the way students in literature classes read and express their ideas in asymmetrical power relations. For my purposes, it helps unpack the various perspectives at work in the way we all read and respond to theory in the practicum. In contrast to the fall 2002 course, in which theoretical assumptions often remained uninterrogated, students in the more recent iterations of the practicum seem willing to debate their assumptions in groups that focus on a specific pedagogical or social problem. Students are asked, for example, to develop a theoretical rationale, individually and in groups, to support their position on issues ranging from the cultural politics of Standard English to the selection of a reader for a first-year composition class.

In one such activity, on responding to student drafts, members of one group identified their different approaches in relation to their disciplines. The group most concerned with grammar and structure suggested that this was because they were literature majors; they contrasted themselves with creative writers who, they argued, are focused on more ethereal concerns. This activity led to a series of animated discussions about the relationship between theory and disciplinary identities.

The point of such activities is to make explicit complex relationships between theory and practice that too often remain undeveloped and, therefore, uninterrogated in the graduate seminar. As the instructor in these dissensus-based discussions, I am often in a position to offer questions that facilitate rethinkings of the theoretical assumptions circulating in the class. While it may appear natural for students to select a pedagogical approach based on experience, the focus of theorizing in the course is to engage in a radical rethinking of assumptions in light of new concerns. Moreover, theorizing becomes an important means through which students consider possible disparities between their own experiences and those of the individuals they will be teaching.

I have also found it useful to introduce alternative perspectives that might complicate commonly held theoretical assumptions. Students are encouraged, for example, to read their arguments in relation to institutional documents such as the university's writing policy and the Writing Program Administration Outcome Statement. Like Freire's literacy instructors, these documents encourage students to mediate between their own experiences and the pedagogical assumptions of people outside the class. In such cases, students are encouraged to avoid the tendency to use theory to validate preexisting assumptions and to relate their assumptions to the specific context in which they are teaching.

I have no illusions that simply restructuring the major class assignments and calling attention to different perspectives on theory will effectively dispel all problematic perceptions of theory and its relationship to practice. And I am not sanguine about the prospect that these practices will somehow counter the institutional factors that contribute to misperceptions of composition theory. What I have noticed, however, is that by demonstrating that *theory* is a problematic and contentious term, and in structuring the course to encourage students' active engagement with it, participants in the practicum are much more likely to clarify not only their practices but also the theoretical assumptions that inform them. Ultimately, I am optimistic that by encouraging teaching assistants to theorize, they will be better situated to adapt to the ever-changing contexts that will continue to shape their engagements with first-year writing students.

Works Cited

Berthoff, Ann E. "Is Teaching Still Possible? Writing, Meaning, and Higher Order Reasoning." *Cross-Talk in Comp Theory: A Reader.* Ed. Victor Villanueva, Jr. Urbana, IL: National Council of Teachers of English, 1997. 307–21.

Bizzell, Patricia. Foreword. *Constructing Knowledges: The Politics of Theory-Building and Pedagogy in Composition.* Sidney I. Dobrin. Albany: State U of New York P, 1997. 1–4.

Dobrin, Sidney I. *Constructing Knowledges: The Politics of Theory-Building and Pedagogy in Composition.* Albany: State U of New York P, 1997.

Eakin, Emily. "The Latest Theory Is That Theory Doesn't Matter." *New York Times* 19 Apr. 2003: D1.

Freire, Paulo. *Pedagogy of the City.* New York: Continuum, 1993.

Lundsford, Andrea. "Cognitive Development and the Basic Writer." *Cross-Talk in Comp Theory: A Reader.* Ed. Victor Villanueva, Jr. Urbana, IL: National Council of Teachers of English, 1997. 277–88.

Rose, Mike. *Lives on the Boundary: A Moving Account of the Struggles and Achievements of America's Educationally Unprepared.* New York: Penguin, 1990.

Tate, Gary, Amy Rupiper, and Kurt Schick, eds. *A Guide to Composition Pedagogies.* New York: Oxford UP, 2001.

Trimbur, John. "Consensus and Difference in Collaborative Learning." *Cross-Talk in Comp Theory: A Reader.* Ed. Victor Villanueva, Jr. Urbana, IL: National Council of Teachers of English, 1997. 439–56.

Villanueva, Victor, Jr., ed. *Cross-Talk in Comp Theory: A Reader.* Urbana, IL: National Council of Teachers of English, 1997.

CHAPTER TEN

Theory in a TA Composition Pedagogy Course: Not If, but How

RUTH OVERMAN FISCHER
George Mason University

Were I to survey those among us who have taught a course in composition pedagogy to teaching assistants and come up against resistance to theory, I suspect that I would find that resistance a given in varying degrees. And if we consider the sixty-six essays dealing with the most prominent current theoretical perspectives in composition studies in Kennedy's *Theorizing Composition: A Critical Sourcebook of Theory and Scholarship in Contemporary Composition Studies*, it's no wonder. Who among us might resist such a plethora of thought ourselves?

My own initiation into this group occurred one fall several years ago when I taught my first graduate-level course in the teaching of writing—English 615: Proseminar in Composition Instruction—to incoming teaching assistants. I was excited at the prospect of the work we would do, grounding composition theory in whatever experience with practice the students had had. I fashioned my course along the lines of the design of my predecessor's course. I naively assumed that the TAs would share my excitement about this journey into theory and its implications for their classroom practice.

I was wrong. Of the class of fifteen students, most expressed dislike for the theoretical frames in which I had attempted to place course discussions; the only two I can recall who seemed to actually enjoy theory were students in the final stages of the MA in the teaching of writing and literature program, a woman in her late thirties and a man, also in his late thirties, who was also completing course requirements for a certification in Teaching English as a Second Language offered by our linguistics program. In addition, this class balked at my not giving them a class-by-class list of "things to do in the English 101 classroom." I had misjudged both the pedagogical and the rhetorical situations and, by the time I figured out the extent of the resistance, I was unable to find a way to mollify its effects and redirect our energies.

As I reflected on the experience with these TAs, several issues emerged. First was a combination of the negative effects of my not having taught the course before and my naiveté about the makeup and needs of this particular group of students. I obviously had not made a compelling case for the importance of theory/theorizing in their future thinking as teachers of English 101. In addition, they were not PhD students in rhetoric and composition (Mason does not have such a program) but were instead, except for the two mentioned earlier, students in the MFA program in fiction, non-fiction, or poetry. Only one was actually teaching English 101 at the time she was taking the course; the rest were tutors in the university writing center and would not be in their own classrooms until the fall of the following year. Consequently, discussions about course design, syllabus construction, and assignment sequencing and their rationales were not relevant to the TAs' need for "in the moment" strategies for working one-on-one with students in the writing center. In addition, they were at the beginning stage of their MFA programs and undoubtedly had some anxiety about what their other course work would be like.

I also discovered that—not surprising, when I think about it—some of the MFA students were not as interested in teaching English 101—or learning the theory behind that teaching—as they were in producing their own writing, and therefore had little time or tolerance for a pedagogy course that required the kind of rigor that warranted granting three graduate credits. Others viewed theory through the lens of previous experience with literary theory from undergraduate courses and brought with them their resistance to what they considered the esoterica of theoretical discussions. Why, they figured, would theories of writing not be just as esoteric? Like many graduate students from programs around the country—if the anecdotes I have heard from colleagues are any indication—for them theory was not a priority among academic interests.

Given the interdisciplinary nature of our field and the fact that no grand Theory pulls us together into one harmonious whole, such resistance among our TAs might even be understandable. Kennedy notes that

> Composition Studies has emerged as a highly interdisciplinary field that draws on the scholarship of many other specialties and has a discourse in which multiple perspectives find expression. It has rejected a central, objective representation; instead it proposes a plurality of possible approaches, with different vocabularies, different metaphors, and different frames of reference. (ix–x).

And yet, despite the fact that no grand Theory of composition studies exists, we know that influences of theory *on* composition have an impact on all aspects of the teaching of writing. Such "theory" may be tacit and unarticulated, based on the ways we were taught how to write in an academic setting—a situation that seems to me all the more reason such an articulation is necessary. Consequently, it is important that theory (of the small *t* variety mentioned in Dobrin's *Constructing Knowledges: The Politics of Theory-Building and Pedagogy in Composition*) be a part of any course on composition pedagogy. The question then becomes not if but how we can help our TAs see theory as a valid part of their development as teachers of writing to undergraduates in our general education writing courses.

In this essay, I address reasons I have found for resistance to theory based on further experience with our TAs and conversations with my colleagues who teach them. I then suggest, through a description of the TA teaching preparation model currently in place in the English department at George Mason University, ways to ameliorate that resistance. This description includes the selection process, the training schedule, and a course design in which a sequencing of pedagogical experiences based on hands-on experience and course-based instruction attempts both to promote an awareness among the TAs of the ongoing dialogue between practice and theory and to invite them to initiate their own dialogue.

Defining Theory

What do we mean by the term *theory* anyway? The term res-
onates differently for each of our disciplinary communities. As
one with training in applied linguistics (ESL) and composition,
both of which have a strong focus on teaching, I see theory in relation to my teaching practices as a way of planning, enacting, evaluating, and revising what I do in the classroom.

Dobrin sees theory as providing "a framework within which
[one] can operate, ask questions, even alter or refine principles of
that theory based on new experience, new observation. . . .
[T]heory leaves room for revision." (9). Zebroski views theory as
heuristic "used to mediate our world view and our practices" (7),
which may or may not affect practice. But while theory and practice "are separable in principle, [they are] also answerable to each
other over time" (10). Teachers "work in the spirit of theory
[when they] use theory, as a way to puzzle through classroom
enigmas, as a mediation of thought, as an instrument for envisioning the class and its relations to the student's experience and
the world" (9–10).

Phelps counters Zebroski's view that theory need not contribute to practice when she writes:

> [T]heory doesn't exist for its own sake, or shouldn't. . . . [I]t is
> a form of intelligibility that the theorist tries to give to per-
> sonal dilemmas, deeply felt[,] . . . a way to make sense of life.
> For oneself, for others. In composition, theory is irrevocably
> committed to practice: begins there and returns in recursive
> loops. (*Composition as a Human Science*, viii)

For Phelps, "teaching [writing] is a praxis that applies organized
inquiry (research and theory) and personal reflection in order to
help the developing person move through literacy toward reflection (71).

Bizzell provides a transition to a way to approach theory as
an ongoing attitude or activity. Adding the *-ing* suffix, she defines
theorizing as "thinking about what one is doing—reflecting on
practice . . . in a systematic way, . . . using the ideas of other
thinkers wherever they might be helpful. . . . [T]heorizing may not
dictate practice, but it may guide it" (2–3).

Theory and theorizing, then, can be seen as an ongoing habit of mind, an attitude of movement toward making sense, a systematic means of constructing a rationale for our practice. It is in this sense that I use the term *theory* in this essay.

Characterizing Resistance

Interactions concerning this resistance with TAs and the colleagues who teach them have provided me several insights about possible reasons for such resistance. First, our TAs, especially those in the MFA program, tend to have a "natural" affinity for and facility with the English language and have internalized strategies for communicating purposefully (and successfully) in writing, be it through fiction, poetry, or nonfiction. Without reflection, however, this affinity and these strategies do not serve them well in their role as tutor and then as teacher. In fact, I suspect they think that delving into what makes their writing work in ways that would serve them as teachers might somehow "mess up their muse" by asking them to analyze too closely how they write. Their successes with literacy over the years have not required them to be analytical about the reasons for those successes; they have not needed to figure out *how* they write well. And so when they are asked to consider how writing can be taught to English 101 students, who may not have had many writing successes and may have even developed an aversion to writing (their own resistance), TAs are being asked to be analytical about processes that have become a tacit part of who they are. The overwhelming majority of our TAs were exempted from the first-year composition course at their undergraduate institutions because they tested out or presented a sufficiently high AP score. Consequently, they will be teaching a course they have not experienced themselves, one they may even consider "remedial."

Not surprisingly, then, TAs have pragmatic concerns about the first-year composition course they will be teaching. These concerns range from the way the course is set up—what kinds of written assignments, how many, when due, how long, what readings, what textbook—to classroom management issues—how to get students to join in class discussion or work in groups or do the assignments—to grading issues—how to respond to their writing, how to grade, how to handle rewriting. In addition, in our composition program, teachers are expected to design their own English 101s in line with our stated program goals, and so TAs are expected to design their courses as well. Therefore, asking TAs to delay addressing these concerns with forays into theory, even if we see these forays as foundational to addressing their issues in a systematic way, raises their level of anxiety.

Some TAs in the MFA program have little interest in teaching beyond their graduate work. Consequently, their concerns with English 101 are purely pragmatic; their teaching is paying for their graduate degree. (By the way, this statement is intended as an observation, not a judgment.) In any case, such an attitude can lead to resistance to theory/izing because doing so, they perceive, takes valuable time and energy from their own development as writers.[1]

A corollary to this lack of commitment to teaching is a lack of understanding of teaching as both an art and a craft. TAs often see teaching more as a list of activities designed to fill the available time than as the development of teacher–student relationships that foster the writing development of their students. They do not realize that, as a discipline whose primary aim is theorized teaching, composition studies is a robust and valid discipline, and a course in writing pedagogy is far more than technical training. As Josh (who along with Eric and Sylvia were TAs who contributed their thinking to this essay) noted, "When I thought of theory for teaching composition, actually teaching writing, I couldn't help but think there was a bit of misrepresentation there."

TAs' previous experiences in other venues with the concept of theory may also predispose them to suspect the value of theory in teaching. As Eric put it, "Theory out of context quickly leads to hot air." They may not see their resistance to theory as itself a theoretical stance or that a theoretical agenda, articulated or not, is at work in any educational setting. According to Josh,

> After all, there are the basics you can teach of composing a good paper (grammar, punctuation, word choice, etc.) but the rest is mostly up to the individual to discover themselves. Blam! I find that my feelings were, in fact, part of a theory of composition. And the complex world of teaching composition was now open.

Or TAs may have an idea that theory is supposed to be some-what esoteric and disconnected from the practical, and so they do not recognize themselves in the act of theorizing—that is, they do not realize that their "movement toward making sense" is indeed theorizing, as well as theory building. Sylvia, for example, "confesses" that

> for every single reading, including the ideas about the theory practice theory arc, I was searching for clues about what I would DO in the classroom—the thinking was, to me, the primer for the action. We [were] all theorizing but with a very specific focus on action. I wanted theories, but theories that I could test again and again and use in the classroom—practical (practice!) theories! ("Sylvia's answers")

Training TAs at Mason

While resistance to theory in a writing pedagogy course may never be completely eliminated, one possibility for reducing its presence and effects is a holistic model of TA selection and train-ing[2] that demonstrates a profound interest in and support for the teaching of writing in an institution's general education curricu-lum. The faculty development process for teaching assistants in the graduate English program at George Mason University is such a model. The process begins even before applicants are chosen to be TAs and extends over the first two years of their teaching assistantship. Within the English department, TAs are expected to "fulfill a major responsibility to those who use the services of the Writing Center and take undergraduate courses in writing and lit-erature. . . . [A]ppointments go to those who most clearly demon-strate the potential to fulfill this major responsibility" (Miller).

The Selection Process

Of the thirty-four TA slots within the graduate English programs, thirty-two are allocated for the Master of Fine Arts students (thir-teen for fiction, thirteen for poetry, and six for nonfiction) and two slots for the Master of Arts program (half to each of four tracks: literature, professional writing and editing, linguistics, and the teaching of writing and literature). MFA (or MA) faculty identify applicants who seem to be the best candidates for the MFA (or MA) program based on the development of their work. These applicants are interviewed for TA appointments by the director of graduate writing programs and either the director of composition or the director of the writing center.

Several days before the interview, the candidates are sent three student writing samples, which reflect as closely as possible the kinds of writing TAs see in the writing center and later in the English 101 classroom. These samples demonstrate deficiencies at both the global level (such as critical thinking, solid claims and evidence, and organization consistent with the perceived assignment) and the local level (sentence structure, grammar, and mechanics). In addition, because Mason has an extensive population of nonnative speakers of English, we include one essay marked by ESL errors at both the global and local levels. Candidates are expected to discuss the writer's purpose and sense of each essay as well as the essay's strengths and weaknesses, in order of importance. Based on this discussion, they provide feedback to the writer. Since candidates may have had little or no experience teaching writing or working with student writers, we do not expect them to speak the discourse of composition studies; rather, we look for responses that indicate good instincts and a sensitivity in helping a student process a paper.

Teaching assistantships are awarded based on the evaluation by the MFA/MA faculty of the candidate's writing and application and the evaluation by the interviewers. A vote of confidence, however, is necessary from either the director of the writing center or the director of composition. As Bill Miller, the director of graduate writing programs, notes, "We, the MFA faculty, also want good classroom teachers. . . . The input of our compositionists is paramount to a candidate's getting an appointment."

Following this selection process, candidates chosen to be TAs begin a series of pedagogical experiences, both hands-on (tutoring in the writing center as well as teaching English 101: Composition and English 201: Reading and Writing about Texts) and academic (English 615: Proseminar in Composition Instruction and English

610: Proseminar in Teaching the Reading of Literature). I next briefly describe what TAs do in the writing center (WC), because their experiences there provide a foundation for English 615.

Tutoring in the Writing Center

During the week before the beginning of classes, TAs meet with the WC director to begin getting situated to the tutoring experience. They also attend the annual orientation and participate in the holistic scoring session of the English 101 proficiency exams taken during summer orientation sessions. After a second week of tutor training, they begin their two semesters in the writing center.

In addition to scheduling and conferencing with WC clients, TAs are encouraged to use the professional resources available to them in the WC and the department, such as journals and faculty, to support their growth as teachers. In addition to tutoring sessions, they are involved in other projects, such as developing workshops for in-center and in-class presentations for interested faculty, maintaining the WC Web site, and online conferencing with students on OWL, the online writing lab.

English 615: Proseminar in Composition Instruction (3 credits)

English 615 enters the picture the second semester, during which TAs continue to tutor in the WC. Unlike the scheduling of the 615 class I described in my introduction, the course has been moved from their first semester as TAs, when they will be working in the WC, to the second semester. This change was instituted to allow TAs one semester to gain experience working with student writers at Mason without the rigor of a pedagogy course and to provide an experiential base for their teaching of English 101 the following semester.

Currently, the teaching of 615 alternates between the director of the writing center and the director of composition.[3] While the particulars of the course design may vary, both directors recognize the value of the lived experience as writer and as student as the basis for theorizing about the teaching of writing. Fully aware of the potential for TA resistance to theory, both directors have been revising the ways in which theory is presented so that it is inter-woven as organically as possible into the course. In addition, TAs are asked to consider different theoretical perspectives in light of their reflected-on experience with an eye for the implications for course design and classroom practice. Also of importance is help-ing the TAs develop an appreciation of composition studies as a robust and valid discipline with a body of theoretical perspectives and research.

We can see how WC director Terry Zawacki presents theory from the beginning of the course.[4] In the section of her syllabus on course goals, she states:

> Louise Phelps, a noted composition theorist, talks about the "PTP arc"—from practice to theory to practice. "The rela-tionship between theory and practice at any point," she writes, "is not a simple one-way influence, but a dialectic. Theoretical ideas filter into practice and are in turn affected by it. What distinguishes the terminus of the arc is that at some depth, theory (explicit formulations of deep structures) acquires the power to counter strong tacit assumptions with new conceptions" (in Anson, *Writing and Response*, 45).
>
> From your years of experience as writers and students of writing, you've already acquired a body of assumptions about writing practices whether articulated or not. Part of our work (and fun, I hope) in the course will be to talk about those assumptions, connect them to practice (e.g., what kinds of teaching strategies, assignment designs, response patterns, evaluative criteria "feel" most right to you), and situate prac-tice within theoretical perspectives and research on compos-ing. My goal is to help you see which theories and practices best reflect your own teaching style and philosophy as well as the aims of required freshman composition.

We see that theory is not a hidden agenda in this course. Not only did Terry let her students know that theory would be an integral part of the course, but she also provided them a model for theo-rizing—Phelps's PTP arc.

Opportunities to interact with theory were provided through course assignments. The first assignment was a position paper in which the TAs used their own experiences with writing, their pre-vious experiences tutoring in the WC, and other teaching experi-ences as a basis for considering such topics as the needs of college writers, their own emerging questions about the teaching of writing, and their goals for the undergraduate writers and the writing course. This writing was a benchmark of TAs' emerging theories about the teaching of writing at the beginning of 615.

Beginning in the fifth week, the TAs began a series of teaching demonstrations in which they presented a teaching practice of special interest to them. In addition to an oral overview that placed the topic within the context of 615, each TA provided an engaging activity for the 615 class, followed by a discussion period. The week following the presentation, the TA submitted a paper, which included a written version of the overview and context, a description of the activity, a reflection on the presentation itself, and a list of works consulted or cited.

An observation of an English 101 class session put TAs in the site of the action. They described what happened, how it happened, and, as nearly as possible, why it happened through a discussion of the lesson in the context of the teacher's syllabus and their own connection with course readings and discussions and, if relevant, their tutoring experiences.

Throughout the course, TAs were expected to participate in an electronic forum called Townhall. They were to write two responses to a prompt based on class readings and discussion, one between Thursday and Sunday and one between Monday and Wednesday. The latter entry was intended as a response to other class members' entries. Townhall provided a space for an exchange of ideas and a chance to note one another's perspectives on theoretical and professional issues. These interactions were also sites of theorizing. Terry's prompt topics ranged from global issues, such as writing in academic discourse and valuing diverse voices while upholding institutional standards, to local issues, such as teaching arrangement, style, the sentence, and the paragraph; responding to student writers; dealing with grammar; and sequencing assignments.

The last major assignment for the course was a final position paper on the teaching of writing, which in addition to a reflection on their initial position at the beginning of the course asked the TAs to provide a rationale and context for their English 101 syllabus, including the ways in which that syllabus enacted the student learning goals for English 101, assignments and assignment sequencing, and textbook choice. They were encouraged to draw on such areas as course readings and discussion, previous tutoring and teaching experience, other syllabi reviewed, class observation, informal discussions with other TAs currently teaching, and their own experiences as writers and students in writing courses.

Conclusion

So there you have it—one way to craft a course in composition pedagogy designed to reduce resistance to theory even as it makes theory and theorizing an integral part of the course. But Terry's 615 did not exist in a vacuum. Her course was part of a sequence of events—a selection process that demonstrated a departmental culture that values the teaching of writing to undergraduates in general education, experience that gave TAs one-on-one tutoring experience with Mason students, and their course in composition pedagogy that was placed at a point in their training that allowed them to build on that experience as they worked toward their own English 101 course. As we saw, Terry set up her English 615 proseminar in a way that expected theorizing to be part of the process of TA development by providing opportunities to theorize along the way and reflect on students' tacit assumptions about teaching in general and the teaching of writing in particular.

But how did Terry's TAs respond to the push to theorize? If the friendly banter on Townhall was any indication, they seemed to be having a great time, as if they had been theorizing all their lives (which, I suggest, they had been about one area of their lives or another). According to Eric,

> Exposure to theory at the very least offers a frame of reference for future experience. Empowering for my cohorts. It gave us a vernacular and set of ideas with which to discuss comp teaching, that few of us had wrestled with before. Without those ideas and their attendant names, we'd have had little in the way of points of departure for our discussions.

Josh contends that

> [e]veryone in the class treated theory as a good support for teaching. . . . The theory helped define why you wanted to do

something, thus the something didn't seem so trivial and directionless. [While not everyone agreed with every theory] after conglomerating pieces that were sincere to their methods, they had their own unique theory for what they wanted to do.

Sylvia realized:

> What this class taught me was that I'll need to allow for change as I come to edit my theories about teaching when those ideas are confronted with the reality of the practice of teaching. (Final Position paper)

I'll let these TAs have the last word.

Notes

1. I am reminded of Zebroski's account of a student whose attitude was one of "didn't you know that this course was supposed to be the easy three hours you get for taking on the dirty job of teaching composition?" (120).

2. I used the term *training* advisedly. I prefer the term *development*, with its implication of ongoing movement in thinking, but I use the more common term in this essay.

3. WC director Terry Zawacki's course is the focus of this essay.

4. I am most grateful to my colleague Terry Zawacki for allowing me access to her syllabus and related course materials and for granting permission to use them in the preparation of this essay, and to Josh, Eric, and Sylvia for sharing their thoughts with me.

Works Cited

Bizzell, Patricia. Foreword. *Constructing Knowledges: The Politics of Theory-Building and Pedagogy in Composition.* Sidney Dobrin. Albany: State U of New York P, 1997. 1–4.

Dobrin, Sidney I. *Constructing Knowledges: The Politics of Theory-Building and Pedagogy in Composition.* Albany: State U of New York P, 1997.

Eric. "The Essay RE 615." E-mail to Ruth Fischer. 28 Sept. 2003.

Josh. "The Essay RE 615." E-mail to Ruth Fischer. 9 Sept. 2003.

Kennedy, Mary Lynch, ed. Preface. *Theorizing Composition: A Critical Sourcebook of Theory and Scholarship in Contemporary Composition Studies.* Westport, CT: Greenwood, 1998. ix–xiii.

Miller, William. "The TA Selection Process." E-mail to Ruth Fischer. 19 Feb. 2003.

Phelps, Louise Wetherbee. *Composition as a Human Science: Contributions to the Self-Understanding of a Discipline.* New York: Oxford UP, 1988.

———. "Images of Student Writing: The Deep Structure of Teacher Response." *Writing and Response: Theory, Practice, and Research.* Ed. Chris M. Anson. Urbana, IL: National Council of Teachers of English, 1989. 37–67.

Sylvia. "Final Position Paper." Unpublished essay, 2003.

———. "Sylvia's answers to your questions." E-mail to Ruth Fischer. 15 Oct. 2003.

Zebroski, James Thomas. *Thinking through Theory: Vygotskian Perspectives on the Teaching of Writing.* Portsmouth, NH: Boynton/Cook, 1994.

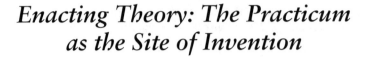

CHAPTER ELEVEN

Enacting Theory: The Practicum as the Site of Invention

MARY LOU ODOM, MICHAEL BERNARD-DONALS,
AND STEPHANIE L. KERSCHBAUM
University of Wisconsin–Madison

There's an ironic twist in the fact that the tension between theory and practice that characterizes (some might say "plagues") the field of composition/rhetoric studies plays itself out most uncomfortably in a place where our work matters the most: our training of teachers of first-year college writing. But evidence of this tension is apparent everywhere. Consider the graduate student from a highly ranked Southern California public university who complains she learned nothing about the teaching of writing in the required practicum, though she did learn quite a bit about pragmatism and the power–knowledge nexus. Or the first-year faculty member at a state university in the South who, when asked what he knew of the theoretical underpinnings of his teaching method—learned in a practicum with one of the leading lights of process-oriented expressivism in the Northeast—realized with some horror that the answer was "nothing."[1] There's irony involved because when pressed, most teachers and theorists of writing suggest that the tension between practice and theory is what keeps us honest: it forces us, unlike many in other subdisciplines of English studies, to be continuously vigilant about the "why," about the reasons behind our teaching practices and the material consequences of our theoretical considerations. Yet the fact that many practica seem to dwell so heavily on either the theory *or* the practice of teaching writing suggests that ultimately we're doing the greatest damage to new teachers when they need most to understand the relation, rather than the divide, between theory and practice: as they begin teaching first-year writing.

The problem resides partly in the fact that both new teachers and many who have worked in the field for a long time misunderstand the relation between theory and practice. In spite of the focus so many smart thinkers in the field have placed on developing just such an understanding in the last twenty years, [2] English studies in general has done a poor job of making clear why theory matters. It seemed for a long time to many graduate students (and the faculty members they became) that the theories of discourse that came to be known as "deconstruction" in the 1980s and the cultural studies– and Marxist-inflected work of the 1990s were fields unto themselves. The work of examining texts, and the contexts in which these texts were written and, later, read, sometimes seemed unconnected to the texts they meant to understand, so much so that an entire field of study became devoted to the rise, dynamics, and fall not of literary studies but of "critical theory".[3] In composition studies, this misunderstanding made itself plain in the 1980s and 1990s in books published by the Modern Language Association and Oxford University Press as introductions to the field, but in which the practice of teaching seemed nearly invisible among many valuable essays on the various approaches to the teaching of writing and to the field of composition/rhetoric studies more generally.[4] It's no surprise, then, that the practica designed to introduce graduate students to the teaching of writing either ignored these theoretical forays altogether or focused attention on them as if doing so would instantly translate into good teaching practice.

More recently, rather than seeing theory as the intellectual foundation on which teaching gets done—or worse, as an unnecessary intellectual endeavor divorced from the actual work of the classroom—the relation between theory and practice has been understood more productively in terms of enactment. Teaching— or, more properly speaking, pedagogy—is the enactment of a theoretical position. To put it another way, what we teach our students is a consequence of what we understand writing to be. Such a position rearticulates the relation between theory and practice not so much as a tension but instead as dialectic, in which each has consequences for the other, and in which neither the theoretical understanding of pedagogy nor the practical understanding of theory gains the upper hand. In this case, what we teach enacts an understanding of writing, of argument, and of rhetoric.

It is with this reconsideration of the relation between theory and practice that the English department at the University of Wisconsin–Madison reconfigured its first-year writing program. Simply put, the program attempts to instill in first-year students a sense that writing has consequences—that our language has practical effects on what we do in our everyday lives—and that those consequences require individuals to take responsibility for how each of us understands the world and our place in it. To provide the program's first-year teachers with a sense of what this means—and, most important, what this means for the student writers in the teachers' classrooms—the director of the program and the graduate student assistant directors, over the course of several years, developed a teaching practicum that favors neither theory nor practice but that instead sees the theory–practice dialectic as opening up rather than foreclosing possible courses of action. The practicum enacts a theory of argument that is later taken up by instructors and modeled in their own classrooms for their students, a theory that sees practice as the constant reevaluation of theory. The course is neither an introduction to comp theory nor a how-to course for first-time teachers, but a course that focuses on what could be called the discursive consequences of argument. In this essay, we describe the practicum, explain how the new teachers in it adopt the model of argument as practice, and then suggest the extent to which the program has succeeded in promulgating a theory and practice of writing that works to encourage student writers and their teachers to see the ethical and practical consequences of writing.

The Program

Before the 2000–01 academic year, each teacher in the first-year writing program at the University of Wisconsin developed and taught a course (English 100) based loosely on the idea of academic literacy. However, the faculty member directing the program and its teacher training had left the university two years earlier, and staff meetings—during which instructors discussed the teaching of writing and worked through syllabi and assignments—had subsequently lost their shape. While the program was guided by the principles of the university's general education "Communications A" component (requiring that students gain an introduction to writing expository and argumentative essays, critical reading and thinking skills, and the process of revision, culminating in twenty-five to thirty pages of polished prose), neither the CommA requirements nor the first-year writing program emphasized just what was meant by "expository and argumentative" prose. As a result, teachers were free to teach any model of exposition and argumentation they felt was effective in the classroom, and thus there were almost as many teaching practices and ideas of writing within the program in any given semester as there were sections (fifty) and teachers of first-year composition.

In the twelve months leading up to the 2000–01 academic year, the director and graduate student co-directors of the program, in consultation with key members of the composition/rhetoric faculty in the department, endeavored to develop a workable idea of argument that could be both taught in the first-year classroom and developed as a theoretical practice on the part of its instructors. Based on Stephen Toulmin's *The Uses of Argument* (and what we'll call, throughout the chapter, the "Toulmin model"), we developed a course on the writing of argument that meant to lead first-year students to see the analysis of written arguments as a tool for the invention of their own arguments. In a three-assignment sequence, teachers begin with a problem, case, or controversy—ideally, one that is historically current. Teachers then work with their students to understand how to address the controversy (if not come to some resolution of it) by teasing out the competing claims made by various individuals or groups with a stake in the issue, the ways in which those claims are supported by paying close attention to what counts as evidence to various parties involved, and how those claims could be supported by what Toulmin calls their warrants (or what, in an Aristotelian model, would be called the argument's major premise).

In the first assignment, students argue for a best resolution to the case or controversy, or—as an alternative—make clear the

DON'T CALL IT THAT

points on which the controversy rests. In the second assignment, teachers work with students to understand the assumptions that must be shared by the parties in the argument for the argument to proceed (what Toulmin calls "backing"). In addition, students learn to investigate the disciplinary conventions in which those assumptions are made clear, as well as the questions that might be asked about those assumptions in order to see them, too, as "arguable." In that second assignment, teachers ask students to choose one of the assumptions on which their argument rested and investigate the extent to which its stability depends on the language used to establish it. An argument over how best to solve the Israeli–Palestinian conflict, for example, might rest on the grounding assumption that territorial claims trump other, more complicated political or religious ones. Students might then be asked to question the nature of those territorial claims—from theological, political, historical, anthropological, or ethical disciplinary perspectives—and subsequently to make an argument for the extent to which territory (the land) can be used to make political or other arguments. In a third assignment, by means developed independently by each instructor, students and instructors examine the ethical consequences of some facet of the arguments they've worked on during the first ten weeks of the semester.

The program provides instructors with a model syllabus that outlines the terms to be introduced during the first several weeks of the course and that becomes less and less detailed as the semester goes on. New instructors attend a weeklong orientation before their first semester of teaching during which they are introduced to those terms and develop the first five to six weeks of their course. As instructors do this, they choose a controversy or case, research the lines of argument that might be pursued by students, and develop a series of writing assignments intended to move students from analyzing arguments to producing arguments of their own. What this means, then, is that the practicum—which meets for the first eight to nine weeks of the instructors' first semester of teaching—must not only serve as a sounding board for new teachers, but must also be a forum in which they work to understand the theory of argument themselves in order to model it for their students in their assignments and in their teaching. Instructors move from following a fairly detailed plan for the course in the first weeks of the term to developing—on their own terms—a sense of the consequences of argument toward the end of the semester. In this way, the practicum, which in effect replaced staff meetings for first-year instructors, has become the institutional location in which the program's leaders (its director and two assistant directors) model the theory of argument that formed the program's core as they teach it to new instructors, and in which instructors themselves develop strategies to take up the vocabulary and rhetorical moves involved in Toulmin's idea of argument.

The model of argument we've worked out in our program is not a simple one: all of the terms in that model (*claim, support/ evidence, warrant, counterargument, backing/grounding*) are complicated and shift as students recognize the extent to which any one of them is understood only in contingent contexts. What we have found is that the most valuable work of the practicum is helping teachers "translate" the model of argument we teach them into terms they can then model for their students. The practicum is set up so that the instructors address the components of the model syllabus three to four weeks ahead of their students: while their students are being introduced to the terms of argument, in the practicum teachers are developing strategies to help them understand the relationship between claims and warrants and how formulating warrants as questions will help them develop lines of inquiry and claims of their own. While the students are beginning their second unit, the teachers are developing the link between the second unit (on assumptions) and the third unit (on the ethical and political consequences of argument). This means that the work of the practicum involves a very real struggle to understand how Toulmin's terms are consequent for the construction of argument, or, to put it in far more pedestrian terms, how the writing of an argument enacts an understanding (what we might call a theory) of its terms.

Data Collection

To better understand this enactment, we turn to a study that draws on two related bodies of data. The primary data source consists of audiotaped and transcribed sessions of the weekly practicum meetings during the fall 2002 semester. In this study, the practicum is neither treated as nor perceived to be a transparent site: the practicum itself is a classroom, and ultimately, on the interactions of instructors before they enter their own classrooms, they are students themselves. Furthermore, the administrators in the English 100 program are themselves practitioners enacting their own theory of how to indoctrinate instructors in their program to meet their goals.

The practicum is grounded in certain theoretical premises. First, we assume that instructors need to learn, discuss, and even try out certain theoretical approaches to teaching argument before they engage in such teaching in their own classrooms. Second, we assume that following the trajectory of the English 100 course syllabus is an effective way to create such an opportunity for instructors. As a result of this approach, each session of the practicum has an agenda reflecting what is to be the focus of the course in the immediate future. Discussion of how best to assign, teach, and grade components of the course's model syllabus is common, but often the instructors find themselves "learning" the theoretical underpinning of the model just as their students will.

The practicum's structure encourages teacher reflection—reflection considered as an instrumental and legitimate form of professional knowledge (Schön, *Educating*, *Reflective Practitioner*; Goodman and Goodman; Yancey). This reflection is augmented by the second data source—audiotaped and transcribed interviews conducted with a small sample (four) of instructors participating in the practicum. Since instructors come to the English 100 program with varied personalities, academic profiles, and teaching experiences, the focal instructors were chosen in order to maintain gender and experiential balance. Additionally, two instructors were chosen because of their dominant presence during the seminars (subsequently reflected in their high proportion of talk in the practicum transcripts), and two, conversely, were chosen because of their reticence and hence minimal presence in the transcripts. Instructors were asked a standard set of questions, along with questions specific to each individual based on his or her actions in English 790 (the practicum).

We approached all of these transcripts with an eye toward understanding how instructors made use of the practicum to engage with the theory of argument put forth in the English 100 program. Particularly with the practicum transcripts, we identified moments in which teachers' reflective talk described the Toulmin model's place in their plans for, reports of action in, and reflections on classroom practice. Additionally, the transcripts were examined to ascertain not how these instructors eventually *used* the Toulmin model in their classrooms, but rather how they went about *envisioning and understanding* its use for themselves and their students.

Efforts to identify and categorize these actions as they were manifested in the practicum became an early step in seeking to understand teachers' positions in attempts to integrate Toulmin's theory of argument into practice. First, the data were combed for any instance in which instructors made mention of, engaged in any activity related to, or reflected on personal or student experiences with the Toulmin model of argumentation used in the model syllabus. This preliminary step ensured that every possible moment in which the teachers acted with some regard for the theory or for their own practice was considered, even if their mention of action, or the action itself, was not explicit. What resulted was a series of moments in which teachers, theory, and practice exist alongside one another. Ultimately, it became clear that the theory–practice relationship is characterized by dual, potentially competing processes as instructors learn and teach simultaneously; the analysis thus examines the new instructors in the seminar from this dual-role position: that of both teacher and learner.

In fact, what the data suggest is that through the practicum's efforts to facilitate the uptake of a model of argument based on Toulmin's ideas, instructors must first adopt a number of strategies to establish a coherent theory of argument that is practicable. More specifically, the data suggest different ways in which the instructors "take up" argument as both a theory and a practice; often this uptake involves the instructors' negotiation of their own difficulties with the theory and their subsequent development of means by which they will teach it to their students. Ultimately, then, the practicum enacts the theory of argument with and for the instructors; they in turn enact argument with and for their students.

The Practicum

These strategies of uptake are varied and numerous and, as such, often defy explicit categorization. What is perhaps more important than naming every strategy occurring in the continuum of the instructors' efforts, however, is understanding the actual nature of the continuum itself. In other words, what is apparent in examining the development of these instructors over the course of the eight-week practicum is that their shift between the roles of learner and teacher occurs not at once but rather in incremental steps characterized by an evolution of their facility with the model. For those instructors who eventually became adept with the course's underlying theory, it is their progression from struggling with the model to renaming it or reshaping it for their own purposes that stands as evidence that the practicum has indeed been a site for them to make practicable a theory of argument.

This trend occurred throughout the eight weeks of the practicum but was particularly apparent during sessions in which instructors engaged in activities for applying the model much like those their own students would have to do. The discussion that follows examines exchanges in two such sessions of the practicum. These sessions occurred during the first and fifth weeks of the semester, and they involved the instructors and administrators working through arguments from the instructors' own course texts.

In the first meeting of English 790, for example, administrators led the instructors in exercises in argument analysis, just as the instructors had done or would soon do with their students in their own classes. At the administrators' request, instructors volunteered to describe their course debate and the argument of one of their chosen texts for the first unit. The class as a whole then analyzed the argument of the text according to the Toulmin model by identifying the argument's claim, supports, warrants, and grounding. As the class worked toward this goal, it was clear that a number of the instructors were still struggling to gain command of the terms used in the Toulmin model. In the following excerpt, "Peter"[5] and the other instructors in the practicum attempt to talk through an analysis of Peter's first Unit 1 text. This text argued that the events of September 11, 2001, may have spelled the end of an age dominated by ironic sensibility. With the program's assistant director (MLO) leading the discussion, the group began the process of analyzing one claim from that argument—the claim that "Irony makes it impossible to know the difference between a joke and a menace."[6]

> MLO: What's a piece of support that might go along with that claim?
>
> PETER: Um, well, this point about Marx I would take as a piece of support. He's saying, "Who would believe that history is tragedy and then farce except for someone who never took anything seriously?" I mean, do people know what I'm saying? Isn't that kind of the support of that? . . . "If you're an ironist and you believe in Marx therefore you can't take anything seriously" is what he's saying. . . . See, it's kind of convoluted, right?

What is perhaps most immediately apparent in Peter's efforts to align his text with the components of the Toulmin model is that he repeatedly turns to his classmates and the administrator for feedback on his thoughts. He demonstrates that while he has a strong sense of his text's argument and a great deal of familiarity with the subject matter, the application of the model is not yet an automatic or uncomplicated process for him. He draws on the similarly evolving knowledge of the other instructors for both support and assistance in developing his understanding of how to put this theory of argument into practice.

Peter's role as a learner attempting to make sense of the Toulmin model is clear. But this is only one part of the complex position he occupies with regard to taking up the course's theory for argument. Even as he attempts, and in some instances seems to struggle with, his own understanding of the model, he must also consider his imminent obligation to make it accessible and understandable to his own students. MLO helps him in this direction by responding to his assessment of the argument as "convoluted" as the exchange continues and as other instructors begin to chime in with their own thoughts:

> MLO: Yeah, it is [convoluted]. But your students are going to have to figure it out, so that's okay.

PETER: Mm-hm.

MLO: Have you decided which piece of support you want to go with? Do you want to say, "Ironists are Marxists who don't take things seriously?"

PETER: Yeah. This is really interesting 'cause I had to do this with them 'cause his argument is so weak in here.

MLO: Okay.

PETER: Another thing his support is—he says that "movies featuring characters who see dead people or TV hosts who talk to the other side suggest that death was not to be seen as real." It's a totally stupid point, you know. [. . .] This is hard, I think. What do you think, Mary Lou? You think that's okay? Just go with the first part about Marx?

Once again Peter looks for help in mapping out the parts of his text's argument. More important, however, he also begins to connect his experience in the practicum, specifically his own difficulty applying the Toulmin model to his text, with the experience he and his students have in the classroom. This dual role is evident in that not only can Peter suggest possible answers to the questions posed by the administrator, but he can also identify potential problems with or alternatives to his own answers. This is an important aspect of Peter's uptake strategy; he combines his own learning of the theory with looking ahead to the special challenges the theory might pose for his students and for himself as a teacher.

Of course, Peter is not alone in the practicum or in the engagement of uptake strategies; his fellow instructors both benefit from and play a role in his learning (and their own). This situation is an important one for instructors because it allows them to collaboratively work through the theory for themselves even as it provides insight into what may transpire in their own classrooms as their students do the same. Furthermore, as other instructors express their thoughts and concerns about the analysis Peter began, they voice additional concerns and problems that may prove relevant for their students. The attempt to apply the Toulmin model to Peter's text continues as the administrator moves the discussion forward with the claim, support, and warrant that Peter and his peers developed for the text in question:

MLO: All right. So "Irony makes it impossible to know the difference between a joke and a menace." And he's supporting that by saying that "Pop cultural phenomena—like movies—are examples of not taking things seriously." Okay? What's a warrant for this argument?

MOLLY: Actually, that's what—I was just thinking about this, and I'm not sure it works, because it's saying that those who do not take things seriously are being ironic.

PETER: That's a warrant?

MOLLY: But it doesn't—that warrant is very—you can definitely argue with that.

MLO: Mm-hm.

ERIC: Couldn't you also say that there's an assumption that not taking things seriously *means* you can't tell the difference between a joke and a menace? [Peter: Yeah, yeah, true.] That means that.

PETER: You know, one of the things that I find confusing is the difference between warrant and sort of—I don't know—assumptions or something.

This exchange reinforces the practicum's function as a site where theory is practiced—where instructors work alongside one another and with the course administrators to enact for themselves the program's chosen model of argument before enacting it with their students. Here, Peter is joined in his efforts in this enactment by other instructors, whose own unique insights on and questions about the theory add to their collective understanding about not only the model but also the challenges any learner might face with it.

Of further importance here is the confusion Peter expresses over finer points of the vocabulary of the Toulmin model. Such uncertainty about this major aspect of analyzing argument with this approach repeatedly proves to be a primary challenge in the program's use of this theory. Instructors in the practicum (and in the follow-up interviews conducted for this study) often refer to Toulmin's terminology as the major source of difficulty for their students as well as for themselves. Such confusion certainly is apparent in practicum discussions with Peter and his peers. Despite these challenges, the fact that the instructors have experienced this confusion for themselves before tackling it with their students represents precisely the benefit of a practicum of this nature. As the instructors attempt individually and as a group to work through their uptake of the model, their voices play out logistical scenarios and potential complications in a setting similar, yet prior, to their own classrooms. These actions are an important part of the instructors' initial experience with the program's theory—the experience of a learner—yet they are also critical to the eventual growth of these teachers.

So how do these instructors, when encountering a glitch in their use of the theory, negotiate the model so that it ultimately can be valuable for themselves and their students? This negotiation can occur by means of several strategies, but more important than any one of these is the fact that to create and make use of such strategies, a certain degree of proficiency with the model is first necessary. How this proficiency is achieved is something Peter demonstrates near the end of the exercise on his course text. After discussing the differences between warrants and grounding, and after devising several possible warrants for the claim made in Peter's text, the instructors begin to examine the appropriateness of those warrants. MLO facilitates this discussion by pointing to one of the suggested warrants and querying the group.

> MLO: Okay, and what about the other one? Does that also work—the belief that irony equates to just not being serious?
>
> PETER: They work in almost some sort of geometry proof kind of way.
>
> MLO: Uh huh.
>
> PETER: I mean, they really build on each other like the transitive property or whatever.
>
> ERIC: Like change or something like that?
>
> PETER: Yeah, change, yeah. "If a equals b, and b equals c, then a equals c." . . .

To determine whether the warrant he and the other instructors devised was a workable one, Peter employs a strategy whereby he puts the model into new terms—terms that reinforce his existing understanding of the model and appear to make it more immediately usable for him.

This example of Peter's strategy for "practicing" the theory grounding this program illuminates several moves that are key for these instructors' successful experiences in the practicum. First, we see that Peter's understanding of the role of a warrant in analyzing argument has become clearer—so clear, in fact, that he can now explain it in other, very different terms. Specifically, Peter in this instance has gone so far as to reach into another discipline altogether for help in articulating the relationship of the components of the Toulmin model. Second, we see Eric picking up on this strategy himself and making further sense of Peter's analogy to the transitive property.

Peter himself ultimately expresses the value of this exercise in enacting the program's theory. As the group prepares to move on to another topic, Peter thanks MLO for "indulging" the lengthy analysis of his argument and notes that while he knew the argument in his text was a flawed one, the exercise had been beneficial in assisting him in "putting language to the fact that there are so few supports in this piece." Peter then articulates an important shift in his thinking and in the roles he fulfills as a participant in the practicum. He moves from reflecting on his own enhanced knowledge of the Toulmin model to looking ahead to its value for his teaching: "It's going to be interesting to look at it from an argument analysis [perspective]—just sort of saying, what does he [the author] offer? Nothing. Just a bunch of claims." Peter has moved from his initial confusion over the model's complexity to an appreciation of what this same complexity might eventually offer him as a teacher.

To be sure, Peter's own uncertainty with the model has not been eradicated entirely. Indeed, much as his students' will likely be, Peter's process of learning to use this model to the fullest will be an emergent one that evolves in fits and starts. What his experience to this point in the practicum has done, however, is to instill in him a budding comprehension of all that enacting the theory can entail; his ability and willingness to recast the model's language and relationships in his own terms is evidence of that. Thus, he moves forward prepared to engage in yet another way of enacting the theory—that of teaching it to his own students.

That these instructors manipulate elements of a theory as a means to better learn it should indicate that this strategy may have its place in the other role they occupy—that of teacher—as well. In other words, it perhaps should come as no surprise that the instructors, as they become more engaged in shaping their own pedagogies and developing assignments and expectations unique to their own classes, are inclined further to reshape, recast, and even challenge the constraints of the Toulmin model and the program's model syllabus itself.

Such an impulse is borne out in various ways throughout the semester, but the instructors continue, just as they did in that first week, to use the practicum as a site where this reshaping can be tested and explored. But whereas the first sessions saw this reshaping as a more tentative means of learning the Toulmin model, in later sessions the instructors are far more confident and purposeful in offering their own take on this theory. The fifth of the practicum's eight sessions, for example, led by the director of English 100 (MBD), focused on how instructors (and in turn their students) might use the warrant of their course debate as a point of entry into the research question that would drive their second unit assignments. Additionally, discussion ensued about other issues relevant to the teaching of research writing.

> MBD: One of the things you have to decide is how much work you need to do before your library date.[7] . . . What you do in the first three weeks before that point is to begin introducing search terms that [students] may find useful, so that when they get into that [library] workshop, they can start punching things in.
>
> PETER: Yeah. Like, I encourage them to conceive of their three drafts in the second paper differently in that the first draft may operate a lot like an annotated bibliography—with a jumping off point of their argument in Unit 1, the warrants and groundings that they discovered about that, and then, just a little bit of riffing on how these articles might then problematize and/or back up their warrants and groundings in Unit 1.

Peter is once again a prominent speaker in the practicum, but the nature of his comments here differs drastically from those in the practicum's first week. Peter now speaks not out of confusion or to question the Toulmin model but instead to offer something of his own approach to teaching with it. Rather than focusing primarily on understanding the model and its terminology, Peter explains to MBD and to his fellow instructors how he is using the very terminology that once so perplexed him to enrich the research process for his students.

Eric expresses a similar desire to shape the course theory and syllabus in his own particular way. After MBD discusses how students can be guided into developing and exploring authentic research questions, Eric reveals his own plans for the progression of assignments in his course and the way he envisions the Toulmin model playing out in the debate he and his students are exploring.

> MBD: So long as they can make their way from the question that they've latched on to to the research that they're finding, or even just to the question that they started with, they're going to have a really neat contour. . . . This is a very far-flung place from where they started and yet, they have a disciplinary lens, they're starting to focus their questions, they're beginning to hit something that's interesting to them, and all of a sudden, this thing that they started with, which may have been boring, isn't so boring. . . . Okay, questions about this?

> ERIC: Can some of this be delayed to Unit 3, in terms of the way that they look at some of these questions from incredibly disparate perspectives? My Unit 2 topic is nuclear proliferation and who determines who has these capabilities. . . . That's kind of the warrant underneath the question of "Why are we interested in Iraq right now?" Unit 3 I was considering a much more open-ended question about the consequences of this debate in different fields than they might be interested in. With Unit 2, I was still much more interested in them doing research and understanding the history of the international policies themselves as they relate to nuclear warfare. In other words, I wasn't planning on letting them go into this many potential questions, although it could still happen, but kind of not foregrounding that sort of approach.

Much as Peter showed his own development as a teacher comfortable with using the Toulmin model, Eric too demonstrates that he now engages with the model at a much deeper level than he did in the early practicum sessions. Eric has even extended his comfort level with enacting the course theory to envisioning its role in his assignment trajectory differently than the program's model syllabus initially lays it out.

Discussion

The data show various ways that instructors' experiences in the practicum encourage various roles and positions with regard to the material they are teaching. For instance, Peter is at times a student, learning the model of argument alongside his peers; at other times, Peter takes on the authority of the teacher, speaking to others about how he is using the model in conceiving writing tasks and research goals. As we note earlier, this is suggestive of the role the practicum plays in instructors' development: it enables their understanding of the ways in which the terms of argument lead them to develop a *theory* of argument. This theory generating has numerous consequences for the teaching of the course, which we describe in more detail below.

Our model of teaching argument presumes that having a language for argument is akin to knowing how to use argument. Thomas Kuhn writes that "discovering a new sort of phenomenon is necessarily a complex event, one which involves recognizing both *that* something is and *what* it is" (55). Our instructors cannot teach argument without a language with which to describe it—i.e., recognizing *that* it exists. What remains is for them to determine precisely *what* these terms are and how they can be used.

In practical terms, this means that our practicum gives instructors that language through Toulmin's model of argument. It also goes a step further by providing a space where instructors can practice it, test it out, develop definitions for terms, and so on. As we note, throughout the space of the practicum, instructors worked to recast the language of argument provided by the program (and Stephen Toulmin) into terms they themselves found practicable.

This generation of terms is a significant move toward developing a rhetorical practice of argument. As instructors move toward the third unit of the course, the program pushes them to take on a more active role in articulating their goals for their students. The program does this precisely by leaving relatively open the third (and final) unit of the semester, which focuses on the consequences of argument. As instructors flesh out the Toulmin model, they are thus forced to acknowledge the ways that understanding what argument *is* is akin to understanding its ethical and consequential impact.

The practicum plays an important role in scaffolding Peter's learning with regard to the Toulmin model of argument. There are two primary rhetorical strategies evident in the data that suggest how the practicum enabled this work: by providing collaboration with peers and administrators through which instructors question their orientation to the theoretical model they'll be enacting, and by facilitating the translation of the model into other, more practicable, terms.

First, we address the idea that the practicum provides a collaborative atmosphere for instructors to question the model's language for describing argument. In Peter's case, he looks to both the program administrators and to peers to help him flesh out the terms he is using and how those terms allow him to talk about argumentation. In the first practicum session, for example, Peter explicitly requests confirmation from his peers about whether what he is describing does, in fact, fit the definition of *support*. As he begins somewhat tentatively, "Um, well, this point about Marx I would take as a piece of support," and then as he describes the "support" in more detail, he looks to others in the room: "I mean, do people know what I'm saying? Isn't that kind of the support of that?" We argue that this look to his peers is part of a shared process of meaning making going on in the classroom. In other words, Peter questions whether others share his definition of support and, in so doing, works to see if what he is describing matches others' models of what "support" indexes.

We also see collaboration enabling Peter's development of other terms in the model, as he puts pressure on the notion of "warrant." When Molly suggests, "Actually, that's what—I was just thinking about this, and I'm not sure it works, because it's saying that those who do not take things seriously are being ironic," Peter's follow-up is "That's a warrant?"—a statement that suggests he is still working out the model on a definitional level. While Molly has indeed suggested a "warrant"—a connection between the claim and support—Peter is still focused on understanding how the information she has provided aligns with terms from Toulmin's model of argument.

When Eric suggests that the warrant could be rephrased as a kind of "assumption," Peter then asks aloud, "You know, one of the things that I find confusing is the difference between warrant and sort of—I don't know—assumptions or something." He is now engaging with *other* terms that may help him understand what a warrant is—is a warrant an *assumption*, or is it something else? This move is significant, we think, because Peter is moving from simply trying to match lines from the text with the terms ("Is this a support?") to using language to help him develop definitions for the terms in Toulmin's model of argument.

A second element of the practicum we'd like to highlight here involves how Peter (and other instructors as well) worked to translate the language provided in the model into language they found more practicable in the classroom. Instructors frequently commented on one another's ideas, using those ideas to identify connections or to establish relationships between ideas. A representative example of this is the work Peter and Eric did together in describing the transitive model for argument. Their work in this instance involved the creation of what Aristotle called *phronesis*, practical wisdom, in which the theoretical premises of any art or science—in this case, rhetoric—were made applicable to specific cases, and in which the conceptual apparatus was made concrete in the language of the everyday. Understanding, for example, that the language of Toulmin's model of argument involves a notion of change or transitivity (a concept not inherent to the model itself) was negotiated between Eric and Peter in the context of the practicum. As the creation of a practicable notion of an argument's underpinnings—in this case, the argument's warrant—such moments are available only in the classroom space of the practicum and, we would add, in the English 100 classroom as the instructors bring what they've negotiated about argument into their teaching of writing.

There's a sense in which this translation of theoretical concepts into other, more practical, language could be said to be reductive, and the mathematical example used by Peter—and sometimes by program administrators—seems to be just that. In another sense, however, it is only through such translations that Eric and Peter understand the notion of transitivity and change at all. (And given the complexity of Toulmin's notion of argument, and his insistence on the notion of change inherent in it, it's not clear at all whether this reduction is a loss, or whether it amounts to a surplus of knowledge made possible only in the context of the practicum.) To put this as simply as possible, far from learning how to "use" Toulmin's theory of argument so it can be taught in the classroom, these instructors are instead forging a language through which to understand that theory on their own terms so that they can then make those redefined terms available for their students. The instructors are practicing the theory of argument in the practicum just as they and their students will later practice it in the English 100 classroom.

Conclusion

What can we say about the success of this model of the practicum? How well does it introduce instructors to a model of argument whose theoretical premises are soundly established and linked to other notions of rhetoric and writing and whose practicability is also well-enough established that instructors are able to use it to teach writing to first-year students? We can answer this question in two ways. The first is objective: Do first-year students come out of the writing class, English 100, having succeeded in writing sound, interesting, and fluent argumentative papers? Have the methods we've attempted to inculcate in the practicum been borne out in the first-year students' success as writers of argument? The second way to assess the program's goals might be called procedural: Do first-year students understand and feel willing to engage with the complexity of argument in the same way that the instructors have felt willing to do in the practicum?

By using the objective measure, it's difficult to determine whether the program has been a success. Certainly, we have numbers on which to make some guesses: while the grades received by students in English 100 have dropped over the five years during which the shift to Toulmin and the current practicum has occurred, the mean student evaluation score for the course has risen substantially over the same time.[8] This suggests—though it may not mean—that students have responded positively to the demands of the course and have found their writing to have improved, in spite of what they report as an increased rigor in the class and an increase in the amount of time they spend doing the work. In addition, a longitudinal study done under the auspices of the university's Verbal Assessment Committee—which was charged to measure the success of the university's two required communications courses (CommA and CommB)—notes that students who have completed the CommA requirement feel more successful as writers in their second writing course, though their grades in that second course are not statistically any higher than those who were exempted from the first course.[9] Because we do not collect portfolios or do other long-term assessments of student writing, we cannot say whether the change in our approach to teacher training reflected in the practicum has brought about a marked improvement in student writing or in students' understanding of argument.

On the second criterion, however, it's possible to say that the practicum as it has emerged in our program is a success, in the sense that first-year students have been provided a model of argument that is not so much a template that can be overlaid onto their own written arguments but that functions, rather, as a discursive practice in which they engage together to build a language through which to understand and write arguments. While it might be hard to measure in any quantitative way such a statement, what we have seen as we've observed first-year teachers in the classroom does in fact bear this out. Instructors work collaboratively with their students to question the premises of arguments, both those written by more or less "professional" writers on the subjects of disagreement that form the core of the units, and those written by the students themselves as they stake out positions on those subjects of disagreement and analyze what assumptions and warrants underpin those positions. In addition, instructors work to help students develop a language to discuss those arguments. In visit after visit—each first-year instructor is observed, as a matter of program policy, twice during their first semester of teaching—we have seen instructors modeling their struggles with the language and practice of argument, whether in front of the classroom at the chalkboard discussing the positions it's possible to take on a controversial issue (such as how the events of 9/11 have forced a return to serious discourse), or working with students in groups as they come up with arguments of their own. In some instances, instructors use the very language they developed in collaboration with their fellow teachers in the space of the practicum; in other instances, they collaborate with their students to come up with alternative terms, sometimes for use in the class as a whole and sometimes with individual students.

More to the point, when instructors return to teach English 100 for a second time, they may not necessarily return to the model of argument—Stephen Toulmin's or the derivation of it we work with in English 100—but they do begin from the premises of the argumentative project laid out in the practicum to develop a vocabulary of argument and an accompanying epistemology, anything from Aristotle's enthymeme, to stasis theory, to Burke's pentad, or a hybrid of two or more of these and other notions of argument. In other words, the practicum as we've tried to develop it here is inextricably a course in the theory of argument, but it's not an introduction to argument theory. It is, instead, a *practicum* in the strongest sense of the term: a location where instructors engage the practice of the theory of argument, as well as strategies that make that practice visible in writing (both the students' and the instructor's). As we continue to work through this model of the practicum, we are at least satisfied that its premise—that one learns argument best by engaging in the practice of argument in a community where it matters, in effect, that argument involve an ethical commitment to engagement with others—is fully sound.

Notes

1. The authors could recount dozens of such stories, both from graduate students and from faculty members trained in some of the leading composition programs in the country. These are just two; those who told the stories prefer to remain anonymous.

2. This list includes, among others, Louise Phelps's *Composition as a Human Science*; the work of Jim Berlin, particularly *Rhetoric, Poetics, and Cultures*; Patricia Bizzell's *Academic Discourse and Critical Consciousness* and many of her essays; John Schilb's *Between the Lines*; and Lester Faigley's *Fragments of Rationality*.

3. See, as just one obvious example, Jeff Williams, ed., *The States of Theory,* a special issue of *the minnesota review.*

4. See Clifford and Schilb's *Writing Theory and Critical Theory*, Anne Ruggles Gere's *Into the Field*, and Harkin and Schilb's *Contending with Words.*

5. The names of all instructors in the practicum have been changed to pseudonyms in this essay.

6. Transcripts have been edited for readability. For example, hesitations and repeated words and syllables have been omitted when not relevant to meaning.

7. Each section of English 100 spends one class period in a research workshop led by one of the undergraduate library's reference librarians.

8. An informal survey conducted at the end of the 2001–02 academic year found that while the average GPA of students completing English 100 had dropped by nearly two-tenths rather consistently over the previous five years, the average student evaluation score for the instructor had risen consistently by the same amount (two-tenths) over the same period.

9. See "Outcomes Associated with the General Education Communication-B Requirement" issued by the Verbal Assessment Committee, especially page 45.

Works Cited

Berlin, James A. *Rhetoric, Poetics, and Cultures: Refiguring College English Studies.* Urbana, IL: National Council of Teachers of English, 1996.

Bizzell, Patricia. *Academic Discourse and Critical Consciousness.* Pittsburgh: U of Pittsburgh P, 1992.

Clifford, John, and John Schilb, eds. *Writing Theory and Critical Theory.* New York: Modern Language Association, 1994.

Faigley, Lester. *Fragments of Rationality: Postmodernity and the Subject of Composition.* Pittsburgh: U of Pittsburgh P, 1992.

Gere, Anne Ruggles, ed. *Into the Field: Sites of Composition Studies.* New York: Modern Language Association, 1993.

Goodman, Yetta M., and Kenneth S. Goodman. "Vygotsky in a Whole-Language Perspective." *Vygotsky and Education: Instructional Implications and Applications of Sociohistorical Psychology.* Ed. Luis C. Moll. New York: Cambridge UP, 1990. 223–50.

Harkin, Patricia, and John Schilb, eds. *Contending with Words: Composition and Rhetoric in a Postmodern Age.* New York: Modern Language Association, 1991.

Kuhn, Thomas S. *The Structure of Scientific Revolutions.* 2nd ed. Chicago: U of Chicago P, 1970.

Phelps, Louise Wetherbee. *Composition as a Human Science: Contributions to the Self-Understanding of a Discipline.* New York: Oxford UP, 1988.

Schilb, John. *Between the Lines: Relating Composition Theory and Literary Theory.* Portsmouth, NH: Boynton/Cook, 1996.

Schön, Donald A. *Educating the Reflective Practitioner: Toward a New Design for Teaching and Learning in the Professions.* San Francisco: Jossey-Bass, 1987.

———. *The Reflective Practitioner: How Professionals Think in Action.* New York: Basic Books, 1983.

Toulmin, Stephen. *The Uses of Argument.* Cambridge: Cambridge UP, 1988.

Verbal Assessment Committee, University of Wisconsin–Madison. "Outcomes Associated with the General Education Communication-B Requirement." Draft. 1 Sept. 2001. University of Wisconsin–Madison.

Williams, Jeffrey, ed. *The States of Theory.* Spec. issue of *the minnesota review* ns 41.2 (Fall 1993/Spring 1994): 1–338.

Yancey, Kathleen Blake. "Foreword: Only Connect." *Practice in Context: Situating the Work of Writing Teachers.* Ed. Cindy Moore and Peggy O'Neill. Urbana, IL: National Council of Teachers of English, 2002.

CHAPTER TWELVE

Burkean Ruminations on How, When, and Where Teacher Knowledge Originates

DAVID STACEY

Humboldt State University

A major characteristic of the modern movement in writing instruction is graduate teacher training. Until relatively recently, advanced studies in English did not train graduate students to teach composition, the activity that often occupies the largest part of their early professional careers in tenure-track positions at regional or state colleges and universities. It used to be that after having little or no training in how to teach writing, new assistant professors would flounder through their very first experiences with teaching writing. This has changed, of course, in the past twenty-five or so years. There are now graduate programs, conferences and journals, and awards and endowed chairs devoted specifically to rhetoric and composition. A whole new professional edifice has been constructed within, and sometimes outside of, the English degree, so that it is now rare, even for a new holder of a PhD in literature, to be unable to point to some preparatory work in writing instruction. No one should have to "re-tool" anymore, or teach themselves, on the job, how to teach writing, as some of the major figures in contemporary composition theory had to do, as Patrick Bizzaro reports.

Still, there is a kind of re-tooling often taking place. Many new assistant professors find the most challenging part of their work not in first-year composition but in sophomore- or junior-level work with education majors, "single subject" degree students— people studying to be teachers, including incoming MA students with teacher training backgrounds who want to be teaching assistants in a local writing program. Teaching new teachers is often what we have *not* been trained to do, and it can be a major part of the daily work in applied composition studies. The point to be made is twofold: as composition specialists, we are often not concerned merely with first-year writing. Very often we do indeed have second- and third- and fourth-year students, as well as graduate students, so our sun does not rise and fall on FYC (first-year comp) alone—and these students are often in training to be teachers of English in middle and high schools. Second: are we not propagating a fundamental "trained incapacity," as Kenneth Burke (*Permanence* 7–11) would call it, in rhetoric and composition when we focus exclusively on FYC, composition theory, and the politics of writing instruction, only to discover when we actually start working in the field that we are working not only with first-year students in the writing classroom but also with junior- and senior- and masters-level students in teacher training?

To be trained, counterproductively, *away* from doing something well. This is an irony of efficiency, we might call it, a type of "perspective by incongruity" that Burke valued throughout his career. Originating in the sociological writing of Thorstein Veblen, "trained incapacity" became for Burke the basis of a strain of thought that has come to be identified in his earlier writings as a proto-deconstructive appreciation of the times when an insight actually functions as a blindness (*Permanence and Change*, 7–17). In contemporary composition, we congratulate ourselves on developing a field of study that actually prepares graduate students to be writing teachers, but many of us go forth after advanced study to work in English departments at universities that were once "normal schools," where teacher credentialing is an extremely important aspect of what we do. The very thing that makes us good at FYC—a sophisticated working knowledge of new theories of literacy and pedagogy—makes us not so good at the other: dealing with what might be called (again with reference to the early Burke) an "attitude toward theory" that we can encounter among English education majors and other kinds of teachers-in-training.

An interesting instance of how both this trained incapacity and this attitude toward theory come about is a situation recounted by James Gray in his fascinating memoir of the origins of the National Writing Project (NWP), *Teachers at the Center*. He recounts an important shift in his own apprenticeship as a teacher, from an emphasis on love of reading, which he cares about, to scholarship, which he dislikes. A small detail in an overall wonderful story, perhaps, but in the course of describing his own apprenticeship, Gray discusses how much he loves reading and how he then discovers that he has an aversion to scholarship: and this discovery is the very prompt that motivates him to become a *teacher*, rather than a "researcher" or "scholar" or "professor."

Is this an important part of how "teacher" is constructed in our professional practices? Are we witnessing what a Burkean analyst might call a "ritual drama," a myth of origin? Imagine the following transaction as part of a Browningesque dramatic dialogue about teacher training:

Q: How do you become a teacher?
A: Well . . . read a lot and love doing it. When you hit scholarship, veer off. Then you're ready. Get to work.

This imagined ur-scene seems to me to be an instantiation of our cultural idea of what is "natural" in our commonsense concept of "teacher." People who want to work with knowledge and other people do teaching; people who want to work with knowledge and ideas do scholarship, or research, or "theory." We might even say that in James Gray's memoir, this type of transaction is a moment or occasion of pre-theory. It's a kind of formula or scheme for those structural binaries that would-be teachers read about, or *feel*, uncomfortably, when they find themselves "doing theory" in my third-year English ed course, Introduction to Composition Theory, or in my graduate level Master of Arts in the Teaching of Writing (MATW) course, Seminar in Teaching Writing. Here's the binary:

Love of reading = teaching (good)

Love of scholarship = not-teaching (bad)

I mention the discomfort of education majors in my courses because their anxiety around theory is, I am arguing here, precisely symptomatic of the problem of a trained incapacity in PhD-level composition studies. Kris Halstrom, a graduate student in my English 611 Teaching Writing seminar last fall, devoted her course paper to this issue, especially as it pertains to that kind of politically aware teaching called "critical pedagogy." In summarizing some of the research she did for her essay, she makes an astute observation:

> In the November 1998 issue of *The Journal of Critical Pedagogy*, Barry Kanpol explains critical pedagogy to beginning teachers and answers three of the "central themes" of skeptics. One question has to do with who speaks and for whom. How can a middle class professor claim to speak on behalf of oppressed, marginalized people? And when a college teacher uses the "opaque" academic jargon critical theory is so good at inviting, doesn't this obscure the message, and even dominate those outside of that discourse community? And, how can it possibly work in the classroom, good as its intentions may be? Kanpol answers that "any one has a right to struggle for democracy," from any social class. A teacher's good intentions, he says, are enough to legitimate their work on behalf of others. As for the off-putting jargon of critical theory, he supports it as "a new and vibrant language to challenge old forms" of speech and thought.

Ms. Halstrom and many other graduate students struggle with the problem of difficult ideas expressed in difficult language. As it happens, I agree with Kanpol about the actual viability of critical theory in teacher training, but he might be letting himself and the rest of us "critical" pedagogues off too easy. Certainly Ms. Halstrom is not happy with Kanpol's notion that difficulty = vibrancy, as she went on to worry the issue of theory throughout the rest of her essay. As with most if not all new teachers passionately interested in the well-being of her students, however, Ms. Halstrom wants to find some kind of balance between the kind of knowledge a teacher gets from experience, what Stephen North famously calls the "lore" that comes from "practitioner inquiry," and the more abstract, perhaps thornier, quasi-scientific, philosophical or theoretical ideas of critical pedagogy. And the most significant part of the trouble she discovers here, with or in "theory," is very often specifically regarded as a problem of or with *language*.

A second autobiographical situation described in Gray's book highlights the serious problems inherent in the widely perceived opacity, or even irrelevance, of theoretical language. This time Gray lets Marjorie Kaiser, professor of education at the University of Louisville, enact the dramatistic rite of passage in teacher training, the conditioning moment when "teaching" is hived off from "scholarship." Describing her and a colleague's discovery of the work of the National Writing Project in Louisville in the early 1980s, she recounts:

> We did not know much about the Bay Area Writing Project at that time. Berkeley was not spending its limited funds on publications. In fact, most of the material we eventually received from Jim Gray was mimeographed. What I did know was what I had been doing: team teaching graduate courses with faculty in rhetoric who did not share my view of the value of teacher knowledge and the validity of wisdom that comes from classroom experience and from reflection on that experience. Rather, my team-teaching partner felt a responsibility to inform teachers of rhetorical theories that often had little connection to classroom practice. (60)

As it happens, being a product (graduate) of that very rhet and comp program developed in the late 1970s and early 1980s at Louisville (one of the first such programs in the country), I know the principal actors involved here—even the unnamed colleague who was apparently too interested in rhetoric or theory for his students' good. And I think I inherit, alas, by some sort of generative grammar, the situation Kaiser describes: I find myself today in my teaching of would-be teachers, especially in the MA-level seminar, trying to inform students of rhetorical theories that (they are often not shy about telling me) sometimes seem to have little ostensible connection to classroom practice.

This indicates to me that there is, to invoke Burke again, a set of problematic relationships implicit in our cluster of generative terms—*teaching, scholarship, research, reading, theory*—as these are configured in the founding mandate of the NWP, as well as in our work with teachers-in-training in rhetoric and composition. If there are contradictory energies in the core of our disciplinary constitution that seem at times to bubble up in interesting if not always productive forms of graduate-level student resistance, then a good set of questions to confront right away in the training of a teacher in a seminar in teaching writing is: How, when, where does lore (a composition studies term), or reflective teacher knowledge (the founding concept of the National Writing Project), figure into this cluster of terms? How do we get students who have never taught a first-year writing class (at least independently) involved in the kind of knowledge produced by actual teaching? And what is the relationship of this teaching knowledge to Theory (with a capital "T," as writers such as Gerald Graff and James Zebroski like to inflect the term)?

This set of questions brings us to a Burkean kind of conundrum, a puzzle about beginnings not unlike Stanley Fish's pragmatic quandary about how to join a community (when in order to belong to it you have to somehow be always already inside it). If teachers learn from teach*ing*, if Marjorie Kaiser is right to privilege "teacher knowledge and the validity of wisdom that comes from classroom experience and from reflection on that experience," how does one *begin* to be a teacher? Further, how do we in comp studies want to handle the concomitant discounting by Gray, Kaiser, and others of a body of theory about rhetoric, communication, learning, and language that we have developed? I don't happen to agree—in substance—that these theories have little connection to classroom practice, but I cannot discount this perception, because it constitutes a rather powerful paradox of substance, which brings us to yet another relevant term from Burke. What I think happens right here in Kaiser's account (and in many another daily dramat[ist]ic rite in the everyday social life of academia) is a significant problem of definition, indeed a paradox of substance: If one learns to teach by teaching, then how does a teacher become a teacher? Where do you start? What is the origin? Don't you have to learn how to be a teacher before you become a teacher? How can you reflect on an experience before you've had the experience?

Please don't mistake my claim that this is an important, essentializing paradox for an argument against what Kaiser and Gray and many others call "teacher knowledge." The ideas and actualities of "teachers teaching teachers" are powerfully appealing on many different levels, and I am not disputing the basic idea that teachers learn best from one another, especially when they write together. It could indeed be said that this question, "How does a teacher learn to teach?," is merely a theoretical "chicken and egg" riddle, and therefore not all that important in light of the many important achievements of the NWP. For the reasons discussed previously, however, I think it really is important. Many students resist theoretical opacity when they encounter it in a seminar on teaching writing, but the kind of knowledge embodied in such language does reside at the heart of the Masters in Teaching Writing degree at Humboldt State University and similar degree programs at other, similar, regional universities. If theory is eschewed, more or less reflexively, as something that rebuffs teachers before they "get to practice," then there is a problem, and it seriously affects the relationship between two different academic fields or disciplines, English education and composition studies.

In an influential essay on a "theory of theory" for composition studies, James Zebroski comes very close to identifying this problem as the essential, hugely damaging thing I think it is:

> I would argue that the great fault in composition is between the disciplinary practices (but also some teaching and writing practices) that have funneled into composition from English and the humanities (i.e., scholarship) and the disciplinary practices funneled into composition through education, especially English Education, from the social sciences (research). (44)

The relationship between these two fields is beyond the scope of my purpose here, but in the remaining space of this essay I can at least outline in broad strokes a practicable, experimental, indeed experiential argument "for theory," with a consideration of one possibility of a disciplinary rapprochement: some tentative inquiries into new ways teachers have of telling stories about themselves and their work. My intent as a compositionist is to try to arrange a meeting halfway between theory and practice (Zebroski's "scholarship" and "research") by emphasizing a scholarly, research, and pedagogical interest and method that is common among scholars, researchers, and teachers in English studies, English education, and composition studies.

Storytelling is of course important to everything we do as teachers because it plays so major a role in our culture. Many of our attitudes toward theory are, I believe, deeply embedded in our practical experiences of listening to and telling stories. I first heard about a specifically *digital* kind of storytelling at the November 2000 national conference of the National Writing Project in Baltimore, where I attended two sessions on this interesting and truly new form of narration. Here is how its advocates describe digital storytelling (DS):

> Digital stories are short video projects that bring together multi-media, including still images, voice, video, music, sound, text, animation, artifacts, and other materials. Stories can be created, displayed, and disseminated using personal computers and relatively simple software. The three main components of digital storytelling—story, multimedia, and digital technology—result in dynamic, powerful, context rich presentations. The format and medium, which can be produced on CD-ROM and published and disseminated on the World Wide Web, personal computers, and video screen displays, make them accessible to a broad audience. (Conference Handout, *Center for Digital Storytelling*)

Digital stories are usually produced in QuickTime movie format. The two practitioners of digital storytelling who have done the most to promote it within the NWP are Caleb Paull in Berkeley, California, and Corey Harbaugh from the Third Coast Writing Project in (and around) Kalamazoo, Michigan. Its basic elements are not complicated:

Basic Digital Storytelling Steps

- ◆ Write a script or outline about the story you want to tell.
- ◆ Capture your images with a digital or video camera. Film is OK too—then consider using PhotoCD to save scanning time.
- ◆ Process your images and save at a high resolution.
- ◆ Create a storyboard with your pictures.
- ◆ Put your images together creating a movie or slideshow.
- ◆ Add sound to your pictures.

- Compress your master movie to a downloadable size on the Web.

- For additional technical help, see the Web Review article *Editing Shortcuts and File Conversion.* (*Webreview: Cross-Training for Web Teams.*)

One of the most attractive elements of DS is immediately apparent. Here is a democratization of technology not just dreamt about but achieved, for DS arises alongside a widening access to the material means of editing visual narrative—anyone with a relatively new computer can do it (see *Webreview*). My first impression of DS is that it is significant not merely because it is fun to do; nor is it only for teachers. But writing teachers should be learning about composing in multimedia, as Chris Anson, Gunther Kress, and others have been saying for some time now, because it is technologically upon us. As a new and potentially defamiliarizing means of storytelling, it can only intensify the most profound purpose of narrative:

> [T]he development of a professional identity is inextricable from personal identity and . . . when personal and professional development are brought into dialogue, when teachers are given the opportunity to compose and reflect on their own stories of learning and of selfhood within a supportive and challenging community, then teachers can begin to resist and revise the scripting narratives of the culture and begin to compose new narratives of identity and practice. They can begin to author their own development. (*UNL Teacher College*).

If those of us who manage seminars in teaching writing can place our trust in "stories of learning and selfhood," I believe we may be able to overcome deleterious attitudes toward theory in our students and perhaps resolve some of the problems arising from our trained incapacity. We would see ourselves as trying to get new writing teachers engaged in "author[ing] their own development" from the very point of their entrance into the field. This is not a simple or idealistic solution, for two reasons.

First, when we consider how important storytelling is to the development of a professional, not merely personal, identity, we will still be concerned about the origins of teacher knowledge.

New teachers may not have that body of teaching experience to reflect on that constitutes the kind of teacher knowledge championed by NWP. Nevertheless, they do, of course, possess a deeply intuitive experience of storytelling. In a sense, then, all we would have to do is "add digital" to how we already work with storytelling in teacher preparation. But there is a second catch. When we look at teacher narratives written by experienced teachers, we often find a serious problem, as Mark Dressman points out repeatedly in his research into teacher narratives: an immediate and overwhelming emphasis on the positive, indeed idealistic, aspects of teaching. This occurs at the expense of nothing less than the very development of a professional identity we hope to cultivate in the first place.

That there was something a bit too idealistic was certainly my initial impression of digital stories I viewed at the NWP annual conference. The QuickTime presentations I watched were interesting, highly engaging depictions of individual and collaborative experiences, brimming with energy and enthusiasm for both the process of working with technology and the experiences and challenges of teaching. They were impressive, especially as vehicles of personal expression, as a new "means of production" for expressive discourse. In fact, the most noticeable feature of each video I saw was its overall celebratory nature; this was so noticeable that I began to wonder if perhaps the common thread of idealistic celebration of teacher identity might not be some kind of sacrifice of content to learning curve. Was this a kind of emergent formula, perhaps a marker of genre, in digital storytelling? Did an overly idealistic message have something to do with technique rather than content?

I doubt it. Throughout his work in writing with computers, Myron Tuman insists that a proper use of technology is signified when a teacher does what he or she always did in the classroom, only more so, as it were. The digital difference, according to Tuman, is quantitative and extensional, rather than qualitative and revolutionary. When we move into new technologies, a great deal of our practice will change, of course, but there need not be any *qualitative* break in "what we do" as human beings teaching and learning. This is Tuman's consistent theme. What Dressman ("Theory *into* Practice?") points out about teacher narratives in general, then, probably applies to digital storytelling as surely as it applies to narratives told by teachers in the mono-medium of print. When teachers compose stories to show their teaching lives, their narratives are often overly idealistic.

Dressman finds in his research that teachers confine themselves too quickly and too thoroughly to a conventional "story of successful practice" ("Theory *into* Practice?" 50). Dressman does to the teacher narrative something akin to what Mary Louise Pratt did to the science of linguistics in her noted article "Linguistic Utopias": languages conceived of as stable over time and across communities are idealistic projections; they exist only "in the head." In like fashion, Dressman characterizes teacher narratives as idealist projections of internalized expectations rather than as representations of real—often uncontrolled and uncontrollable—experience. Further, they rely on nineteenth-century notions of novelistic mimesis for their effect. They virtually follow a formula: "The teachers in the story tried something new and were a great success; try it, and you'll be successful too" ("Theory *into* Practice?" 1).

This is significant, and unfortunate, according to Dressman, because it sets up emotionally defeating experiences. Teachers interpret the ins and outs of actual practice as failure and then blame themselves:

> What . . . those models [of good practice in the standard conventional form of the best practice teacher narrative in, say, *Language Arts*] share is an uncomplicated belief that, to teach effectively, one always moves from abstract, big ideas about what "should be" (the skill of "using adjectives," or the principles of "process writing" or a "literature based curriculum," for example) to their practical implementation. One always moves from "theory *into* practice," in other words, never in the opposite direction—and, most certainly, never without direction. . . . [O]ur idealism . . . can be so illuminating that it can blind us to other possible interpretations of the unexpected, and keep even the best practitioners feeling inadequate. ("Mrs. Wilson's University" 502)

Dressman pinpoints the issue: *theory in one direction only* blinds teachers to their own realistic and actual, rather than idealized and conventionally internalized, "success." It shuts down "other possible interpretations" ("Mrs. Wilson's University" 502). In one sense, then, the solution to this type of trained incapacity is simple: stop thinking of English 611, the teaching seminar, and the study of rhetorical, literary, and pedagogical theory therein, as "theory first." This is difficult to do only if we confine our thinking (and reading and writing) to what Burke (*Permanence and Change*) calls "temporal priority," instead of thinking, always also, in terms of "logical priority," and moving back and forth between these two primary principles of organization. In one possible vocabulary of teacher knowledge, we might say that we are being *unnecessarily chronological* and *insufficiently topical*. When we think of preparing would-be teachers in our usual, commonsense ways—i.e., "first you find out about how to be a teacher, then you go out there and become a teacher"—we're being too linear. We're hung up by origins thinking, relying on a myth of presence, trying to be foundational. And, perhaps paradoxically, if and as we try to escape abstract, abstruse, or otherwise difficult "theory," what we are actually getting away from are the actualities of practice or lived experience.

Frank Farmer's understanding of a "sense of theory," which he derives from Bakhtin, might help us implement Dressman's antifoundational critique of the teaching narrative. If I find in my teaching seminar that graduate students seem to prefer what Farmer calls the "answerable, unrepeatable eventness" of concrete experience (15) to the opacity of theoretical language, I might nonetheless use storytelling as the way to create a more appealing theory—practice dynamic for these students. If my students are pragmatists—antitheorist, as Farmer explains—they still seem to believe (and commonsensibly so) that a teaching seminar exists to establish a groundwork for teaching practice. Then again, they are also antipragmatists as well, for the notion that here is where you learn to teach *before* you actually teach is foundational, theory-in-one-direction thinking. For students who shy away from reading and writing that strikes them as too "scholarly" or "critical" or "theoretical," then, Farmer's nuanced attempt to rescue a practicable form of deductive hypothesis from the postmodernist ruins of foundational reasoning can be of some help: "[A] sense of theory is present in every utterance . . . [;] some notion of truth—however constrained, tenuous or fragile—accompanies every act of saying" (12).

A new theory–practice dynamic would be complex, with regard to the theoretical foundations of a typical teaching seminar, when we consider with Dressman that a Habermasian "success orientation" imbues much of our commonsense thinking about the goals and objectives of teaching. Dressman's response to the idealism he finds beating away so powerfully at the heart of typical teacher stories is simultaneously pragmatic and rhetorical, a privileging of experience aimed at reinvigorating a sense of theory.

"[N]arratives that include the twists and turns of practice are more powerful and persuasive than narratives that report only success" says Dressman ("Theory *into* Practice?" 1). For teacher trainees who have yet to encounter actual practice, the "twists and turns" that would complicate "success" could come from— where else but?—theory, or rather *a sense of theory*—a notion that you can be more or less true to experience so long as you are . . . more rather than less true to experience. This is a somewhat Burkean, roundabout way of agreeing with David Bartholomae. Learning to teach is very like learning to write, in that a narrative account of either process (that includes the twists and turns of practice) is more likely to be a "chronicle of loss, violence and compromise" (142) than a story that reports only success.

It matters then, very much, how you interpret the stuff of life that constitutes the content of your story, and you can't interpret that story without taking up some position that is in some sense *outside*—tenuously, provisionally—distant, critical, theoretical. Perhaps this explains resistance on the part of teachers-who-are-still-students, for who wants to complicate success? Especially before one has actually had any! In any case, critical reflection is, as we know, conventionally seen as "that which breaks up narratives." A convenient, very accessible "sense of theory" I have often used to begin the seminar is Gerald Graff's:

> What we have come to call "theory," I would suggest, is the kind of reflective discourse about practices that is generated when a consensus that was once taken for granted in a community breaks down. When this happens, assumptions that had

previously gone without saying as "the normal state of affairs"
. . . have to be explicitly formulated and argued about. (32).

To speak deconstructively, as it were, an even more basic definition of *theory* might be the "troping" or turning, or transforming, of presence into distance. If, then, with Dressman, we would
be true in our stories to the twists and turns of actual experience,
or in his terms, "the random, unpredictable, and unsettling occur-
rences of life in classrooms" ("Theory *into* Practice?")—thereby
creating new plots for teaching in the classroom, on the page, or in
QuickTime—we will need, as Farmer puts it, if not theory itself
then at least a *sense* of theory, a sense that, in Graff's words,
"assumptions that had previously gone without saying as 'the normal state of affairs' . . . have to be explicitly formulated and argued
about." In my experience, students seem able to appreciate and
enjoy Graff's neat conceptualization, even though "defamiliariza-
tion," or that which "was the normal state of affairs," often needs
to be talked about, sometimes with a discussion of Althusser's definitions of "ideology," before and during the writing and reading
and revising of stories. This is so because, of course, narratives are
always preanalytic, which is to say that a story's continuity is borrowed from the flow of experience. The felt sense of unity in a narrative is a product of the genre. Whatever interrupts narratives, as
"that which now needs to be talked about," will always destroy
the illusion of presence that stories provide, and whatever creates
this kind of distance is usually what we ascribe the meaning of
"critical" to. Therefore, if we conclude with Dressman that we do
not need to be linear in our conception of theory, that theory and
practice always interact with each other, then we can also conclude, with other education theorists, that it is feasible and practicable to have would-be teachers tell stories. But further, we can
and should look for ways to interrupt those stories:

> "[S]torytelling, when accompanied by opportunities to exam-
> ine critically those stories [told by would-be teachers during
> their methods and preservice courses] in dialogue with others,
> help[s] them to resist other stories that would narrow and con-
> strain their identities and their notions of language and learn-
> ing. Students . . . place their own narratives alongside, rather

than subordinate to, other narratives from their education classes or from interactions with veteran teachers. By grasping the ideologies and the social contingencies that had shaped their own education, they became able to shape their own stories. (Ritchie and Wilson, qtd. in Sullivan 204)

Ritchie and Wilson also agree that students can and should be encouraged to tell stories about learning in their own lives. Students can be encouraged to see themselves as teachers by telling stories about themselves in all kinds of learning situations; this is how they actually develop into teachers. What is important here, again, is that the enterprise not be limited to or by an expressive purpose, or generic emphasis on success. These advocates of teacher narratives seek to emphasize the validity of personal experience in relation to "ideology" and "social contingency," what Dressman, after Bourdieu, conceives of as the back-and-forth interaction of theory and practice, the "reflexive, reciprocal relationship that exists between what they [teachers] believe, or hold to be true in principle, and what they more intuitively, habitually know they must do in order to prevail" ("Theory *into* Practice?" 58).

One way to integrate storytelling into the teaching seminar is by assigning observation projects. Each fall term, incoming MATW students in my English 611 seek out an experienced teacher of first-year composition who will allow them to attend his or her classes. After some theoretical discussion of "participant observation" and the rudiments of ethnographic data collection, students visit the classes ten times, keep an observation journal, and then recount their experiences to the rest of the class. Orally and in online discussion forums, a student describes incidents and impressions, using a loose form of ethnographic field notes as recognizable, if relatively informal, evidential support within a narrative framework.

This observation takes place at the same time that students are consulting theoreticians of multiculturalism, community, and public life, such as Min-Zahn Lu, Richard Sennett, and Joseph Harris; "reflective" compositionists such as Kathleen Blake Yancey; and writers working with "contact zones," such as Mary Louise Pratt, Gloria Anzaldúa, Patricia Bizzell, and David Bartholomae. The common element among them is that these writers are all involved in theorizing *experience*. A valuable text to accompany these readings and writings is Haswell and Lu's collection of writing-teacher narratives, *Comp Tales: An Introduction to College Composition through Its Stories*, because it anticipates the form and even format of a common kind of anecdote, one that these students are moving toward as they assume the generic, knowledge, and discourse conventions of the narratives that will accompany their new social roles as writing teachers.

Finally, however, Resa Crane Bizzaro provides the prompt for what I have found to be the most useful conception of "preservice" student teacher storytelling: the "entrance-to-the-profession narrative." Drawing on a series of interviews she and Patrick Bizzaro conducted with several notable figures in the field of composition studies, Crane Bizzaro situates her own exploration into her once-hidden identity as a Native American next to their biographical accounts. Her conclusions:

> From my perspective, community renewal must begin with an examination of the paths of individual scholars who must then be heard as part of the collective history of the field of composition studies. This "retelling" of the history of composition studies has two purposes: to flesh out stories of how individuals who contributed significantly to composition theory entered the field and to analyze their narratives paratactically with our own personal narratives to reinvigorate and renew our own composition community. . . . For all of us, the political act of self-determination in the classroom, in the profession, and in our society is also a moral responsibility. (496)

Not a literacy biography or autoethnography but an entrance-into-the-profession narrative. And from the very start, precisely because these would-be teachers lack actual teaching experience, they begin to shape a crucial "act of self-determination" through their own teaching stories by simultaneously setting them alongside the stories of actual practitioners in *Comp Tales* and next to stories of actual theorists, in the research by Bizzaro and Crane Bizzaro. This, finally, is the most powerful approach to my own trained incapacity that I have discovered, because it allows me to do the most I can do to get students who have never taught a first-year writing class involved in the kind of knowledge produced by actual teaching.

Works Cited

Althusser, Louis. "Ideology and Ideological State Apparatuses (Notes towards an Investigation)." *Lenin and Philosophy, and Other Essays.* 2nd ed. London: New Left, 1977.

Anson, Chris M. "Distant Voices: Teaching Writing in a Culture of Technology." *College English* 61.3 (1999): 61–80.

Bartholomae, David. "Inventing the University." *When a Writer Can't Write: Studies in Writer's Block and Other Composing-Process Problems.* Ed. Mike Rose. New York: Guildford, 1985. 134–65.

Bizzaro, Patrick. "What I Learned in Grad School, or Literary Training and the Theorizing of Composition." *College Composition and Communication* 50.4 (1999): 722–42.

Bizzaro, Resa Crane. "Making Places as Teacher-Scholars in Composition Studies: Comparing Transition Narratives." *College Composition and Communication* 53.3 (2002): 487–506.

Burke, Kenneth A. *Grammar of Motives.* Berkeley: U of California P, 1969.

———. *Permanence and Change: An Anatomy of Purpose.* 3rd ed. Berkeley: U of California P, 1984.

Center for Digital Storytelling. 23 June 2005 http://www.storycenter.org.

Dressman, Mark. "Mrs. Wilson's University: A Case Study in the Ironies of Good Practice." *Language Arts* 76.6 (1999): 500–509.

———. "Theory *into* Practice? Reading against the Grain of Good Practice Narratives." *Language Arts* 78.1 (2000): 50–61.

Farmer, Frank. *Saying and Silence: Listening to Composition with Bakhtin.* Logan: Utah State UP, 2001.

Fish, Stanley. "Critical Self-Consciousness, or Can We Know What We're Doing." *Doing What Comes Naturally: Change, Rhetoric, and the Practice of Theory in Literary and Legal Studies.* Durham: Duke UP, 1989. 436–67.

Graff, Gerald. "Debate the Canon in Class." *Harpers* 282.1691 (April 1991): 17–44.

Gray, James. *Teachers at the Center: A Memoir of the Early Years of the National Writing Project.* Berkeley, CA: National Writing Project, 2000.

Halstrom, Kris. Term Paper for English 611. Humboldt State University, 2001.

Harbaugh, Corey. *A Story of Hands*. 23 June 2005 http://www.wmich.edu/thirdcoastwp/corey.html.

Haswell, Richard H., and Min-Zhan Lu. *Comp Tales: An Introduction to College Composition through Its Stories*. New York: Longman, 2000.

Kress, Gunther. "'English' at the Crossroads: Rethinking Curricula of Communication in the Context of the Turn to the Visual." *Passions, Pedagogies, and 21st Century Technologies*. Ed. Gail E. Hawisher and Cynthia L. Selfe. Logan: Utah State UP/Urbana, IL: National Council of Teachers of English, 1999. 66–88.

North, Stephen M. *The Making of Knowledge in Composition: Portrait of an Emerging Field*. Upper Montclair, NJ: Boynton/Cook, 1987.

Paull, Caleb, Corey Harbaugh, Susan Willis, Colleen Myers, Ann Gardner, Beth Calloway, and Sharon Bishop. "Digital Storytelling: A New Multimedia Presentation Format." Annual Conference of the National Writing Project. Baltimore. 16 Nov. 2001.

Pratt, Mary Louise. "Linguistic Utopias." *The Linguistics of Writing: Arguments between Language and Literature*. Ed. Nigel Fabb et al. Manchester, UK: Manchester UP, 1987. 48–66.

Ritchie, Joy S., and David E. Wilson, with Ruth Kupfer et al. *Teacher Narrative as Critical Inquiry: Rewriting the Script*. New York: Teachers College Press, 2000.

Sullivan, James D. Rev. of *Teacher Narrative as Critical Inquiry: Rewriting the Script*, by Joy S. Ritchie and David E. Wilson. *Teaching English in the Two-Year College* 29.2 (2001): 204–6.

Tuman, Myron C. *CriticalThinking.com: A Guide to Deep Thinking in a Shallow Age*. N.p.: Xlibris, 2002.

UNL Teacher College. http://tc.unl.edu/dwilson/tnci.html.

Webreview: Cross-Training for Web Teams. http://www.webreview.com/1999/07_23/designers/07_23_99_3.shtml.

Zebroski, James. "Toward a Theory of Theory for Composition Studies." *Under Construction: Working at the Intersections of Composition Theory, Research and Practice*. Ed. Christine Farris and Chris Anson. Logan: Utah State UP, 30–48.

CHAPTER THIRTEEN

The Teaching Practicum as a Site of Inquiry and Action

JOANNE ADDISON
University of Colorado–Denver

Many of us have engaged in debates concerning the legitimacy of the teaching practicum within our departments and universities. Most often these debates center on the necessity of the teaching practicum, how many credit hours the practicum should be worth, whether these hours will be placed under the same grading rubric as other graduate courses, whether these hours will count toward a student's required course work, and whether those teaching the practicum should be allowed to count it as part of their regular teaching load. These debates seem to leave little time for discussion of the actual content of composition practica, evidenced by the lack of articles and book-length works on composition practica in a field largely defined by its commitment to the teaching of writing.

It's easy to say these debates are rooted in the misguided beliefs of others concerning the legitimacy of teaching practica in particular and, by extension, the role of first-year composition and the field of rhetoric and composition in U.S. universities. But these debates do not originate solely or even primarily from the skepticism of our colleagues. To a certain extent, these debates arise as part of our institutional struggles over financial and cultural capital—in terms of who has the authority to make these kinds of decisions, what the financial impact of these decisions will be, and the status of rhetoric and composition as a field within both English departments and academia as a whole. More important, these debates arise from our own collectively ambivalent feelings about first-year composition, its role in maintaining our livelihood as a field, and just what it is that we should be training graduate students to do in our practicum. This ambivalence, while sometimes leading to constructive debate and other times to dogmatic positions, also opens us to the very criticisms that challenge the necessity for the composition teaching practicum. These criticisms occur not just in departmental meetings, college hallways, and the academic press, but also in the popular press.

The attention given to college-level writing instruction by the popular press is not surprising given the importance of reading and writing in today's economy. One of the more recent and thorough explorations of the importance of successful literacy acquisition is Deborah Brandt's *Literacy in American Lives*:

> Unending cycles of competition and change keep raising the stakes for literacy achievement. In fact, as literacy has gotten implicated in almost all of the ways that money is now made in America, the reading and writing skills of the population have become grounds for unprecedented encroachment and concern by those who profit from what those skills produce. . . . [L]ike other commodities with private and public value, it is a grounds for potential exploitations, injustice, and struggle as well as potential hope, satisfaction, and reward. (2–3)

The role of the composition practicum in these cycles of competition and change as well as the ways in which the composition practicum can function as a site of theoretical and empirical work that explores this struggle are the focus of this chapter. In beginning here, we must recognize that the teaching practicum and our fight for its legitimacy are part of the ongoing commodification described previously, because those of us who earn a livelihood from teaching writing have a vested interest in the continuation of first-year composition programs—the composition practicum being one of the most important tools for its continuation.

Composition and the Popular Press

While most popular press accounts of what is and isn't working in college writing programs center on first-year composition courses, directly implicated in these critiques is the composition teaching practicum. It is important to note that many articles written about college writing programs are prompted by press releases from organizations that benefit from the failures (or perceived failures) of our educational institutions. This is not to say that these organizations want our educational institutions to fail, just that they benefit when they do fail (or are perceived to be failing). An example of one such organization is the College Board. Everyone from the Associated Press (Feller) to the National Writing Project, *USA Today* ("Elevate Writing Instruction") to *The Hispanic Outlook in Higher Education* (Martinez and Martinez), published articles on the College Board's report of the National Commission on Writing titled *The Neglected "R."* This report discusses the inadequacy of undergraduate writing programs, the problem of leaving the teaching of writing to inexperienced graduate students, and the need for improved teacher preparation at the college level. Similarly, the results of a recent survey conducted by ACT concerning the teaching of grammar ("Survey Shows") appeared in many general newspapers such as the *Chicago Sun-Times* (Rossi) and the *Los Angeles Times* ("High School") after ACT disseminated its own press release.

Of course, if all students could achieve a specific level of writing before entering college, there would be little need for testing organizations like the College Board because we wouldn't need ACT scores to tell us if our students are competent writers. Therefore, the College Board directly benefits from disseminating the conclusions of their own writing commission and research projects, sometimes fostering a widespread belief in the inadequacies of our educational systems. While it is easy to criticize this report based solely on the grounds that it is published by the very organization that will financially benefit from its findings, we must keep in mind that prominent members of the field of rhetoric and composition, including Jacqueline Jones Royster, Richard Sterling, and David M. Bloome, sit on this commission's National Advisory Panel. Further, many of our colleagues have worked for and shaped the policies and actions of ACT in one way or another—from grading exams to sitting on advisory panels—and numerous factors play into the failures or perceived failures of our educational institutions, including the ways in which compositionists respond to criticisms of writing programs by means of our teaching practicum, if we respond at all.

In this essay, I'd like to explore one specific issue related to teaching composition, an issue recently refueled by the reports mentioned earlier, because it is represented in the academic and popular press in relation to what we do and don't do in the composition teaching practicum—grammar instruction. I have chosen this specific focus because of the amount of attention it receives in both popular and academic circles and the ways it exemplifies developments and lack of developments in the field of rhetoric and composition.[1]

Grammar: To Teach or Not to Teach

Dennis Baron's 2003 article in the *Chronicle of Higher Education* sums up well the position of many compositionists: "teaching grammar does not lead to better writing." Baron's article was written in response to the widely disseminated results of a survey conducted by ACT ("Survey Shows") wherein ACT found that "college professors rank grammar as the most important skill for students entering college, while high school teachers consider it the least important" (qtd. in Baron). As mentioned earlier, the results of this survey appeared in many general newspapers, although responses to the survey results were concentrated in more insular academic publications. In talking about grammar teaching, here I am referring specifically to questions about the efficacy of teaching grammar from a traditional prescriptive perspective. Baron's argument, that teaching grammar does not lead to better writing and thus grammar instruction should not be a point of major emphasis in writing classes or a major focus of writing instructors, is, perhaps, all too familiar. In fact, it has become so familiar that this sentiment has spilled over to include work aimed at improving syntactic complexity on both a linguistic and a rhetorical level. As Robert Connors noted in "The Erasure of the Sentence:" "When preparing to write this essay, I asked a number of friends and colleagues in composition studies what had ever happened to sentence-combining. At least half of them replied that it had lost currency because it had been shown not to work, not to help students write better" (119). Connors goes on to explain that in fact rigorous empirical research on a number of sentence-based instructional techniques, including sentence combining, have been shown to improve writing ability. George Hillocks's comprehensive meta-analysis on composition research offers an even more thorough review of the findings of research in this area.

It is curious that current writing program practices do not reflect this research and that instead of debating the most effective sentence-based approaches to improving writing, we spend our time refuting the efficacy of teaching grammar, finding ways to circumvent teaching grammar, or engaging in grammar-based teaching practices that, unlike sentence combining, have not been proven to work. For example, as Larry Beason points out in *Voices from the Field*, a Bedford/St. Martin's publication, over the last twenty years many compositionists have held strongly to the belief that grammar should be taught in context: "It has become, in fact, a cliché that often fails to inspire teachers to seek out or create innovative approaches to grammar teaching."

Not only has this mantra helped lead to the end of exploration in this area by individual teachers, but even if empirical research proved teaching grammar in context to be an effective approach, increased class sizes and demands placed on both adjuncts and full-time faculty prevent this approach from being feasible. In the *Times Educational Supplement*, Richard Hudson and Geoff Barton respond to this approach by saying:

> The reality was that it proved impossible to achieve this level of customized response, and little of the feedback could be described as genuinely grammatical in nature. More seriously, the approach left pupils without any overarching understanding of grammar, no template on which to work. While for some educationists this was held up as liberating—the analogy being that you do not have to be able to service a car in order to drive one—grammar could not be marginalized from English for long. You might not need to know how to service the car, but you do have to know the difference between a door, a clutch and a steering wheel. (6)

With the impossibility of teaching grammar in context in any sort of comprehensive and effective way, many of us have turned to the "minilecture" (or turned to our writing centers to provide minilectures). Teachers who have been enrolled in a composition practicum are very familiar with the minilecture concept. The minilecture seems to embody our struggle with grammar; many of us think grammar is important but don't want to teach it and yet feel some duty to do something about it—thus the minilecture. I think it is practices such as the minilecture that Rodney Huddleston and Geoffrey Pullum refer to in their *Chronicle of Higher Education* article when they say: "Instead of systematic teaching of syntactic analysis, what tends to be found in colleges and universities today, mostly within writing programs, is a modest amount of trivialized and routinized grammar."

Back to the Practicum

How can the composition practicum be used to help us move beyond simplistic debates about the teaching of grammar that are all too often misconstrued in the literacy marketplace? In order to further this discussion, I'd like to begin not with Baron's line of argument—which seems to do little more than add fuel to the fire and lead to more frustration than hope—but rather with Robert Connors's line of argument. In "The Erasure of the Sentence," Connors asserts that we should be questioning why compositionists have abandoned research on sentence-based teaching methods, especially those shown to improve student writing. Here, a response to the ACT report would begin not with a focus on reiterating the conclusion that direct grammar instruction doesn't lead to better writing. Rather, based on our field's own forgotten research, this response would question why ACT chose to focus on direct grammar instruction in its press release and redirect the debate toward an emphasis on sentence-based rhetorics that can improve syntactic fluency, or the ability to recognize and choose among a number of linguistic options leading to improved rhetorical effects. And this response would occur in every popular outlet in which the report was discussed.

Further, this is the very type of response that graduate students in our composition practica should be taught to explore. This exploration should encompass not just practical teaching matters but also matters of institutional critique and the politicized role of literacy instruction in the United States today. In other words, furthering the discussion on grammar instruction ought to involve the very type of theorizing and experimentation that is generally the focus of graduate instruction. Let's make sure not only that our students are informed of the complexities of an issue like the teaching of grammar but also that we help them create habits of mind that lead to questioning and exploration. The issue of whether to teach grammar, and the financial and cultural ramifications of such a choice, can be woven throughout the course of a practicum in ways that help our students learn how to build useful theories and systematically test classroom practices as they come to create their own understandings of one of the most widely discussed issues related to writing improvement. Following are steps that can be taken in incorporating this strategy into a teaching practicum:

1. Before the semester begins, the practicum teacher should decide on two or three grammar texts and/or sentence-based rhetorics that teaching assistants will use with their students. Suggestions include Daiker, Kerek, and Morenberg's *The Writer's Options* and Kolln's *Rhetorical Grammar*. If you would like students to compare these approaches to a more traditional approach, a grammar handbook can be used to develop a minilecture/worksheet series. Teams of students should be assigned to use one of these approaches (i.e., students should work in teams of two, three, or four, depending on the size of the practicum, throughout the semester on this component of the course).

2. During a presemester orientation, or during one of the first practicum sessions, students should be shown how these approaches work and how to fully integrate them into a composition class.

3. Students should be given a framework for analyzing the effectiveness of whatever approach they are using. This should be relatively simple but systematic classroom-based research that allows students to test whether the approach used is actually

improving student writing. Books such as *The Art of Class-room Inquiry* (Hubbard and Power) can be a helpful resource in this. In the interest of time, a framework for analysis should be developed by the teacher of the practicum for the students—the primary goal here is not to teach the students how to conduct rigorous academic research (although validity and reliability should be built into even the simplest framework) but to help create habits of mind that lead to systematic questioning of educational practices.

4. At some point in the semester, students should read popular and academic accounts of the role of the teaching of grammar in the composition classroom. You can begin with the sources cited in this chapter, asking students to bring in one or two more academic and popular reports on this issue and making enough copies of their material to share with all other members of the practicum. This will result in a good collection of material with minimal research from the students (I am mindful of the many things that must be covered in a teaching practicum, and making this component manageable is a priority if it is to be successful).

5. At the end of the semester, each student can write a report on the success/failure of the approach they employed and the ways in which their work during the semester supports and/ or undermines the academic and popular material they read earlier.

6. You may want each team of students to produce a piece of col-laborative writing based on their research, perhaps the type of policy statement concerning the teaching of grammar that would be presented to a department or school district or in a mock press release modeled on those found on the College Board, National Council of Teachers of English, or National Writing Project Web sites.

I want to conclude by making clear that I'm not suggesting a wholesale return to forgotten strategies aimed at improving writing, such as sentence combining, as a panacea. Rather, I am using this as an example of the need to teach our graduate students ways to understand and respond to public and academic critiques of writing instruction in useful and forward-looking ways. To do so, we can use our teaching practica as sites of inquiry and action as we work with our students to engage and alter debates on literacy development.

Notes

1. An article published in the *New York Times* (Markoff), for example, briefly chronicles the development of grammar checkers, a development that came to a halt with the inclusion of a grammar checker in the versions of Word produced by Microsoft in the early 1990s. Once control of grammar checkers was basically left in the hands of Microsoft, the opportunity to make this technology useful for writing instruction, and to learn more about how our language works, was lost. We are in a similar situation with writing software because very little is produced by writing teachers and more and more by a few private companies. Most of us have become content to adapt to the software available instead of insisting on the institutional support needed to develop our own software—as argued for by Paul LeBlanc in *Writing Teachers Writing Software*. Once again, this situation leads to a loss of learning opportunities for those of us in writing studies.

Works Cited

Baron, Dennis. "Teaching Grammar Doesn't Lead to Better Writing." *Chronicle of Higher Education* 16 May 2003: 20.

Beason, Larry. "Teaching Grammar in 2002." *Voices from the Field* 25 Oct. 2003. 30 June 2005 http://www.bedfordstmartins.com/voices/beason_01.html.

Brandt, Deborah. *Literacy in American Lives*. Cambridge: Cambridge UP, 2001.

Connors, Robert J. "The Erasure of the Sentence." *College Composition and Communication* 52 (2000): 96–128.

Daiker, Donald A., Andrew Kerek, and Max Morenberg. *The Writer's Options: Combining to Composing*. 3rd ed. New York: Harper & Row, 1986.

"Elevate Writing Instruction." *USA Today* 7 May 2003: 10A.

Feller, Ben. "Writing Revolution Needed, Commission Finds." *Associated Press.* 25 Apr. 2003: BC Cycle.

"High School English Teachers Just Don't Get It No More." *Los Angeles Times* 15 May 2003: B18.

Hillocks, George, Jr. *Research on Written Composition.* Urbana, IL: ERIC Clearinghouse on Reading and Communication Skills and National Conference on Research in English, 1986.

Hubbard, Ruth Shagoury, and Brenda Miller Power. *The Art of Classroom Inquiry: A Handbook for Teacher-Researchers.* Rev. ed. Portsmouth, NH: Heinemann, 2003.

Huddleston, Rodney, and Geoffrey Pullum. "Of Grammatophobia." *The Chronicle of Higher Education* 3 Jan. 2003: B20.

Hudson, Richard, and Geoff Barton. "Glamour or Grind?" *Times Educational Supplement* 1 Feb. 2002: 6.

Kolln, Martha. *Rhetorical Grammar: Grammatical Choices, Rhetorical Effects.* 4th ed. New York: Longman, 2003.

LeBlanc, Paul. *Writing Teachers Writing Software: Creating Our Place in the Electronic Age.* Urbana, IL: National Council of Teachers of English/Houghton, MI: *Computers in Composition,* 1993.

Markoff, John. "A Computer Scientist's Lament: Grammar Has Lost Its Technological Edge." *New York Times* 15 Apr. 2002: C4.

Martinez, Tony P., and Alison P. Martinez. "The Neglected 'R.'" *Hispanic Outlook in Higher Education* 8 Sept. 2003: 19.

The National Commission on Writing in America's Schools and Colleges. *The Neglected "R": The Need for a Writing Revolution.* New York: College Entrance Examination Board, 2003.

National Writing Project. 30 June 2005 http://www.writingproject.org.

Rossi, Rosalind. "Grammar Valued More in College Than in High School." *Chicago Sun-Times* 9 Apr. 2003. 30 June 2005 http://www.suntimes.com/output/education/cst-nws-gram09.html.

"Survey Shows Writing Skills Most Important to College Teachers Not Always Emphasized in High School Instruction." *ACT Newsroom* 8 Apr. 2003. 30 June 2005 http://www.act.org/news/releases/2003/4–08-03.html.

CHAPTER FOURTEEN

The New Media Instructor: Cultural Capital and Writing Instruction

JEFF RICE
Wayne State University

My interests in technology and writing concentrate around a pedagogical as well as a professional question: What might we mean if we used the phrase "an instructor of new media" in place of "an instructor of writing"? What I mean by the phrase "new media" is the application of new communicative technologies for the purpose of writing. These technologies include, but are not limited to, hypertext, MOO, Flash, Weblogs, QuickTime, and e-mail. In the English graduate program, the writing practicum structures curricula that teach what new instructors should know in order to teach writing: theory, assessment, grammar, citation, revision, and organization. Seldom, however, is new media a part of such study. When I ask if the instructor of writing should (or can) be called an instructor of new media, I am, in effect, asking how we as a field teach graduate students about writing and what kinds of knowledges are needed to teach writing. In other words, I am asking a question about cultural capital.

My question involves how composition studies constructs its own sense of cultural capital and how technology acquisition (and thus new media knowledge) fits into such an understanding. Pierre Bourdieu defines cultural capital as the relationship between knowledge and economic control; accumulation of various cultural knowledges (culture capital) ensures people some degree of control and influence in their lives, as well as how they are controlled. As schools control the dissemination of knowledge, Bourdieu argues, so too do they control who gains access to that knowledge, who will use that knowledge to better himself or herself economically, and who will remain economically marginal because of a lack of knowledge.

> By traditionally defining the educational system as the group of institutional or routine mechanisms by means of which is operated what Durkheim calls "the conservation of a culture inherited from the past," i.e., the transmission from generation to generation of accumulated information, classical theories tend to dissociate the function of cultural reproduction proper to all educational systems from their function of social reproduction. (Bourdieu 488)

Unlike Bourdieu, I am not interested in focusing on the economic aspect of cultural capital but rather on why and how composition studies minimizes technology as part of a cultural capital (needed knowledge) necessary for writing instruction. I borrow from Bourdieu to better understand James Berlin's position that "English teachers are the bankers, the keepers and dispensers, of certain portions of this cultural capital. Their value to society is defined in terms of the investment and reproduction of this cultural capital" (Berlin 15). How we become English teachers, and how we view technology in relationship to how we teach, then, depends on how such values are reproduced. For writing instruction, the practicum signifies this place of reproduction.

Two well-designed, recently published texts making their way into graduate practica highlight my point. Gary Tate, Amy Rupiper, and Kurt Schick's *A Guide to Composition Pedagogies* positions its essay on technology last in the collection of brief descriptions of various composition approaches. This essay, Charles Moran's summary of e-mail, hypertext, and word processing, includes few references to current work in these areas and discusses only one essay on hypertext. Moran's survey provides just enough information to address technology's importance to writing, but so little as to leave readers wondering what exactly they should know. Gary Olson's collection, *Rhetoric and Composition as Intellectual Work*, also positions technology and writing last among the included essays. Unlike Moran's essay, Cynthia Selfe and Richard Selfe's "The Intellectual Work of Computers and Composition Studies" is more inclusive. Focusing largely on scholarly work dealing with sociology, ethnography, and other

culturally related issues, the essay (written by two important figures involved in composition and technology), however, leaves
rhetoric unmentioned. That technology involves rhetorical production might be assumed, but the rich bibliography accompanying the essay leaves out many new media writers who are
concerned with such issues. Apparently, neither composition
scholars nor new instructors assigned this book need to know
about such work.

If I were to follow John Guillory's position that cultural capital is tied to academic notions of canon, I might find the choice of
such texts on practica reading lists suspect for the little space
devoted to writing and technology. Guillory's argument focuses
on how a group of texts becomes institutionalized in instruction,
thus affecting the kinds of knowledge various institutions are
capable of producing:

> The distinction between the canonical and the noncanonical
> can be seen not as the form in which judgments are actually
> made about individual works, but as an effect of the syllabus
> as an institutional instrument, the fact that works not
> included on a given syllabus appear to have no status at all.
> (Guillory 30)

In composition studies, the canon includes not just specific authors
(as is often the case in literary studies) but, more important, specific pedagogical approaches (expressivist, cognitive, feminist,
etc.). These approaches, in turn, become institutionalized as composition studies itself. As Charles Altieri writes, "Works we can-
onize tend to project ideals," and those ideals translate as
pedagogy (135). Thus, the texts read in composition practica don't
raise as much concern as the subsequent pedagogical approach
responsible for diminishing technology's importance to writing
instruction.

The most dominant composition approach to teaching writing, I contend, is expressivism. My concern, though, is not with
assignments taught in expressivist-influenced classrooms or even
with expressivist assignments given in various practica.[1] Instead, I
ask how an ideology of expressivism has led composition studies
to emphasize a specific form of cultural capital, one that minimizes a need to know much, if anything, about technology and,

consequently, new media. To demonstrate my claim, I turn first to the practicum's dependence on a composition canon.

The Composition Canon

Guillory's analysis of the literary canon can be generalized to the concerns of composition studies and the formation of its own canon. Guillory argues that the institutionalization of specific works into a canon marks a hegemonic process (hegemony indicating a rule of one body over another in such a way as to seem natural and accepted by the ruled body). In academia, hegemony takes place when one body of knowledge becomes accepted in the discipline as the discipline itself: "Canonical and noncanonical works are by definition mutually exclusive; they confront each other in an internally divided curriculum in the same way that hegemonic culture confronts nonhegemonic subcultures in the larger social order" (20). Unlike Guillory, though, my naming of a composition canon deals more with specific theoretical movements or ideas that have become canonized, not with the canonization of specific authors or texts (which for Guillory is an issue related to the "culture wars" and the need to integrate multiethnic authors into literature curricula). The composition canon is also created less through the syllabus, as Guillory notes regarding literary study, and more through the practicum, which has become the tool for disseminating knowledge regarding how to teach rhetoric and composition. The practicum produces a specific type of rhetoric and composition instructor, one whose specialty tends to exclude technology. As Berlin writes, "A college curriculum is a device for encouraging the production of a certain kind of graduate, in effect, a certain kind of person" (17). The practicum, as one such device, typically requires comprehensive study of most, if not all, of the following subjects:

Classical and modern rhetoric
History of rhetoric and composition
Expressivism (also labeled—correctly or not—as process theory)
Assessment
Classroom practice

While these subjects constitute the dominant areas of study within the practicum, other areas may also be included: literacy studies, cultural studies, poststructuralism, feminism, computers and writing, service-learning writing, and the newer area of eco-criticism. Thus, it is not an uncommon expectation that students in the practicum be versed in some variation of Kenneth Burke's *A Grammar of Motives*, Aristotle's *Rhetoric*, Mina Shaughnessy's *Errors and Expectations*, Nancy Sommers's "Responding to Student Writing," David Bartholomae's "Inventing the University," and Peter Elbow's *Writing without Teachers*. Knowledge of these texts produces cultural awareness and a common language from which future instructors work. Underemphasized in this process, however, is technology. While many practica allow technology readings to be included (as marked by the computers and writing mentioned previously), most often, as I indicated by my early text examples, those readings are limited or left as an afterthought (the last reading in a course).[2]

The reason for this discrepancy stems from the broader issue of knowledge production, a point we can identify as related to composition studies' tenuous affiliation with theory. After all, the inclusion of technology in writing instruction is itself a theoretical position (how and why we use technology derives from various theoretical ideas). Until the early 1960s, composition studies, as Stephen North notes, based its hiring practices and research methods on "lore," the anecdotal recounting of classroom experience (this happened to me; therefore, it must be true for all cases). Before the 1960s, English studies deemed composition an unintellectual endeavor[3] with little theoretical basis. Edward P. J. Corbett commented on the effect of the 1960s on composition training:

> But for the teaching of writing, which supported [departments'] graduate students, usually the only training [graduate students] got was in a rather desultory practicum which met once a week and which dealt chiefly with the nuts-and-bolts aspects of the writing course. (445)

The empirical research begun by the 1963 publications of Richard Braddock, Richard Lloyd-Jones, and Lowell Schoer's *Research in Written Composition* and Albert Kitzhaber's *Themes*,

Theories, and Therapy attempted to change experiences like that of Corbett's and prompted the beginning of what North calls composition with a capital C. In other words, empirical research emphasized that writing instructors accumulate knowledge in order to become professionals in the field of composition studies. Personal experience would not suffice by itself; instead, instructors needed to work from theoretical positions as to why one method worked in place of another.

Thus, with the construction of theory came the need for cultural capital. Theory, as Gregory Ulmer has noted, is always based on *knowledge* of previous theory: "In each case the theorist generates a new theory based on the authority of another theory whose argument is accepted as a literal rather than a figurative analogy" (9). Theory depends on some form of previous theoretical knowledge. Robert Connors argues that composition studies was designed to be untheoretical because it emerged out of a historical tradition (borrowed from the German university model) that undervalued rhetoric as intellectual work:

> To the increasingly powerful acolytes of the German system, however, rhetoric was at best a suspect and unscientific study, one seemingly unredeemable by research, and at worst simply unscholarly drudge work. It could not be buried and it would not go away, but neither could it be saved as "real scholarship." (62)

Eventually, Connors notes, the work demanded in composition courses focused on the "encouragement of student self-expression" and the close "individualized contact between teacher and student" (67) as opposed to scholarly research. These two factors contributed to the perception of composition as merely the production of *writings* as opposed to the production of knowledge about writing.

Adding to Connors's observations, I propose that even though, as North claims, 1960s composition studies recognized the need to theorize its work and thus reinvent itself, it still kept alive this early anti-intellectual agenda Connors describes. Composition studies did so through the introduction of expressivism (represented in the works of Peter Elbow [*Writing without Teachers*],

William Coles, and Donald Murray). Begun in the late 1960s, expressivism stressed the importance of self-expression in place of theorization.[4] Indeed, expressivism's emphasis on "write what you know" rejected the acquisition of cultural capital for knowledge production (the research model) and emphasized a model similar to what Connors identifies as a devalued practice. As expressivism teaches, knowledge will come from within because it emerges from an individual, not a collective, experience. Peter Elbow writes in his influential *Writing without Teachers*, "The better you get at feeling how your words affect consciousness, the better you will be at deciding *for yourself* whether your words are any good" (104–5, Elbow's italics). According to Elbow's teaching, everything is based on personal experience, not knowledge construction. No writer (nor piece of information) can contradict or supplement another writer's experience: "But you are always wrong [in critique of another's writing] in that you can never quarrel with their experience—never quarrel even with their report of their experience" (106).

While its supposedly anti-institutional agenda appeared, for its time, revolutionary for rejecting the educational system's research demands (the very demands North feels are vital for the field's identification), expressivism has in fact served the institution by supporting an anti-intellectual workforce. Knowledge of technology involves maintaining a standard of academic currency. The expressivist ideology, on the other hand, downplays academic currency's importance for teaching.[5] Expressivist-inspired teachers only have to know how to coax out a student's true feelings in order to be effective teachers. The implications for technology acquisition, then, are large. One does not need to learn the pedagogical value of using technology in writing instruction, nor does one need to learn about technology. For software and textbook publishers (and, as I note at the end of this essay, for WebCT), expressivist pedagogy has helped create and support a workforce not obligated to know how to use technology-based tools in order to be effective teachers. Such knowledge is antithetical to the expressivist agenda because one would have to learn outside of individualized, human experience. Even if expressivism isn't the dominant form of composition introduced in a given practicum, its ideology, I contend, is. How that ideology influences exposure to and understanding of technology affects how a writing instructor views new media practices. To make this point more explicit, I detail two influential expressivist writers and their approaches to writing instruction.

Expressivism

To better understand expressivist pedagogy's influence on the construction of an antitechnology ideology in composition studies and how that attitude manifests in the practicum, I turn to two expressivist writers: William Coles and Peter Elbow. Early in his now classic *The Plural I*, William Coles describes his introduction to writing instruction:

> There were no guidelines given any of us who were involved in the teaching of Humanities I, as the required freshman composition course at Case Institute of Technology was called in the 1960s, no set texts that any of us were expected to deal with, no minimum number of papers the students had to write. In developing a plan for my two sections of the course, therefore, I was free to imagine that I was being original. (5)

Coles entered writing instruction without a canon. "No set texts" guided his teaching. Since he had no canonical texts to depend on for pedagogical direction, Coles opted to transfer a noncanonical (or nontext) system of learning to his own teaching practices. In *The Plural I*, Coles does not introduce students to specific writers or texts so that they can learn how writing looks or works. Instead, he lets students write about the ideas they already have regarding a given subject. Through discussion of such writing, students learn from their own work what they need to know. "The approach—it sounds so simple—was one based on making the students' writing (and not something else), and the students' writing as a form of language using, the center of a course" (6). In a sense, there exists a parallel between Coles's approach to teaching writing and the type of writing he asks his students to do: write by instinct, not by acquired knowledge. Coles taught without textual advice; his students wrote likewise. "From this point on," Coles tells the students of his first classroom, "the course would provide its own materials" (10).

Coles's pedagogy is replicated in Peter Elbow's concept of freewriting. Freewriting, Elbow instructs writers, means jotting down ideas of how one *might* approach a given topic (don't be critical of your first thoughts; let them just come out), sort through these ideas for the best option, and reshape that kernel of an idea until it's correct. One already possesses knowledge; the trick is in extracting it. In *Writing without Teachers*, Elbow instructs students:

> Suppose you have four hours [to write]. Divide it into four units of an hour. For the first 45 minutes, simply write as quickly as you can, as though you were talking to someone. All the things that come to mind about the matter. You may not be able to write everything you know in that time or you may have written everything you know in the first 10 minutes. Simply keep writing in either case, thinking things out as the words go down onto paper, following your train of thought where it leads, following the words where they lead. (19)

Despite its role as heuristic, freewriting reflects a method of knowledge production absent from the acquisition of any cultural capital. Like Coles, Elbow doesn't want students to research ideas, contextualize their thoughts with other work, or support their ideas with data: "The essential act of experiencing something is wholly internal," Elbow states in *Writing with Power*, "the opening of some slippery gland or the clenching of some hidden muscle" (325). Elbow's rationale explains Coles's frustration with student responses early in *The Plural I*. Coles thinks the students aren't being true to themselves and thus produce flaky answers. But his students are true to what they know; they have yet to experience how ideas are disseminated in writing, film, and television (and we can currently add the online environment). Coles's students define a concept (the amateur assignment, for instance) as if they already possess the cultural capital to do so, when, in fact, they don't. They don't consult writings on amateurism; they don't explore actual incidents of amateurism; they don't interview or study specific amateurs. The students know what an amateur is because they know it. Whatever clichés or stereotypes they've absorbed become their first impressions and, thus, the basis of their writing.

The Ideology of Expressivism

What I learn from Elbow and Coles is how a specific type of teaching practice canonized in the practicum leads to a dominant ideology. Following the work of Gary Olson, I want to name expressivism as an anti-intellectual ideology. Olson traces anti-intellectualism in composition studies to the expressivist movement (exemplified in Wendy Bishop's work) and argues for expanding composition studies to mean more than just the teaching of writing:

> Constituting rhetoric and composition as a discipline whose raison d'être is the teaching of writing—that is, all research, all theory, all scholarship exists for the sole purpose of furthering and refining the teaching of composition—is dangerously and unacceptably narrow and even, in some people's eyes, anti-intellectual. (24)

Anti-intellectualism, of course, is not a new area of distress for higher education. Richard Hofstadter raised similar concern in the 1960s by tracing post–World War II anti-intellectual sentiment to nineteenth-century schooling practices that discouraged intellectual inquiry and new knowledge acquisition. Particularly through the heroes it built within an emerging, popular literature, the educational system emphasized figures who cared little for books and "naturally" knew what they needed to know (much like Elbow's imaginary student writer who already knows everything but just needs to know how to get that knowledge on paper, or like Coles's writers):

> American heroes were notable as simple, sincere men of high character. Washington, a central figure in this literature, was portrayed in some of the books as an example both of the self-made man and of the practical man with little use for the intellectual life. "He was more solid than brilliant, and had more judgment than genius. He had great dread of public life, cared little for books, and possessed no library," said a history book of the 1880s and 1890s. (Hofstadter 307)

What Hofstadter traces to the nineteenth century resurfaces as an ideology of late 1960s expressivism. Indeed, W. Ross Winterowd draws identical parallels to expressivism's inheritance of antibook

Romanticism: "'Up! Up! my Friend, and quit your books'" (122) Winterowd quotes Wordsworth. "Like Emerson, Wordsworth— widely read in both classical and modern literature—repeatedly proclaims his distrust of books and his faith in nature" (121). Such ideas manifest in the American Romantic tradition as well, like Walt Whitman exclaiming, "A morning-glory at my window satisfies me more than the metaphysics of books" (43). The book as technology produced nineteenth-century disdain for intellectualism much as current expressivist ideology does for learning technology.[6]

My interest in this critique of expressivism is not to accuse the profession of still teaching expressivist writing. Instead, I ask why this theory of writing dominates the ways we think of ourselves as teachers, and specifically how it shapes a current ideology that places little importance on understanding technology. When it comes to new media, and more specifically to the integration of technology into writing instruction, we position ourselves as already having the prerequisite cultural capital (defined as "personal experience") to make sense of it even though considerable numbers of our profession still do not understand how technology is constructed. The legacy of expressivism thus has become the main influence on contemporary attitudes regarding new media and technology. We have adopted an expressivist ideology regarding our own learning processes.

Pedagogy without Expressivism/
The Language of New Media

How, then, does an expressivist ideology influence eventual teaching with technology? Because of the minimal importance granted technology in many practica, when instructors turn to new media applications, they often do so from an expressivist position. The work initially introduced by educators such as Coles and Elbow has since transformed into an anti-intellectual (and thus antitechnology) composition ideology taught in practica and eventually put into classroom practice. Typically, this ideology has downplayed the importance of theory to writing instruction, but it has also limited our ability to learn new technologies conducive to writing pedagogy. Thus, when Sid Dobrin recounts how specific ideologies are privileged in composition studies, we can expand his argument to that of learning new technologies:

> Growing disdain for theory is becoming a crucial component in the creeping anti-intellectualism that now surrounds discussions of the academy. Within composition, the question of which sorts of knowledge to privilege over others has become a conversation that is central to the development of the field's identity as well to that of the academy as a whole. (16)

The best example of this privileging exists in how writing instructors eventually teach with technology. When writing instruction introduces technology into its curriculum, the tendency is to privilege a lack of knowledge acquisition. The best examples of this practice come from the massive adaption of prepackaged "managed" software programs such as WebCT and Blackboard, which require little technological knowledge from users, or the insistence that students who work with new media in writing classrooms do not need to understand how new media languages (like HTML) operate.

This ideology extends even into composition studies' subdiscipline of computers and writing because its teachers often have been trained first as compositionists. I want to briefly explore how the ideology of expressivism manifests in current teaching with technology. My first example comes from *Kairos*, the online academic journal for computers and writing. Writings featured in *Kairos* at times minimize knowledge of technology in favor of prepackaged systems. In *Kairos* 4.1, Barbara Monroe, for instance, describes how her students learn to write hypertext only through eNotebook, a program for making Web pages that does not require any knowledge of HTML. Monroe stresses the difficulty involved in teaching HTML and recommends the "document conversion" method supported by programs like eNotebook: "that is, first writing and revising the argument as a traditional academic essay and then translating that essay into hypertext." In Monroe's comment, I hear expressivist ideology; one doesn't need *to know* something not already inherent in one's writing (like learning a markup language).[7]

Monroe argues against knowing how to write HTML because the software can convert a word-processing document into the markup language for the student. Likewise, the TechRhet discussion list, a listserv devoted to those who are involved in computers and writing, has found itself several times over the last few years engaged in debate over whether HTML should be taught; most often the "not" argument prevails.[8] Those within the computers and writing community who reject teaching new media languages simultaneously with writing base their objection on either the difficulty in doing so or the lack of necessity. After all, programs do exist that can make Web pages. Why should students know how to do it themselves? In other words, knowledge exists elsewhere; why should we acquire it?

Indeed, this has been the philosophy behind the financially successful course management system WebCT. WebCT (like Blackboard) "manages" technology for its users so that they do not need to learn it themselves. Consequently, WebCT controls how knowledge is created and disseminated. The company describes its services accordingly:

> WebCT's *Professional Services Organization* has the resources, skills and experience to help your institution effectively address these issues. We know the WebCT course management system better than anyone and have a dedicated group of people who have direct, on-campus experience deploying e-learning solutions. This combination of knowledge and experience allows us to assist institutions in addressing each of these critical issues at a level of depth and clarity no one else can. (*WebCT*)

The company's rhetoric emphasizes the importance of using preexisting structures (its own creations based on its own experience) in place of self-creation. WebCT taps into an ideology that disdains learning outside of personal experience and thus fits nicely in the expressivist domain.

And here is the major contradiction within the expressivist ideology. Not only are intellectualism and new learning sacrificed in this model, but so is the personal experience expressivism cherishes. Without learning new tasks conducive to innovations in communication, such as working in new media environments, where does this experience come from? Without learning HTML, for instance, how does personal experience expressed in hypertext develop when, in fact, an outside force "manages" technology for the writer?

My interest is not in arguing for the teaching of HTML.[9] Instead, I'm arguing against the ideology implicit in contemporary composition attitudes regarding technology. Such an ideology assumes that communication occurs on its own without knowledge regarding how the communicative tools work. We assume that the machine—the notebook, the typewriter, the computer, the managed system—will perform the technical aspects of writing for us. Yet the introduction of many new media languages has changed the situation. Unlike the computer, for instance, HTML, Flash, Perl, and other new media languages are themselves writing. Writing is transformed based on technological innovation. As Marshall McLuhan and Quentin Fiore wrote in the late 1960s, new media "is forcing us to reconsider and reevaluate practically every thought, every action and every institution formerly taken for granted" (8). Composition studies can no longer take for granted that writing is divorced from the language of new media, nor can it deny its students and teachers the ability to acquire extended cultural capital in the area of new media.

I propose that composition studies reevaluate its practica to better reflect the writing done in new media. In many ways, we work in a situation akin to Eric Havelock's description of ancient Greece, a populace that knew about the new technology of writing (i.e., was aware of the need for acquiring new cultural capital) but opted for oral recitation instead: "[In Plato's day,] the educational apparatus, as so often since, lagged behind technological advance, and preferred to adhere to traditional methods of oral instruction when other possibilities were becoming available" (40–41). We cling to those theories and methods relevant to print culture but limit our exposure to innovations in technology. What's important, however, is not just that we incorporate technology into writing instruction but that we understand technology's effect on how we write so that we do not become "managed" either by the corporate or by the anti-intellectual agenda. Convincing departments and administrations to buy technology is no longer the major problem; convincing ourselves to learn technology as we simultaneously learn about writing instruction still is.

Acknowledgment

I thank Michael Barry, John Freeman, Marcel O'Gorman, Nick Rombes, and Rosemary Weatherston (aka The UDM Writing Group) for comments on an earlier draft of this essay.

Notes

1. I am referring to the tendency to assign students in the practicum journal and portfolio projects, two assignments typical in expressivist classrooms.

2. While I acknowledge that this statement may seem to be an unfair generalization, I list here some examples to clarify my point. Note Purdue University's catalog description of its practicum reprinted on a practicum syllabus: "Reading professional literature on the teaching of writing, linguistics, and ESL. Studies of methodologies, issues of assessment, and the relationship between theory and pedagogy." Even though Purdue's reputation includes its writing program's emphasis on technology, no mention of technology exists in the course description (http://www.courses. purdue.edu/cgibin/relay.exe/query?qid=courseDetails&num PerPage=20&page=1&showPrevious=F&showCurrent=T&show Future=T&usePaging=F&adminCampusLocation=westLafayette& academicProgramDesignation=traditional&abbreviation=ENGL& academicInitiative=puWestLafayetteTrdtn&session=2005Fal&course Number=505A. See also the University of Arizona's practicum description: "English 510 introduces students to theories and practices in contemporary composition instruction. Students will read theorists in the teaching of writing, focusing on how theory and practice in writing and writing pedagogy inform each other. We will consider critically and at length both 'process' theory and pedagogy and its apparent morphing into 'postprocess' theory and pedagogy" (www.u.arizona.edu/~rcte/ courses/fall01.htm). The University of Oregon, which runs a computer lab for writing courses, offers no technology instruction in its stated aims for teacher training. Topics covered in its practicum include "The design and purpose of the Writing Program, Teaching argumentative writing, Teaching critical reading, Creating effective writing assignments, Teaching grammar, style, and usage, Evaluating and grading student writing, Discussing class observations" (although this URL is no longer live, it is cached at http://web.archive.org/web/20020204221330/http://www. uoregon.edu/~uocomp/word/semapp.html). None of these examples is meant to isolate these programs as faulty but rather to demonstrate a generalizable trend affecting programs that have deservingly excellent reputations.

3. I don't mean to imply that composition is today accepted across the board as intellectual. But its status has changed dramatically since the 1960s.

4. I am not, obviously, the first to level the charge of anti-intellectual-ism against the expressivists. Peter Elbow acknowledges this critique in *Writing without Teachers*. See the appendix essay in which Elbow argues that his pedagogy is intellectual because it seeks answers to questions. *How* it does that, however, remains, for me, the main reason why expressivism is anti-intellectual.

5. I am differentiating between "ideology" and "practice." I don't mean that instructors interested in expressivism have no interest in technology. I am speaking about the ideology of expressivism, which minimizes research and, thus, academic currency. Academic currency today includes technology.

6. This is not a Luddite position (though at times that might be the case). It is an anti-intellectual position. Learning new technologies involves intellectual work.

7. See also Lisa Hammond Rashley's "Women's Studies 101 on the Web" in *Kairos* 6.1 for a discussion of the instructor's choice of Black-board over learning new media technologies like hypertext (http://english.ttu.edu/kairos/6.1/binder.html?response/wost/index.htm).

8. See, for instance, the "Black Reaper" thread (www.interversity.org/ lists/techrhet/archives/jan2002/threads.html), the "Web Publishing" thread (www.interversity.org/lists/techrhet/archives/may2002/threads.html), and the "Improved Netscape Web Publishing" thread (www.interversity.org/lists/techrhet/archives/apr2002/ threads.html).

9. Reducing the argument to learning or not learning one specific tech-nology is counterproductive. Instead, we need to address *why* we don't learn technology in conjunction with writing instruction.

Works Cited

Altieri, Charles. "An Idea and Ideal of Literary Canon." *Falling into Theory: Conflicting Views on Reading Literature*. Ed. David H. Richter. Boston: Bedford/St. Martin's, 1994.

Aristotle. *The Rhetoric of Aristotle*. Ed. Lane Cooper. Englewood Cliffs, NJ: Prentice Hall, 1960.

Bartholomae, David. "Inventing the University." *Composition in Four Keys: Inquiring into the Field*. Ed. Mark Wiley, Barbara Gleason, and Louise Wetherbee Phelps. Mountain View, CA: Mayfield, 1996. 460–79.

Berlin, James A. *Rhetorics, Poetics, and Cultures: Refiguring College English Studies*. Urbana, IL: National Council of Teachers of English, 1996.

Bourdieu, Pierre. "Cultural Reproduction and Social Reproduction." *Power and Ideology in Education*. Ed. Jerome Karabel and A. H. Halsey. New York: Oxford UP, 1977.

Braddock, Richard, Richard Lloyd-Jones, and Lowell Schoer. *Research in Written Composition*. Champaign, IL: National Council of Teachers of English, 1963.

Burke, Kenneth. *A Grammar of Motives*. 2nd ed. Berkeley: U of California P, 1969.

Coles, William E., Jr. *The Plural I*. Portsmouth, NH: Boynton/Cook, 1988.

Connors, Robert J. "Rhetoric in the Modern University: The Creation of an Underclass." *The Politics of Writing Instruction: Postsecondary*. Ed. Richard H. Bullock and John Trimbur. Portsmouth, NH: Boynton/Cook, 1991. 55–84.

Corbett, Edward P. J. "Teaching Composition: Where We've Been and Where We're Going." *College Composition and Communication* 38.4 (1987): 444–52.

Dobrin, Sidney I. *Constructing Knowledges: The Politics of Theory-Building and Pedagogy in Composition*. Albany: State U of New York P, 1997.

Elbow, Peter. *Writing without Teachers*. New York: Oxford UP, 1973.

———. *Writing with Power: Techniques for Mastering the Writing Process*. New York: Oxford UP, 1981.

Guillory, John. *Cultural Capital: The Problem of Literary Canon Formation*. Chicago: U of Chicago P, 1993.

Havelock, Eric Alfred. *Preface to Plato*. Cambridge: Belknap, 1963.

Hofstadter, Richard. *Anti-intellectualism in American Life*. New York: Knopf, 1963.

Kitzhaber, Albert. *Themes, Theories, and Therapy*. New York: McGraw-Hill, 1963.

McLuhan, Marshall, and Quentin Fiore. *The Medium Is the Massage: An Inventory of Effects*. 1967. San Francisco: Hardwired, 1996.

Monroe, Barbara. "'Compromising' on the Web: Evolving Standards and Pedagogy for an Evolving Rhetoric." *Kairos* 4.1. Winter 1999. 5 Jan. 2003   http://english.ttu.edu/kairos/4.1/binder.html?response/monroe/index.html.

Moran, Charles. "Technology and the Teaching of Writing." *A Guide to Composition Pedagogies*. Ed. Gary Tate, Amy Rupiper, and Kurt Schick. New York: Oxford UP, 2001. 203–23.

Murray, Donald M. *Write to Learn*. New York: Holt, Rinehart and Winston, 1984.

North, Stephen M. *The Making of Knowledge in Composition: Portrait of an Emerging Field*. Upper Montclair, NJ: Boynton/Cook, 1987.

Olson, Gary A., ed. "The Death of Composition as an Intellectual Discipline." *Rhetoric and Composition as Intellectual Work*. Carbondale: Southern Illinois UP, 2002. 23–31.

Rashley, Lisa Hammond. "Women's Studies 101 on the Web." *Kairos* 6.1. Fall 2000. 5 July 2005 http://english.ttu.edu/kairos/6.1/binder.html?response/wost/index.htm.

Selfe, Cynthia L., and Richard J. Selfe. "The Intellectual Work of Computers and Composition Studies." *Rhetoric and Composition as Intellectual Work*. Ed. Gary A. Olson. Carbondale: Southern Illinois UP, 2002. 203–20.

Shaughnessy, Mina P. *Errors and Expectations: A Guide for the Teacher of Basic Writing*. New York: Oxford UP, 1977.

Sommers, Nancy. "Responding to Student Writing." *College Composition and Communication* 33.2 (1982): 148–56.

Tate, Gary, Amy Rupiper, and Kurt Schick. *A Guide to Composition Pedagogies*. New York: Oxford UP, 2001.

Ulmer, Gregory L. *Heuretics: The Logic of Invention*. Baltimore: Johns Hopkins UP, 1994.

WebCT. "WebCT Software and Services." 1 Jan. 2003 http://www.webct.com/products/viewpage?name=products_services.

Whitman, Walt. *Complete Poetry and Selected Prose*. Ed. James E. Miller, Jr. Boston: Houghton Mifflin, 1959.

Winterowd, W. Ross. *The English Department: A Personal and Institutional History*. Carbondale: Southern Illinois UP, 1998.

CHAPTER FIFTEEN

Finding Myself Lost in the Composition Practicum Course

LU ELLEN HUNTLEY

University of North Carolina at Wilmington

This is the Hour of Lead—
Remembered, if outlived,
As Freezing persons recollect the Snow—
First—Chill—then Stupor—then the letting go—
EMILY DICKINSON, "After Great Pain"

My aim is to tell about my experience teaching a graduate composition practicum because it is the roughest semester I have lived through in nearly three decades of teaching. The worst part is that I was ineffective as a teacher, and this made me sick. The best part is that when the semester was over and stress had taken its toll, I was in a downward spiral and took no one down with me. From my perspective, all graduate students fared well, and the class came to closure without a hitch. Students' perceptions, on the other hand, are something I cannot claim to understand.

The context is the University of North Carolina at Wilmington (UNCW), a school of approximately 11,000 students, all of whom must complete six hours of composition, with the exception of a small percentage placing out. This two-semester course work for students includes first-year English 101 and English 201, the academic research component usually completed at sophomore level. The composition program at UNCW has been the purview of the English department since 1978. We have had seven professors serve as directors of the composition program during this time. In addition, by 1989 the English department launched its Master of Arts program. In 1999 a split occurred in the English department;

a creative writing department was formed, soon to offer programs in fine arts on the undergraduate and graduate levels.

I detail this background to assist comprehension of the story.

Losing It

The chair of the English department called me at home to ask if I could meet the following morning with the chair of the creative writing department and our English department graduate studies coordinator. I sensed concern as he said it was about the composition practicum I was teaching. The class that met weekly in a windowless seminar room on Wednesday afternoons from 3:30 until 6:15 had become an anxious place, especially since the course midterm. We were seven weeks into the study of the theory and practice of teaching composition, a required course for teaching assistants preparing to teach first- and second-year composition for the English department. The majority of class members were graduate teaching assistants from the MFA program in the creative writing department. English department graduate TAs were also in the class, as were several graduate students, not TAs, who elected to take the course.

I was the first to arrive for the meeting scheduled in the English department chair's office, an enclosed space large enough for two couches and arranged to accommodate comfortably as many as seven people. That morning the four of us talked behind closed doors. Soft light created by carefully placed table and desk lamps and a torchère helped soothe my empty queasiness. The graduate students had been complaining about the course, its demands, and me. They felt that the midterm had been unfair. Many were fearful of failing and career ruin.

"From the students who have been coming to me, and there have been a lot of them, they don't think the class is preparing them for teaching. Even though I've seen the midterm the students are complaining about and think it's perfectly reasonable, it's not effective when students are this upset," one colleague said.

Another added, "Because you did not assign grades to some of the midterms, some students say they are failing. Students tell me they can't concentrate because the class makes them apprehensive.

Some say they are completely lost. They don't feel they can talk to you. They worry about you observing their classes next semester or asking for job recommendations from you in the future. Some say their job prospects after graduate school will be limited because of their experience in this course. The students who have come to me are really upset. And frankly, I'm concerned about you."

I listened, taking in every word. My stomach growled. I got a hot feeling all over and felt shivers. Directing a question to the chair of the English department, I asked, "Do you think you need to get somebody else to step in and finish teaching the course?"

"No," he said with characteristic assured calm, leaning back in his ergonomic desk chair.

A few seconds of silence and I asked, "What do each of you advise I do at this point?" Each one delivered a version of the same answer: "When you meet the students today, ask them what you and they can do respectively to relieve the anxiety in the class. Have a talk and listen."

Directing Composition

Three years ago I assumed the position of director of composition in our English department at UNCW and, among other responsibilities associated with the post, agreed to teach the spring semester practicum course for teaching assistants, English 503: Theories and Practices of Teaching Composition. Having taught for many years Writing for Teachers, an undergraduate version of the course, I was easily interested in teaching graduate students who were preparing to teach for the English department first- and second-year composition.

When first approached by the then-chair of the English department and asked what I thought about directing our composition program, I was in favor of the idea. Having been a member of the department for eighteen years, beginning as a lecturer teaching four classes of composition a semester and working my way through graduate school and into the ranks, I was confident about assuming the director of composition role. The conversation that day in my office was brief. I did not ask a lot of questions.

The thought of serving the English department in this way seemed reasonable. The colleague currently serving as director of composition had been in the administrative post for five years, an extended term from the typical four-year stint. He and his wife, another colleague in the department, were soon to have their first child. By agreeing to take over at this point, I could help. Too willingly saying yes to solve a problem and saying it too often is an established pattern that was going to turn on me this time. Soon enough this goodwill behavior would cause me to crash-land.

I knew that over the years the director of composition role within our English department had become more complicated since the addition of our masters program in 1989 and especially so when the creative writing faculty split from the English department, forming the creative writing department in 1999. Soon after, the Master of Fine Arts program emerged from the newly formed department with tremendous support from the university. Results of the departmental division are still playing out. Most relevant to the director of composition narrative has been the number of MFA teaching assistants joining the ranks with the English department teaching assistants. This combined group from a two-year MA program and a three-year MFA program comprises the individuals for whom the director of composition arranges English department mentors, makes up the population of the composition practicum course, and becomes those individuals whom the composition director will follow for classroom teaching observations.

When I became composition director in 2001, I inherited a group of graduate students who had taken the practicum course the previous spring and were teaching on their own for the first time. I was to observe each of these new teachers twice a semester. In addition was a group of MFA graduate students who were in their second year of teaching; I was to observe these students once a semester. Finally, the group included new TAs from both departments—four from English and seven from creative writing—for whom I made assignments with an English department mentor, an instructor then teaching a composition course. Graduate teaching assistants from two departments, each with its own program demands, one a two-year program, the other a three-year program—this was a confused reality of which I had been unaware. Keeping track of the track(s) and getting to know the new teachers presented challenges. This was a big part of the job as director of composition, but there were other fronts that kept me second-guessing as unpredictable incidents caught me by surprise.

Making Corrections

Two unfortunate but significant events occurred within six months of my stepping into the post of composition director. I write of each incident to illustrate how poor judgment on the part of one or two individuals who teach classes within the composition program can create stress for the person serving as director. This goes with the territory. I relate these incidents because both made me acutely aware of how the actions of others at any time under my direction could emerge out of nowhere and present a problem. I call these events Big Lessons 1 and 2.

> *Big Lesson 1*: A nontraditional student became disturbed in one of the composition classes taught by a graduate teaching assistant when the teacher made the decision at the beginning of the semester to cancel all Friday class sessions and create an online class discussion in lieu of class. The composition class assigned to the teacher was not designated as an online section. The nontraditional student who complained about this change in the class setup reported her displeasure to the provost's office, bypassing the English department and the College of Arts and Sciences. As director of composition, I was one of the last to hear about the student's complaint and the teaching assistant's poor judgment in class management. Yet it was up to me to address the teacher, find out what was going on, make clear the university policy about designated online classes, and get the problem solved.
>
> Reviewing the teacher's one-page syllabus—thin on specifics—I found the policies and procedures to be vague, mostly undetermined. The intention to cancel Friday classes and hold electronic discussions on Thursday evenings seemed

like something decided irrespective of the course syllabus. "The shy students like the opportunity to have conversations online," the teacher assistant told me. "The discussions are much better than in the classroom because everyone gets into it with lots to say."

"It's a great idea to establish class message boards and electronic opportunities to enhance student engagement with material and the ongoing class," I said. "Canceling university-scheduled Friday classes, however, is not an option."

I was the bad person and for several weeks continued getting e-mail messages from students in this class telling me that taking away their online discussions had ruined everything and made it hard for the shy students to participate. Students from this class told me I was unfair; the class wouldn't be the same.

This particular TA was someone with whom I was unfamiliar. Our first interaction happened after the problem occurred. When the provost's office called the English department to inquire about an instructor who was canceling Friday classes, the problem came straight to me. Lesson 1 taught me this: get to know the people I had inherited, review their syllabi pronto, and observe them teaching ASAP. I moved to a higher state of alert.

Big Lesson 2: A common final exam is the culminating experience for undergraduates in our first-semester composition course, and this exam has evolved into one that has all students read and discuss a contemporary article or essay concerning a compelling cultural issue about which they can relate. Students work together on the article in the final days of class. On the day of the exam, students are given a prompt based on the article. They then use the article as a springboard for their own essays. For this exit exam, in-class discussion and reading and writing processes are brought to bear as necessary avenues of preparation for students' compositions. The common final is mandatory; the university sets the exam schedule; students know well in advance of this requirement. There are no exemptions from this exam or exceptions made for students to take this exam early.

A part-time instructor, disgruntled because she was not given classes to teach the next semester, took it upon herself to dismiss her students from taking the English 101 common final exam. Her action in effect invalidated the English 101 experience for her students, creating an unprecedented situation for the composition program, the English department, and the university.

With Big Lesson 1, I solved the problem by meeting with the TA and working through the syllabus, making sure the class got back on track in compliance with university requirements. I bore the brunt of the emotions of a few upset students. The problem was contained. The consequences of Big Lesson 2, however, were more significant and widespread.

After the final exam fiasco, the university aimed to stop payment to the instructor who dismissed students from the common final. The dean of the School of Arts and Sciences called a meeting with the English department chair, the assistant chair, and me to discuss the matter. Once again, someone about whom I knew little was creating havoc. This time it was a part-time instructor. Our dependence on part-time teachers in composition had been increasing incrementally over time, but a problem like this was a first. This incident sent a shock wave through me. An individual teaching in the composition program I was directing willingly derailed our common final examination. I did not know this person, much less this individual's pedagogy or classroom demeanor. Such a vengeful act was mean-spirited and reflected badly on us all, especially our department and the composition program. Lesson 2 reiterated for me Lesson 1: know who is teaching, review their work, and observe them in the classroom. Lesson 2 made me feel like I was driving an eighteen-wheeler unaware of the cargo I was carrying.

This is why I thought teaching the graduate course Theory and Practice of Teaching Composition would help me keep the composition program on the road; teaching teachers about composition theory and practice is familiar territory for me. To my way of thinking, teaching this course would make administrative detail work and the unexpected mishaps of being composition director not seem so hard. The practicum would be a solid place to establish a stronghold. I know my stuff. I had no idea that I was soon to crash and burn.

Teaching the Practicum

From the beginning, it was hard to create conditions for discussion in the graduate class; students found the course readings tedious, intimidating, confusing. The informal response papers students submitted were exploratory, however, and many were beginning to construct good questions. I made copies of the most provocative paper to use in the class because the student expressed well her questions, citing passages from a course text, Lindemann's *A Rhetoric for Writing Teachers*:

> [W]hen Lindemann says, "[w]e can provide . . . guidance . . . by modeling or discussing with students the kinds of goal-based plans we might develop in responding to an assignment . . ." (27), I nod in agreement. Theoretically, this is all sound, but then I remember something: I must put this into practice. Now I'm at a loss again. . . . How do I present material to the class? How do I teach students without boring them? How can I be sure that they understand. . . . This is how I feel now; I'm interested in learning different strategies (and being exposed to teaching plans) that will help me teach students how to organize an idea. Once I have a few strategies, then I think I'll be more comfortable with (and find it helpful) to discuss in great detail the theories and complexities involved in composition. Right now, however, I feel like I'm in over my head.

Here, I thought, was an example of a student struggling in productive ways to make sense of assigned reading. The strength in this and other passages from the paper was the student's ability to pinpoint where she is and how she feels about the material. The paper overall was a model "think piece" or response paper. I felt that the merits of the paper warranted publishing for the class and having the author read it to initiate discussion. My thought was that this would open things up, and we could launch from here into other confusions and questions.

When I got to class that day, I learned the student had dropped the course. I was disheartened. She had felt in over her head, which I thought was a good issue for us to talk about. Her absence was an early warning sign of trouble ahead.

The class meetings began to feel like trying to swim against a riptide with a treacherous undertow. Communication between students during class sessions revealed divisions between graduate students from English and from creative writing. A sensitive student picked up on the problem and initiated a collection of brief biographies—a who's who in the class; another helped create an electronic message board for posting topics and questions on which to hold discussion. These projects were put in place. But the class overall did not invest either for or against course goals. My attempts during class to create conditions for small- and large-group discussion failed. Everything felt forced.

The plan for the midterm exam was for students to compose discussion questions from course readings and use writing processes to refine the best of these, and from here I would frame the midterm. Class members could then choose from their own questions the ones they wanted to write on to demonstrate understanding of and response to the fundamentals of the theory and practice of teaching composition. My efforts to set the process in motion got tangled. Some students contributed good questions, but many students spent a lot of time resisting the course readings. The idea of the midterm became the monster that overshadowed the reality of necessary study. Some in the class seemed to be under the impression that as graduate students they were beyond midterms. All I had in mind was for students to read, think, and discuss ideas fundamental to the discipline. From here we would continue to develop theory-to-practice connections and study our own writing processes.

The midterm had become the monster; as its creator, I was the mad scientist out to gobble up lost children. I, the authority on teaching, overpowered these graduate students. The persona I evinced made it worse. I wanted to give them teaching secrets, demonstrate how to structure composition courses and the classroom to prevent being taken advantage of by students acting "studenty." I would introduce them to composition theory, and we would investigate together a field of study with a remarkable classical tradition, infused with the spirit of democratic ideals. Once we established beginnings for theorizing the teaching of writing in classrooms, we could think pedagogically and figure out the nuts and bolts. When I organized plans for the semester, the midterm exam was to be an exercise for reviewing readings and deepening understanding. I thought class members would assist in creating questions, and the exam would be a co-created text. Despite having explained this to students theoretically and pedagogically early in the semester and at various points as we worked, when it came time to implement, the word *midterm* became a hot button. Earlier explanation—dismissed. Their anxiety over the exam shut down the process of working together.

I am wise to the classroom—composition or otherwise—and what happens there. But I did not know how close I was to depression or that teaching had helped to cover its tracks for many years. Teaching was my life, composition my passion, and I was lost. When this class of graduate students rebelled by shutting down communication, refusing to read, mocking assignments, and complaining loudly to administrators, they helped create a situation that stopped me cold.

In some ways, we were triggers for each other as we manifested obsessive-compulsive tendencies, versions of perfectionism, and passive aggression. When I read and responded to the midterm answers—locating page numbers and passages for students to reread, pointing out understanding that could be developed, and offering suggestions for further consideration—I determined that some papers were not finished enough for a grade and I wrote, "continue to work on this." Knowing that class members were going to put together a final course portfolio, I was comfortable about keeping processes open and about my ability to frame ways to assist student reflection as we continued. Here was the clash. No grade on the midterm and my suggestion to "keep working" translated to some students as a message of failure; for others, it was an insult; and for a few, just too much to ask.

Telling the Truth

The afternoon of the day I met about the practicum with administrators from the English and creative writing departments, I prepared for the 3:15 class meeting. Forget books and plans. I had to give in and admit I was lost; the communication breakdown we were experiencing had broken me. I began by asking the students what I could do to make things better. This is when we had our honest moment.

"As a class we have a problem," I said. "Communication has broken down, and we need to discuss what to do about it." The first student to speak said she thought she was supposed to be learning how to put together a syllabus, but so far the readings in the course hadn't shown how to do that.

Another student said, "Why are we doing what we're doing? I thought teaching was supposed to mean we'd have a tool bag; so far there's not much in mine. I want to know what kinds of assignments to give students, what happens on the first day, these kinds of things, not what we're reading about. I don't get any-thing out of the reading."

"I thought I would finish this class having a syllabus and then have the summer to mold it and have a structure that looks like it will work," another student added.

Still another said, "I thought we would be looking at different approaches and get an overview and take what is applicable to us. And the midterm bummed me out."

At this moment, the tone of the student remarks became more intense, and the discussion opened further.

"I don't understand why we have to 're-do' the midterm. I was so happy to get it over with the first time; I can't imagine going back and even looking at it."

One student became emphatic: "I would have preferred an 'F' on the midterm. I am emotionally tired. What's the point of work-ing on something like this? We need more practical application, a concrete way to make a syllabus. The midterm is not usable. The whole experience was a setback."

At this point, the tone in the conversation between the stu-dents took another turn and a student said, "I've lost trust in this course." This statement was the match lighting the kindling.

"I feel like everything I do in this class is wrong. I can't do anything right. I feel like I have to do a works cited page with the response paper assignment; I am not sure what is expected. These papers are overwhelming, and I'm terrified of the research project. I don't know how to survive."

The conversation had become quite dramatic by this point, but the discourse became more startling when the next student spoke.

"There is a fundamental division between MA and CRW students. All I want is practical knowledge. I didn't come here to teach English 101. I signed a contract and intend to keep up my part of the deal, but I want to be left alone."

Another student added, "This course is a setback. I haven't been able to move forward. Now I don't have the energy for it."

Still another comment: "My main problem is the process is never-ending. I need for the midterm to end. There is nothing dying off in this class. We're always in process."

At this point I said, "Just drop the midterm if you want to; leave it. You'll have plenty to reflect on in your course portfolio. You can choose not to work further on the midterm or complete reflections about it and spend time on other work from the course."

This comment seemed to make the student angrier. She did not want to work further on the midterm, but she did not want to just drop it either.

Finally another student said, "We all value writing, but when I have to work on this course, I am mentally exhausted. Areas of my writing and my life are suffering."

From here, I intervened and asked, "What can I do to make it better?" We determined the following:

Relax the midterm expectation; work on it further or not; feature it in the final course portfolio or not.

Revisit the course calendar and specify dates for class guests (currently teaching TAs) to talk about designing course syllabi.

Make the inquiry project less intimidating.

Be accessible for conferences.

These four points the class made specific are significant because we began to work together rather than at cross-purposes. I had planned all along for teaching assistants from the Departments of English and Creative Writing to come to our class to talk about how they designed course syllabi. This point, then, was already in the works. Also, since the beginning I had encouraged students to think about the inquiry project as a practical investigation into some area of teaching composition that would help them prepare for teaching their own classes. And as for my accessibility, I had been in my office consistently. Students had been reluctant to come there, I think, because I made them uncomfortable. They felt they could not question my authority, and I had overwhelmed them, which is why they sought refuge among themselves or complained to the graduate administrators. Taken together, however, this list constitutes a tangible outcome of our class that day. We needed that. The experience of the discussion was another thing we needed; it cleared the air. The students let out frustrations, and we approached being real.

Examining It

Communication gaps between teachers and students are inevitable regardless of classroom context. Everyone shows up with expectations, realized or not, as well as different sorts of background. It is the work of a teacher to be clear from the beginning how the class operates—establishing parameters, structure, time frames, and policies. Without appearing rigid, a teacher who comes across as firm yet approachable can be effective. Details matter but much depends on the tone set during the initial class sessions. Everybody in the classroom has an agenda. The teacher, however, is the main architect for the project (i.e., the course/class) and the master craftsperson. The students are central because the course is designed with them in mind, but they are not in charge of the original plan.

Regardless of the precision of the syllabus, the clarity of objectives, the integrity of requirements, the cohesiveness of the course of study, or the tone set by the teacher, students key into the overall course on their own terms. This means teachers must be consistent and trust that the course gets off the ground; and as a group, first with our leadership and down the line with students assuming responsibility for the enterprise, we can engage together in the remarkable collective pursuit of making learning a happening. The nature of teaching, however, with all its many variables, depends on reciprocal communication between all involved (i.e., teacher to student[s], student[s] to teacher, student[s] to student[s]). We work on communication, we falter, we make headway, we soar, sometimes we breakdown. We keep going.

In the context of this narrative, the division between MA and CRW graduate students was a factor more severe than I realized going into the course. I might have been able to pick up on the vibe had I been more centered when I first met the class. But I missed it and was not thinking along those lines. The field of composition studies was at the heart of my thinking as I went in to class that first afternoon. To put it bluntly, the professor my students met on opening day was prepared and passionate, unaware that she had ventured onto a fault line. Many students did not want to be there in the first place. The last thing the majority of students wanted to experience was an excitable woman, ready to take them to the field of composition studies. The midterm, already detailed, stands as the culmination of a bad first step, extensive division between CRW and MA students, and graduate student anxiety gone haywire about confronting the unknown.

Most students who spoke during the discussion transcribed in the previous section were CRW students, not English MA students. MA students did speak up during the conversation, but their comments overall were less confused by the composition texts we were studying. There was a struggle about the subject of the course and less willingness to consider common ground from those who represented a creative writing perspective. As the professor, I continued to find myself in the position of defending the course and allowing students' frustrations to keep me on the defensive. In retrospect, the resistant student behavior was successful in thwarting some course aims and assignments (e.g., discussions of composition theory, collaborations about the midterm, interactions between students from different graduate programs). At the same time, because our class reached an emotional abyss, we had an opportunity to witness ourselves in a struggle that could teach us all more than we could have imagined.

Coincidentally, we were reading and trying to discuss *Collision Course: Conflict, Negotiation, and Learning in College Composition* by Russel Durst on the day we had our first real

talk. This text, a study of students and instructors and their varied expectations, was fresh on my mind that day because I had
just reread in Chapter 6, "Persuasion, Politics, and Writing
Instruction," about how students avoided complicated writing
assignments or became angry and emotionally drained from readings about social and political issues in the course text *Rereading
America*. Preferring to steer clear of controversy, students discussed in the Durst text would declare that controversial topics
(e.g., diversity, prejudice) were not important to them (154).
Teaching approaches that lead to questioning and critical attitudes toward U.S. culture bother students when they say they are
in school for pragmatic reasons, not to engage in social awareness
or advocacy.

Similarly, what I kept hearing from many students in the
practicum was that theoretical topics related to the field of composition were not helping them prepare to teach. They did not see
the relevance or practical value of discussing differences between
grammar and usage or identifying distinctions between assessment, evaluation, and grading. Many did not read Durst's book
and therefore never knew or cared that explanations of "mis-
matched" student and teacher goals were reflected in our own
course material. I knew it, and some students caught it; but we
had to leave it at that.

The resistance from CRW or MA students in a course that
provides a theoretical foundation for composition theory and
practice is unfortunate, but the CRW perception that the teaching
of writing need not acknowledge the field of composition/rhetoric
is downright scary. The CRW perception of composition stems
from that department program and emphases valued within it. If
a similar scenario of power structure dissonance between chairs
and directors occurred in connection with any graduate course
other than the practicum, professors would be outraged. Yet the
problematic split between CRW and MA keeps unearthing all
manner of oddity. Newly formed at my institution is the CRW
version of the composition practicum course, although I seriously
doubt that composition theory and practice will make it on the
syllabus. Where this leaves us is anyone's guess. On we go.

At the time I taught this course, I was on the verge of finding
myself lost in a depression my own teaching had served to dis-

guise. We salvaged the course, and students stopped complaining. Most of them are now teaching composition or creative writing courses and still pursuing graduate studies or working as part- or full-time instructors at a university or community college. Interesting to note, when we have openings for positions to teach in our composition program, numerous graduates from our MFA program apply.

I probably will not teach the practicum course again, but if I do, we will read early on "Teachers as Students, Reflecting Resistance" by Douglas Hesse, a short article about ways in which students respond to dissonance and unfamiliar texts or theory. In this article, graduate students may recognize themselves and from here illustrate "the role theory plays in confronting teachers' common sense and . . . [it may remind students] what it is to be a beginner" (226). I would do a lot of things differently if I were to teach again the practicum, but I don't want to think about that now. What I saw in my students allowed me to know anger and sadness in relation to teaching. No other class has ever given such a favor, and "losing" the students in a class opens up a lot of chances for reflection.

In his final course portfolio, one student organized his work by adopting the theme of a single passing day, and says,

> I don't believe any of us who entered English 503 last January can truly say that we haven't been changed by the experience somehow. Part of this lies in the material that we studied over the course of the term, and the perceptible shift in focus from approaching it as a student would any text, to one who examines the material as a template for future endeavors, one that is vitally important to what waits down the road of this path we have undertaken.

The certainty of the course, he says, is that it is not an end, and he anticipates "leaving behind the singular aspect of the student in favor of a new dawn as a teacher." Quoting his favorite author, J. R. R. Tolkein, "Not all who wander are lost. . . ."

When seven students never showed up to retrieve their course portfolios, I was not surprised. What did surprise me was a note written by a class member left in my faculty mailbox some months after the class ended. It suggests we come around in our own way when we are ready.

> Dr. Huntley,
> I just saw you having a workshop with two students in the hallway, and I had a sudden realization of how much I admire and respect you. As I struggle with my own work, day to day, I'm reminded of the things we discussed in our class together, and feel sad that I was too thick to understand it at the time. Isn't that always the way? I'm beaming you very best wishes, and apologies for being such a dunderhead. Sincerely, [Your 503 Student]

Works Cited

Durst, Russel K. *Collision Course: Conflict, Negotiation, and Learning in College Composition*. Urbana, IL: National Council of Teachers of English, 1999.

Hesse, Douglas. "Teachers as Students, Reflecting Resistance." *College Composition and Communication* 44.2 (1993): 224–31.

Lindemann, Erika, with Daniel Anderson. *A Rhetoric for Writing Teachers*. 4th ed. New York: Oxford UP, 2001.

CHAPTER SIXTEEN

Why Not *Call It Practicum?*
It Is *Practice*

DEBORAH MURRAY
Kansas State University

Since reading Robert Tremmel's *Zen and the Practice of Teaching English*, I've come to think about many aspects of my teaching differently. The teaching practicum is a major part of my teaching practice, contributing to my understanding of how novice writers learn how to write and how novice teachers learn how to teach. Rather than focusing on negative connotations of the word *practicum*, I prefer to think about its root word of *practice*: "the doing of something repeatedly or continuously . . . for the purpose . . . of attaining proficiency" (*Oxford English Dictionary Online*). As we teach the practicum, we guide others in this hoped-for attainment of proficiency; moreover, as we guide others, our research and teaching are also enhanced. Our practice, to guide the practice of new teachers, is ongoing: each year we face new students. So that outsiders, both within our departments and within the institution at large, come to value and support our efforts, we need to describe the work of the practicum more completely, establishing a broader context for the professional preparation of the future generation of teachers and scholars.

I've been a member of the English department at Kansas State University for nearly twenty years, first as a graduate student, then as a "temporary" instructor, and now as a "continuing" instructor and director of the writing center. I became an advisor to new graduate teaching assistants in 1989; since that time, I've played an increasingly larger role in the expository writing program at KSU. I've had the opportunity to observe four different WPAs (and a couple of interim directors). Additionally, I've been part of four different composition/rhetoric job searches (two of these hires having since moved on). I have observed individuals with different theoretical approaches and different working styles. From my experience teaching the practicum and watching others do so, it is clear that a strong practicum program is a crucial ingredient of a strong expository writing program and a major contributor to the long-term professional success of GTAs.

Those of us who teach the practicum are primarily responsible for the initial steps in GTAs' professional development as teachers. Most of our graduate students at KSU have never taught before; some of them have never had any professional employment. Not only are practicum teachers helping new teachers survive in the classroom, but we are also contributing to the preparation of a new generation of college faculty. In Robert Boice's essay "Quick Starters: New Faculty Who Succeed," he discusses characteristics of those new faculty who establish a pattern of success early in their careers. Though the group he observed was fairly small, his findings offer insight for our graduate students, people who are certainly "new faculty" early in their career. Rather than wait until someone has a PhD, it makes sense to help those just beginning graduate school become "quick starters."

Many of Boice's findings are thought-provoking, but of the "eight concomitants of quick starts" he lists, I find two especially relevant for the preparation of new teachers: first, new faculty who succeed form a community with others to work on their teaching; and second, new faculty who succeed learn how to plan their courses efficiently. Boice found that quick starters form a teaching community:

> [They] showed a marked disposition to seek advice about teaching, from colleagues, via reading and observing, and from faculty development programs. Specifically, they spent an average of four hours per week in social contacts with colleagues that included discussions about teaching. (113)

The practicum offers the sort of faculty development program described by Boice, providing new teaching professionals with the opportunity to connect with colleagues. By setting up a framework for talking about teaching, reading theory, seeking advice, observing, and being observed, the practicum supports the habits that can lead to professional success.

Boice's other finding that seems significant to the current discussion is that quick starters "evidenced quick transitions away from spending the bulk of work weeks on teaching preparation" (113). With an awareness that one of the primary challenges of new teachers is managing their workload, practicum teachers focus on helping them learn effective strategies for doing their jobs better—and thus more efficiently. Those entering the classroom for the first time are overwhelmed by trying to figure out how to plan a class, and even more overwhelmed by figuring out how to get their grading done. In addition, making the transition to the increased work demanded of graduate courses complicates the balancing act for new graduate students who are also teaching. Those of us teaching the practicum are committed to providing excellent instruction and support for those new to the profession. By providing this support, practicum teachers are also making a substantial difference in the quality of instruction of those students enrolled in our beginning expository writing classes (or comparable classes).

Again, an integral aspect of teaching the practicum is helping new teachers manage their workload. These responsibilities range from helping someone operate the copier to helping a new teacher deal with a difficult student. Most significant to the preparation of new teachers is what happens outside the practicum classroom. It's the observations, file reviews, conferences, and drop-in visits that contribute most to effective preparation of teachers. If practicum teachers are available at teachable moments, new teachers are more likely to benefit from instruction. Late one Friday afternoon, for example, a first-semester teacher ("Susan") stopped by my office to ask some questions about her grading. Susan was grading her first set of essays, and she was second-guessing her judgment. After she had graded a couple of essays, she had consulted with a second-year teacher ("Ann"), who disagreed with the grades Susan had assigned. When I looked at a couple of these essays, however, I could see that Susan's grading was on track. Ann doesn't have much more experience than Susan, but she had been able to convey a great deal of confidence in her judgment; Ann's confidence in her grading prowess led to an undermining of

Susan's confidence in her own instincts. Since I was available late Friday afternoon for a one-hour conference, I was able to reassure Susan about her grading, thus leading to a more productive weekend of grading for her. My drop-in visit with Susan is typical of conferences that practicum teachers have with new GTAs. While it's clear that practicum teachers can't be immediately available to answer every question, it's important that new teachers feel that practicum teachers are generally accessible to them.

Although these drop-in visits are time intensive, time in addition to the time spent planning and teaching the practicum, rather than viewing them as hassles, we should see them as opportunities. This time spent providing guidance at the point of need has multiple benefits. First, a small amount of time spent at the front end saves a great deal of time at the back end; that is, it's easier to deal with a potential problem rather than one that has exploded. Second, in an individual conference a practicum teacher can help put a problem into context so that a new teacher can be reflective, considering larger lessons learned from a situation. Third, helping new teachers be more reflective teaches the teacher: these encounters help experienced teachers reflect more broadly on practical and theoretical implications of new teachers' concerns.

In general, out of a group of ten GTAs, three or four will seek me out fairly regularly each week. These contacts can range from quick two-minute exchanges of information to a one-hour problem-solving session. Notably, those who seek me out generally aren't the worst teachers. New teachers who seek more attention from practicum teachers tend to fall into one of two groups. The first group is generally needy, people who lack confidence and want help solving every problem. Sometimes these needy people simply need to have a brief conversation to bolster their confidence; more often, people in this group can eat up every hour of a day. When dealing with these needy new teachers, practicum teachers have to take care not to become co-dependent, fostering a sense that our job is to solve every teaching problem and co-grade all their students' essays.

The second group of teachers who seek out my attention in drop-in visits is quite different. As quick starters, these new teachers are aware of the potential benefits of establishing a collegial relationship with their peers and supervisors. In addition to asking questions, they often share ideas. These new teachers know the importance of staying in touch and maintaining visibility. I depend on these teachers to help keep me informed about general areas of difficulty the group as a whole might be experiencing. I also depend on them to energize me with their ideas. I look forward to seeing these teachers in my office because I learn from them. While being accessible to interact with new teachers requires extra time, it is crucial to fostering their professional development and it can revitalize practicum teachers.

Being accessible to new teachers takes time, and the question of how much time the teaching practicum should take is at the heart of disagreements in many English departments. Those who administrate an expository writing program have different personalities, different stakes, different statuses, and thus different perspectives, which can be reflected in the words we use to describe the work of those who teach the practicum. Guiding new writing teachers is more than simply *advising, teaching,* or *mentoring,* common terms used to define this work.

Are those in charge of the practicum advisors? *Advising* suggests that those being advised are capable of sorting through advice and deciding a course of action on their own. An *advisor* may be a wise person whose advice should be followed, but the term suggests that those being advised simply have less experience, whereas many first-time teachers have *no* knowledge about writing instruction and *no* experience teaching writing. As undergraduates, several of our graduate students tested out of required writing classes, or they enrolled in honors classes, many of which have a format quite different from that of most required expository writing classes. No matter how smart they might be, new teachers who have never been enrolled in a composition/rhetoric class or an expository writing class need more than advice.

Instead of advisors, are those in charge of the practicum teachers? Like our other classes, the practicum demands preparation, grading, and conferring with students. We want our students to do well, and we do our best to help them do so. For classes other than the practicum, however, if our students' performance falls short, they bear the burden of responsibility. Others aren't affected by their poor performance. If practicum students don't do well, however, their students bear the burden. Sometimes, those "teaching" them end up helping them do their grading; in some cases, we end up taking over a course for them. Last fall, one new graduate student teacher had a family emergency and was unable to complete the final month of the semester. As her "teacher," I took on the responsibility of making sure her classes were covered and her students' essays were graded. Additionally, I conferred with several of her students who felt abandoned by their teacher. In response to their anxiety, I helped them revise their essays for the portfolio exam. Would a teacher for a class other than the practicum have analogous responsibilities?

Instead of teachers, are those in charge of the practicum mentors? A new faculty member is often assigned a faculty mentor. The new member asks for advice, for classroom visitation, and for help with lesson planning. If the new faculty member falls short when fulfilling his or her responsibilities, however, it's not his or her mentor's responsibility. If Professor B doesn't show up for his class, for example, it's not Professor C's job to cover it; if Professor B has problems with his students, it's not Professor C's job to meet with those students and mediate disputes. In those cases, "mentoring" involves a positive, collegial, as-needed advisory relationship. In contrast, practicum teachers are both advisory and supervisory. Rather than a peer relationship, the relationship is hierarchical. Though new teachers are our colleagues, supervising teachers also have the power to take them out of the classroom. While initially primarily concerned with a new teacher's growth and development, a supervising teacher will, if that teacher is not performing at an acceptable level, make arrangements to first, improve the teacher's performance, and then, if necessary, remove that teacher from her or his responsibilities. At a certain point, for those administering the writing program, the needs of the students in that teacher's class become more important than the underperforming teacher's needs. As a less extreme example, through letters of recommendation that teaching supervisors write, we can influence whether graduate students get the jobs or the acceptances into graduate programs they are seeking. While practicum teachers do mentor new teachers, clearly our responsibilities are more comprehensive than the term *mentor* suggests.

If the terms *mentor*, *teacher*, and *advisor* don't effectively capture the work of those involved in planning and teaching the practicum and supervising new teachers, we need to consider other possibilities, such as *executive in charge of professional development* or, more simply, *master teacher*. Our language falls short at this point, but we need to keep searching because we need a productive way of describing this important work so that outsiders can understand what we do and thus see it as a worthy investment of resources.

An evolving expository writing program creates further difficulty in defining the practicum and those who teach it. Different WPAs, different administrative pressures, different graduate students enrolled in a program—all these factors lead to an evolving program. Oftentimes, changes happen gradually without much planning; only after the fact do those involved take the time to reassess their status.

At KSU, since 1988 our supervisory system for GTAs teaching expository writing has had the following format. The director of expository writing (the WPA) is a composition/rhetoric professional, tenure track or tenured. As part of administering the writing program, the WPA is the face of the expository writing program; additionally, this person is in charge of the curriculum, portfolio review system, and a three- to five-day intensive training session in August for beginning teachers. Assisting the WPA have been three to five "advisors."

Though KSU had offered an advisory program for several years before creating a course called the practicum, the course was formalized in response to several factors. Former graduate students enrolled in other programs wanted to be able to demonstrate that they had experienced systematic teacher preparation. Additionally, those who were advisors were doing a great deal of work for which there was no official record. To administrators and outsiders, advisors were being "released" from teaching a course rather than "reassigned" to duties as part of their regular load. Once the practicum was formalized in 1996, graduate students teaching in the department were required to enroll in English 805, Practicum in the Teaching of Expository Writing, for two credit hours each year (though rather than a grade, they are assigned "credit" or "no credit"). As described formally, the course is to provide "instruction in the theory and practice of teaching in a university expository writing program." Although new instructors at KSU (other than graduate students) are required to attend the practicum for two years, they are not required to enroll in English 805.

One area perceived differently by the two WPAs I've worked for is the issue of release time. I am one of the two advisors without a PhD (non-tenure track); the practicum "counts" as a course for me in both the fall and the spring semesters. For tenure-track (or tenured) advisors, the practicum "counts" as one course a year. One of the primary reasons for this flexible accounting is pragmatic. Non-tenure-track advisors have a 4/4 load, and tenure-track advisors have a 3/2 load, so releasing non-tenure-track advisors from one course a semester is not quite as costly as releasing a tenure-track advisor from one course a semester would be. Additionally, tenure-track advisors realize that non-tenure-track teachers would be unwilling to add the practicum to their teaching load if it counted as only half a course each semester. Counting the practicum differently for those at different ranks, however, contributes to the problem of definition. Is it or is it not the same as teaching a class? Is it more onerous or less? Some of us feel that the practicum is more demanding than other courses we teach; other teachers view teaching the practicum as less demanding. These differences should be resolved to help clarify problems of perception.

Before the practicum was a course, it was viewed differently, sometimes as a job requirement, sometimes as a way to help teachers do their job better. Additionally, meeting together regularly to talk about teaching and grading helped our department portfolio system succeed. With more or less standardized assignments and more or less standardized requirements, most teachers in the program were able to arrive at comparable standards for portfolio assessment. Just like the rest of us, graduate students occasionally expressed resentment about being required to meet regularly, but we had fairly good cooperation.

Transforming the advisory program into a course solved some paperwork problems, but it created other problems of perception. Once the regular meetings became a course, the power dynamic changed. The meeting leaders became "teachers" and the new teachers became "students." As students enrolled in the practicum, new teachers seemed to feel freer to cut class or fail to complete assignments. New graduate students put the practicum in the same mix with their other courses, sometimes putting it last during weeks in which they had papers due for their other courses.

While we don't require our new teachers to read much theory, our expository writing program's curriculum and its methods are heavily grounded in theory. The current schedule for the practicum at KSU is structured around our curriculum for Expository Writing 1 and 2, curriculum based on Kinneavy's aims of discourse. Our suggested methods of structuring class time, guiding students through the writing process, and responding to student writing in a way that helps them revise successfully are based on the work of James Britton, James Moffett, Peter Elbow, Lisa Ede, and others. In her essay "Training the Workforce: Overview of GTA Education Curricula," Catherine Latterell (142) provides a continuum for categorizing different curricular approaches:

> "Apprenticeships—Practica—Teaching Methods courses—Theory Seminars"

KSU's practicum program is most accurately categorized with those terms on the left (*Apprenticeships* and *Practica*) rather than those on the right (*Teaching Methods courses* and *Theory seminars*). The amount of Theory with a capital T has varied, depending on the priorities of the WPA. When GTAs are asked to read any Theory, they often resist it as "extra" work, in part because few of our GTAs are composition/rhetoric students.

In the face of this resistance, we are challenged to weave theory into our practice. As former WPA Irene Ward says, "We need to know the theory; they need to trust us that we do; it's efficient. If people want to be good teachers, [they will follow our suggested methods because they] work." We can't rely on new teachers to trust those who mentor them, so rather than bombarding them with theory and methods, we need to present information to them in a way that connects it with information they already know or have found to be true. As a practicum teacher in a collaborative program, it is important for me to be up-to-date on theory, but it seems less important to make sure beginning teachers read all the important background before entering the classroom. On the other hand, I find that our best teachers seek out theory to help answer their questions about teaching because they realize that reading others' work helps them do their job more effectively.

At KSU, our first-year practicum is based on surviving. It can be fairly described as an apprenticeship, in which novice teachers learn from master teachers. First-year teachers are introduced to each assignment two to three weeks before they will be teaching it. Those teaching the practicum demonstrate teaching strategies and activities that work, and we also organize grading practice. In addition, practicum teachers model appropriate classroom management. The second-year practicum is primarily focused on professional development, formalizing a more reflective approach to teaching and culminating in the development of a teaching portfolio. Though the basic structure of the practicum is similar from year to year, each day's activities vary based on the needs of each semester's class. Practicum teachers, like all good teachers, need to be flexible, reacting to students' expressed concerns as well as the new teacher's perceptions of a class's strengths and weaknesses.

One of the ongoing challenges of teaching the practicum is that all KSU graduate students are MA students. The learning curve is steep; new teachers are challenged to learn quickly how to teach effectively. Most graduate students come in as novice teachers: they are introduced to new curriculum in each of their first two semesters (Expository Writing 1 in the fall; Expository Writing 2 in the spring). Then, after teaching for us during their second year as "experienced teachers," our graduates move on. A few teachers remain as adjuncts for a semester or two, but most MA graduates move on to other programs (either for further graduate work or to other teaching or editing jobs). Each year we have a new batch of twenty to twenty-five new teachers, teachers who leave us shortly after learning what we have to teach them. Knowing that our efforts improve the quality of what goes on in approximately 100 expository writing classrooms each semester helps motivate the work of practicum teachers, but in some ways our efforts are like those of Sisyphus pushing the stone up the hill: one step forward, two steps back. The workload of those teaching the practicum is constant. We spend a lot of time and effort contributing to the professional development of graduate students who will teach for us for only four semesters.

The workload of the practicum varies depending on the personalities and varying experience levels of the teachers one is supervising. Being responsible for first-year teachers is more demanding than mentoring more experienced teachers because the process includes as much instruction as evaluation. In addition, first-year teachers have more questions and seek out their supervisors more. Another complicating factor is that if new teachers with concerns can't find their assigned supervisor, they are likely to seek out someone else. Is it just coincidence that the supervisors who tend to be more available are those of nontenured status? Though three of those teaching the practicum and those administering the writing program are tenured or tenure track, two of the core advisors are neither tenured nor tenure track; instead, we are described as "continuing" instructors, individuals who achieved early success as graduate students at KSU, continued to find success as "temporary" instructors, and then were asked to join the program as "advisors" in charge of a group of "advisees," groups varying in size from six to fourteen. Though the optimum number was set at "no more than nine," the total number each of us supervises is usually more than that.

In addition to tenure status, the difference in perception about the time required by the practicum can be related to a faculty member's other work assignments. As well as teaching the practicum, the WPA has other administrative responsibilities, so he or she has more course release time than others teaching the practicum. The practicum responsibilities dovetail with other administrative responsibilities, so a WPA may not feel as overburdened by the work of teaching the practicum. Our current WPA feels that counting the practicum as half a course for tenure-track advisors (including himself) and a full course for non-tenure-track advisors is fair. Other tenure-track advisors have disagreed, and the previous WPA resigned primarily because of this dispute.

From my observations of different WPAs and different practicum teachers, it's clear that a team approach to managing the workload is best. That way individuals can rotate the most demanding roles so no one person is overburdened. Also, with approximately one faculty member for every eight new teachers, the workload is manageable. A large institution such as KSU would require a team of five to seven members, thus requiring more composition/rhetoric faculty members than some English departments are willing to hire. Clearly, the resistance to hiring enough tenure-track composition/rhetoric faculty members is the reason KSU has come to rely on two of us without tenure-track status. An institution could also include other interested faculty members as part of the team rotation, thus making the expository writing program a more integral part of the department's overall mission.

A team approach to running the practicum can help employ the strengths of different types of people. Both Irene Ward (former WPA) and Robin Mosher (the other non-tenure-track practicum teacher) spoke about the importance of considering each team member's strengths and weaknesses. Some people are better at inspiring new teachers, giving them confidence in their ability to be successful in the classroom. That confidence gives GTAs ownership of their teaching. Other people are best at being there at teachable moments, helping new teachers find the vocabulary to explain their judgment about grades or helping them find a particular article that supports an approach they want to experiment with. Other people are best at modeling good classroom management techniques. In the course of teaching the practicum, in addition to presenting material, these teachers can demonstrate how one might best break down large tasks into more manageable steps. A team approach to teaching the practicum and administering a writing program can bring together all those different aspects that lead to effective classroom teaching. The team approach also helps keep those in charge of the practicum engaged and revitalized. Those who are able to succeed long term as practicum teachers need to remain plugged in so they don't get burned out.

While the success of a writing program shouldn't be dependent on a particular individual, those who administer the program should possess certain characteristics, the most important of which is presence. Marshall Gregory's essay "Curriculum, Pedagogy, and Teacherly Ethos" speaks powerfully about this quality of presence (70). Gregory focuses on the enthusiasm and passion that effective teachers convey, on the "'leading out' (from Latin *educare*) that lies as the etymological source of *educate* and that also describes education's most basic aim." Gregory points out that effective teachers "lead students out . . . in order to turn . . . [their] potentialities into realities" (73). Applying Gregory's ideas to mentoring and supervising new teachers works quite well. In this capacity, practicum teachers are translators, helping draw out of new teachers their capacity for teaching others.

Those who educate new teachers need to be available and accessible to them at the point of need. If a new teacher can't find a supervisor when needed, the teachable moment is lost. Also, in addition to being accessible, supervisors need to be good listeners so they can respond based on the new teacher's needs rather than provide a preprogrammed lecture. Practicum teachers need to realize that new teachers often don't know what they need. Sometimes they don't even know what questions to ask. Instead of a theory course or a "how-to-get-your-job-done" course, some graduate students would prefer to have a general gripe session, interspersed with some "tips and tricks" for making their grading easier or classroom performance more entertaining. Practicum teachers can face resistance from students who aren't ready to learn what we're teaching.

Educating new teachers, guiding them as they discover what teaching styles and methods suit them, is an important challenge. As we contribute to the development of a new generation of college faculty, those of us teaching the practicum need to remain focused on the practice—the day-to-day challenges of teaching a writing class. It's helpful to think of practice in the Zen sense, rather than in the much-derided denotative sense of the word *practical*. Only while we are writing, teaching writing, and teaching new teachers how to teach writing can we practice various theoretical approaches.

Writing is hard work and teaching writing is even harder. Those devoted to helping new teachers do their best work fulfill a valuable mission, especially at a large research institution; not only do we help maintain good-quality teaching for first- and second-year college students, but we are also an integral part of the professional development of the next generation of teachers and scholars.

Perhaps one of the reasons our efforts aren't appropriately valued is that we sell ourselves short. At KSU, for a cost of approximately five sections a semester (or FTE of 1.25), those teaching the practicum maintain quality control for approximately 100 sections of expository writing (or FTE of 25). Those teaching these

100 sections are paid at a much lower rate than full-time tenure-track faculty members would be (at an abominably low rate, in fact). For a minimal cost, practicum teachers help maintain the quality of an expository writing program. Moreover, by educating a new generation of faculty members, we contribute to the overall excellence of the profession. Administrators should support these efforts with more money for operating expenses, for professional development, and for more master teachers to supervise and teach new graduate students. We're worth it. Our institutions want us to provide a valuable learning experience for new college students, but they aren't willing to devote adequate resources to these required writing classes. With inadequate funding, the KSU expository writing program has relied on the personal commitment of nontenured, underpaid master teachers to work with tenured faculty members to support the professional development of new writing teachers. What will happen when we retire? What will happen if we quit? Practicum teachers need to make our work more visible: our contribution to the development of future faculty members deserves recognition, reward, and resources.

Works Cited

Boice, Robert. "Quick Starters: New Faculty Who Succeed." *New Directions for Teaching and Learning* 48 (Winter 1991): 111–21.

Gregory, Marshall. "Curriculum, Pedagogy, and Teacherly Ethos." *Pedagogy: Critical Approaches to Teaching Literature, Language, Composition, and Culture* 1 (2001): 69–89.

Kinneavy, James L. *A Theory of Discourse: The Aims of Discourse.* Englewood Cliffs, NJ: Prentice Hall, 1971.

Latterell, Catherine. "Training the Workforce: Overview of GTA Education Curricula." *The Allyn & Bacon Sourcebook for Writing Program Administrators.* Ed. Irene Ward and William J. Carpenter. New York: Longman, 2002. 139–55.

Mosher, Robin. Personal Interview. 27 June 2003.

Tremmel, Robert. *Zen and the Practice of Teaching English.* Portsmouth, NH: Boynton/Cook, 1999.

Ward, Irene. Personal Interview. 27 June 2003.

CHAPTER SEVENTEEN

The GTA Writing Portfolio: An Impact Study of Learning by Writing

ROSEMARY (GATES) WINSLOW
The Catholic University of America

I want to suggest a return to the most basic premise that under-girded modern composition pedagogy—that teachers of writing must write. Yet, how many institutions ask prospective and new teachers of writing to write anything besides academic papers? Of the doctoral pedagogy courses and rationales published as a forum in the fall 1995 *Composition Studies*, most of the fourteen were focused on teaching theory. My own was the only one that included nonacademic writing as a component (Winslow). Nor can I uncover any published research, lore, or recommendations for writing portfolios in the doctoral course since the early days of the process movement, with the sole exception of Lynn Z. Bloom's essay "Finding a Family, Finding a Voice," in which Bloom describes tossing out the prepared syllabus to write and workshop with her students. The near-total absence of portfolios in doctoral pedagogy courses seems especially surprising because portfolios are recommended as the best way of encouraging writing development as well as for assessing readiness for college-level courses, for evaluating writing performances *in* courses, and for measuring performance for exiting college.

For twenty years, I have made nonacademic writing a major part of graduate courses on teaching writing, first as part of National Writing Project summer institutes, then at my own school, and last year at a neighboring one. I kept assigning writing portfolios and work in peer response groups because the vast majority of students commented on how crucial the experience was to their writing, their teaching, and their work with one another. Last spring I decided to do a study to learn what the graduate teaching assistants (GTAs) I have taught think the portfolio experience gave them in these three areas and whether they still consider it of great importance past the end of the course. This chapter describes and reports on that study.

Background: Context, Course, and Assignment

In the early days of process pedagogy, writers who taught writing—people such as Donald Murray, Janet Emig, James Moffett, and Ken Macrorie, to name four prominent founders of modern composition—advocated a pedagogy based on a professional model of how the best writers write. In those days, during the early 1970s, I was studying in the newly inaugurated composition program at SUNY Buffalo. James Moffett's, James Britton's, and Janet Emig's breakthrough work had been recently published and formed the basis of the curriculum. In Charles Cooper's classes, we students, who were mostly secondary English teachers, wrote our way through much of Moffett's spectrum of discourse. We shared our writing in peer groups. We learned how to shift among points of view—we learned what that meant. And we wrote for audience, situation, and an eye to publication. We did case studies of our student writers à la Emig. And perhaps because I had thought of myself as a writer since age six; perhaps because I had written freely, inventing forms and styles outside of school and in; perhaps because I came from a poor family and was aware of different languages and registers; perhaps because I taught a heterogeneous population in a large city school system; perhaps because the Vietnam War, civil rights, and women's rights were then so much a prominent part of daily life, the "writing process" was never, for me, without the rich disjunctions, crossings, and inter-weavings of school, home, church, country, town, city, political, cultural daily life. Writing process was what you did when you wrote, and it was not a simple, straightforward model you could follow or teach easily. What you could do was set up an environment and some assignments to encourage writing. You could also do it, watch it, and learn. But as I remember, we were *taught* that we had to do, watch, listen, and learn, because not very much was known then about how people wrote. Everyone in the profession was in a learning mode and filled with excitement for this new way of teaching and learning, for what we *could* learn about how people wrote so that we could teach more effectively. And it was effective. I remember the great gratitude I felt, for, thanks to process teaching, I had a way to work with my eighth graders, most of whom were still learning Standard English. This had been a shock to me, just as seeing my own father's writing had been a shock in those same years. With a new GED in hand and enrolled in a community college, he had asked me to help him with his English papers; I had not known that he could not tell a fragment from a sentence, nor a semicolon from a colon from a period. Teaching by process had been a godsend. My students were writing a great deal, peer grouping, and learning.

In 1983 I began to teach NWP summer institutes: the three-fold assumptions of the project were that (1) teachers of writing must write, (2) they must know theory and research and *do* research, and (3) they needed to collaboratively share difficulties and expertise in order for a strong writing program to take root and flourish. I found this conjunction to work so well to stimulate ongoing learning that I kept the three principles when I began to teach a course on approaches to teaching writing for graduate students at Catholic University. But it was the set of writing assignments that was most readily transplanted into pedagogy courses for graduate students who were not teaching or were first starting to. In the NWP model, teacher participants wrote three or four pieces on the same topic, chosen by them, from different points of view. Based on Moffett, this assignment was designed to make writing teachers more aware of the complexity of writing acts, of shifting rhetorical moves, changes in voice and purpose— of difficulty, messiness, multiple drafts. The writing was both a counterweight to readings and discussions of process, which can seem neat and generalizable in the abstract, and a counterpart of learning. It was the place where *doing* provided the learning that cannot be had by reading, discussing, or studying. Moffett had called it building a "rhetorical repertoire." As Moffett had proposed, writings were brought to peer groups and workshopped, and this not only helped their own writing, but it also helped the development of a close community of writing teachers who continued to share teaching problems and successes in the months and years beyond participation in the institute.

By 1987, when I began to teach the course to new and prospective teachers, postprocess theories were coming to the fore and spurring research into writing as a social act, both impeded and empowered by race, class, and gender relations and constructs. This newer direction deepened the appreciation of what the portfolio offered: trying out new points of view, changing substantive material for various audiences and purposes, writing out of and for one's own concerns—all these opened up different languages, styles, audiences, purposes, genres, and individual choice and power. Most important, teachers learned to think and teach with a more complex view of what writing was and could do. The portfolio project assisted this more complex view because the project could not be accomplished without growing awareness that people have different processes, identities, concerns, styles, and values. In short, process was visible not so much as a model—a thing—but as an *activity*. It was what people did when they wrote. It became clear that everyone did it somewhat differently, and that with each attempt to write on the topic from another perspective, for another purpose, for a different audience, thinking began again, more decisions had to be made as you went along, and no one else could tell you exactly how to do it. You made it up as you went along, you learned each time, and you learned there was always more to learn. It was important to follow your own path, to write, to have readers along the way, and it was important to keep learning, to keep writing, if you were going to teach this complex activity to others. The learning enabled teachers to place more power in students' hands because they could better guide individuals through their attempts to set down what they were trying to say more effectively and extend their thinking from initial attempts.

From 1987 to 1994, I taught the doctoral pedagogy course at my school every other year. In 1992, I became director of the university writing program and soon found that the no-credit practicum, comprising twice-monthly staff meetings, did not give half the GTAs enough to do even an adequate job of teaching first-year writing. In 1994, I strongly encouraged current and new GTAs to enroll in the pedagogy course, and it was so successful in boosting teaching effectiveness, as measured by the student evaluations I had designed and by my observations of their teaching, that in 1995 the course was made a requirement for all GTAs who taught courses or tutored in the writing center. In the spring and fall of 2002, I also taught the course at neighboring Howard University as part of my work with the professional preparation program our schools were involved in together. The curriculum of readings was largely process oriented, supplemented by essays exploring issues of theory, identity, and diversity. Graduate students at both universities had already taken, or were concurrently taking, at least one course in contemporary critical theory. Therefore, I could count on their awareness that social and political issues and constructs affected language and vice versa. Process did not exist in a vacuum but was instead a matter of writers and writing already partially shaped by communal forces. GTAs' concerns about how to have a voice, an identity, and ideas of their own—and whether they even should—in their own graduate study was often out in the open at the start of the course. This concern was especially prominent and keenly felt by the students at Howard. The concern extended to what they should be doing in their own classrooms: even if they wanted to teach, or were supposed to teach, strictly academic writing, they wondered how exactly to do that. So process pedagogy—how to, undergirded by a variety of theoretical and research bases and readings—provided the main readings. Classical, Toulmin, and Rogerian rhetorics, learned through practice in analysis, provided a way of understanding and teaching argument the GTAs could use with their own first-year writing students. To examine issues of how race and class can enter into rhetorical situations and contexts, three weeks were spent on an intensive analysis of claims, lines of argument using the *koinoi topoi* as constructs, multiple audiences, ethos, logos, pathos, and style in Martin Luther King, Jr.'s "Letter from Birmingham Jail." We looked closely at the network of interaction and frequent fusion of these elements in King's language and moves, including the way he negotiates from the position of Other America to claim a stance in opposition to the local audience, situation, and context by appealing to wider audiences and supervening laws. So that students could be made aware of King's strategies, we analyzed specific language and arrangements of sentences and arguments to discover how King's power and effectiveness were accomplished.

Besides readings and class discussions, I gave weekly assignments: a mix of short writing responses to the readings in order to engage thinking about issues of teaching, and more immediately practical tasks such as designing assignments, doing analyses, making lists of questions and comments to use with peer response groups and in conferences, practicing writing comments on drafts and evaluating essays, and so on. A take-home final examination assisted integration of learning.

The main component of the course was the writing portfolio, worth 40 percent of the grade. Following the NWP design, it comprised three pieces on the same topic, chosen by the student. The portfolio had to contain some narrative, expository, and argumentative writing. That these are not mutually exclusive categories forced students to break down the seemingly disparate categories that textbooks tend to present. All pieces had to be written for specific audiences, and the purposes and intended audiences (specific people or publication outlets) had to be stated on a page prefacing the portfolio. Drafts were attached to the final version, in reverse order of date of composition. Invention and research notes were optional. Two of the three pieces had to go through at least two drafts and one through several drafts, taken as near to publishable shape as possible given the time constraints of a semester. Revision had to show more than word- and sentence-level changes. In addition to a preface statement describing the portfolio, students wrote another page evaluating what they had learned that had already affected their teaching and what they expected would affect it in the future. About the fourth or fifth week of class, we workshopped the first set of drafts together; after that, GTAs were on their own in peer groups. After the first month of classes, I cut the class sessions by half an hour to give time for peer response. Relinquishing class time to peer response signaled that I regarded this activity as just as important as anything done in the classroom. During the third month, students chose one draft to discuss in a conference with me. They prepared a short summary of where they were with all their pieces and brought in questions and problems they were having difficulty with. The conference gave them the experience of conferencing from the student writer's side. They had the option to hold more conferences with me, but very few chose to do so.

Between 1995 and 1999, I allowed one piece of fiction, drama, or poetry as one of the three pieces. Although GTAs liked this option, I thought they did not learn as much about rhetorical strategies. They did not do as much shifting of audience and purpose, because literary genres tend to find their own audiences. Surprising to me, GTAs liked doing three nonliterary modes because they valued having to do "what our students do," which they said was also "writing what we want to write."

The Study Design

In May and June 2003, I collected three kinds of data: anonymous surveys, volunteered interviews, and statements from the portfolios. Thirty-nine survey forms were mailed. Seventeen were completed (40 percent), all from the students who took the class from 1994 through 2002. Some of the mailings were returned due to inaccurate addresses: I know of six returned, but a full count is not available as more came in during the summer while I was away and were not saved. Thus, the response rate was actually much higher than the 40 percent indicated since many did not receive the form. Anonymity was preserved by having the responses mailed to my assistant so that I would not know the return addresses. Fourteen respondents were Catholic University GTAs and three were from Howard.

Seven people volunteered to be interviewed. Thirteen portfolio prefaces were made available for my review. There was some overlap in respondents to the three categories, but none was represented in every category. I eliminated from the study two categories of student: those who were not teaching or tutoring then or subsequently and those who did not do the portfolio project as assigned. There were five GTAs in this latter group: two who did not revise at all, one who pieced together mostly previously published writing, and two who had medical situations that prevented completion in the way and at the time assigned.

The survey form asked first for information on the responder: the year the course was taken; number of semesters in various GTA duties (teaching, tutoring, leading small-group writing workshops for underprepared students) and whether these were at Catholic University or at other institutions; and whether male or female. Originally, I had intended to see if there were differences in male and female responses, but only one respondent checked *male*, and one left the item blank. Next, responders were asked to rank from one to six the importance of six components of the course: readings on writing process; readings on rhetoric; class lectures and discussions; weekly assignments; the portfolio project; and the final exam (years 1999 to 2002) or videotaping and analysis of one's own class or tutoring (years 1994 to 1998). A second page contained thirteen Likert scale items seeking ratings by relative importance of the portfolio work to three areas: teaching, one's own writing, and working with other GTAs. A third page contained seventeen Likert scale items seeking ratings on relative importance of the portfolio work to various aspects of teaching writing. A fourth page asked for free commentary on the portfolio work to teaching, graduate study, and work with peers. If respondents had taken a teaching position elsewhere, I asked for any influence of the portfolio work on that position.

I have already described the content and purpose of the portfolio preface statements. For the interviews, I asked four questions: What was the portfolio like for you? Did the portfolio affect your academic writing? Did the portfolio affect your teaching? Did the portfolio affect your work with other GTAs or colleagues at you current position? Six of the eight interviewees were female and two were male. Four have full-time tenure-track positions at other universities, three are current GTAs, and one is an adjunct at two universities and writing the dissertation. Six were or had been Catholic University GTAs; two were Howard University GTAs. Interviews ranged from thirty minutes to an hour. I conducted six of them, and my assistant, a sixth-year GTA, conducted two. I had planned and offered an anonymous group interview option, to be conducted by my assistant, in hopes of obtaining more balanced findings. It was an opportunity for negative views to come forward. But no one took up this offer.

I was looking for GTAs' assessment of the portfolio's impact in a number of areas of their work life and for change in perceptions from the end of the course through graduate study and on past graduate school. By collecting different kinds of data, some of it anonymously to get a wide view and some of it by volunteers to provide a more in-depth view, some of it at the end of the course and some ranging along eight years of graduate and postgraduate work, I was able to obtain a longitudinal, in-depth perspective on the portfolio's impact.

Results and Discussion

The Survey: A View of Trends

The single most significant and clear finding was the ranking of the six course components on the survey. Eight of the seventeen respondents, a shade over half, ranked the portfolio number one in importance. Two ranked it second, four third, one fourth, two fifth, and none last in importance. The two who ranked it fifth, however, gave long comments at the end of the survey expressing strong learning gains and detailing ways the portfolio work had shaped or dramatically changed their own writing and teaching for the better. Five respondents ranked the readings on writing process the highest and two ranked this category second, making this component a strong second in importance. Readings in rhetoric had two rankings of first and three second. Two respondents ranked class discussions as most important. Clearly, over half the respondents to the survey deemed the portfolio the most important of all course components. But the other rankings indicate what I found the other kinds of data to reveal: GTAs found different aspects most useful depending on their needs, inclinations, preferences, personalities, and styles of teaching.

On the first page of the survey, which pertained to the three areas of impact, items rated very high by more than 50 percent of respondents were co-mentoring, the functioning of the TA community, writing graduate student papers, professional writing, personal writing, and teaching at other colleges. Thus, the three major areas were all rated very high by the majority of respondents. Responses to items on general teaching (classroom, tutoring, leading revision groups) were spread across the range, about equally for high, moderate, and low. These results indicate that the portfolio work had a greater relative impact on GTAs' own writing and on work with other GTAs than it did on their teaching. Two respondents rated all items on this page at the low end except for the three items pertaining to their own writing. Yet both of these ranked the portfolio first in importance of the six course components.

Nevertheless the survey responses showed a strong impact on GTAs' teaching as well, as the page focusing on the impact of seventeen items on specific aspects of teaching writing revealed. More than 70 percent of respondents rated the impact of their portfolio work on the teaching of the following aspects very high: revising strategies, peer response groups, conferencing, and evaluating writing. Of these respondents, between four and seven rated the portfolio "indispensable" to their teaching of all these four aspects. Fifty percent to 65 percent rated the following aspects very high: developing assignments, arrangement, tutoring, and coaching students on making decisions about writing. Audience awareness, style, invention, and polishing drafts were rated very high by one-third, moderate by one-third, and low by one-third. Four items were rated low by about half (eight) of the respondents, moderate by a quarter, and high by about a quarter (three or four respondents). Three of these four items were forming a thesis, developing a thesis, and fitting a thesis to an audience. These results were puzzling until set next to the written comments and the portfolio work. Then it became clear that these items referred to areas of teaching that were understood as having been *un*learned. Multiple drafting and writing for specific audiences and different audiences on the same topic almost always broke down the thesis-driven approach, replacing it with a gradual process of locating the central point in a draft during peer discussion and developing a main point as audience and purpose took shape. Forming and fitting a thesis to an audience as terms presented in textbooks no longer matched the ongoing process of thesis emergence that respondents experienced while doing the portfolio. On the fourth low-rated item, research skills, there were only two very high ratings, with five in the moderate and eight on the low end. This is likely due to the fact the GTAs are already quite knowledgeable researchers. Finally, some items were checked "not applicable" by one to three respondents because some GTAs (the MA students) had been tutors only and not classroom teachers. Finally, in a very few instances on the two pages of Likert items on the survey, an item was left unrated.

Written Comments and Interviews: Digging Deeper

The invited comments on the surveys and the oral interviews yielded a more extensive view of the portfolio project's impact in terms of what was learned and the specific causes behind the learning. Sixteen of the seventeen surveys contained written comments at the end, with eight of these (50 percent) over a page in length. Their content was similar to the interview material and the portfolio prefaces. From all written and interview material, several major themes emerged. I consider these one by one for clarity of naming and describing, although they are mutually interacting and not entirely separable.

OPENING OUT GTAS OWN WRITING

The most strongly stated and pervasive theme of the portfolio prefaces written at the end of the course was the expansion of GTAs' own writing into new areas. The main point of these statements was strengthened and refined over time, most strongly and specifically by GTAs who had finished degrees and were publishing. Eight survey respondents and all seven interviewees emphasized that their own writing improved through the portfolio work. I had not asked for any felt experiences, but several were offered. Four interviewees and two survey respondents said that when they first approached the portfolio assignment, they felt fear and frustration because they had to consider writing in forms and styles they had either never written in or not written in for a long time. Two survey respondents and one interviewee offered that they were delighted or "energized" from the start with the prospect of writing the three pieces. All of these GTAs mentioned ways their peer groups had helped to allay fear by giving "comfort and support" in the early stages. Once the drafting and revising were underway, fear turned to discovery, excitement, and confidence as they realized that writing on a chosen topic for chosen audiences allowed them to "write what we want to write." At the same time, they were keenly aware that they were writing the sorts of things they were asking of their students. This is one of the important ways learning to write was integral to learning to teach writing. As the portfolio writing proceeded, GTAs gained practical knowledge, better understanding of concepts, and confidence in their own writing and teaching abilities. There was not a single comment or interview that did not include some discussion of this progression, even for those initially eager for the work. These portfolio statements are typical: "It felt good to be writing in my own style, my own voice, and I didn't tire of going back and tweaking the paper." "The group sessions helped make me a better writer and a better listener." "At first, I had trouble pushing my academic training aside and letting the creative juices flow. . . . [T]hen I started to have fun." "I now feel there is no such thing as 'wrong' writing." "All of us feared deviating from the academic form." "Never before have I invested so much time in perfecting my writing." "I understand better what it is to write effectively." "My peer group didn't work well, but drafting and revising was incredibly helpful in developing my own writing skills." "As I mentioned in class, writing these papers has been of immeasurable help to me, for I have been writing in such a narrow realm for so long. They opened me to the precise nature of the demands I place on my students. Each of the papers demanded plenty of time and energy. . . . [T]hey also allowed me to be creative."

A major subthread of the opening-out theme was *voice*. Two survey respondents named the term and wrote extensively about it. Five interviewees used the term and spoke at length about their learning, with one claiming that finding his own voice, "that nebulous thing," was his most important learning, and another discovering that she had a "choice of voices." But all other interview and survey comments brought up the topic of voice without naming it—as awareness of role and audience learned by the shifting of rhetorical stances they had to make. GTAs who were code-switchers expressed awareness of expanding their range beyond academic writing as a "form" or a "formula" they had previously learned to fit their ideas and voices into. Discussion of readings throughout the semester on language change, language and power, and genre as social constructions in flux helped these GTAs break out of a sense of "academic form" and a strictly regulated, impersonal, "formulaic" writing as the only "right way." Who speaks in what voice and language and to whom proved a powerful set of interactive ideas, especially for those whose home language was furthest from academic discourse. One former GTA who has been an assistant professor and writing center director at another university for the past five years and who had been a journalist for fifteen years and a writing teacher for ten before taking my course said the portfolio project changed her writing and her teaching: it "opened up my voice."

Peer group work proved to be one of the most valuable experiences for improving GTAs' own writing. All eleven portfolio prefaces mentioned that peers' questions and discussion of drafts made them aware of areas where language and ideas were confusing, had "jumps in thought," had ineffective ideas or style given the chosen audiences, or were ineffectively arranged. Seven expressed appreciation for the different strengths each person brought to the group: "A lot of helpful advice came from conversations with the peer group, who asked me clarifying questions which really made me think about what I had written or was going to write. . . . I did so *much* reworking—structural and style change. . . . [M]y papers were more reader-centered." "The peer group reinforced my opinion that an objective, honest view is invariably useful. . . . Peer group suggestions inspired the very topic for my argument." "The diversity of our skills helped us offer each other constructive criticism." "With each session, my view of my essays changed." Group sessions "helped to make me a better writer" and a "better listener. . . . [T]his will benefit my teaching."

The portfolio work and the peer group writing had showed GTAs how others write and how voice develops through revising.

They saw how it develops as a function of increasing attention to audience as audience and purpose become more clearly identified. Three of the interviewees had published in professional journals since taking the class; three had finished dissertations. These former GTAs talked most extensively about the importance of the portfolio and the peer group experience in terms of knowing what to do and how when they had to revise for dissertation committees and editors. Survey comments showed this too. The range of comments on surveys and in interviews from those who were at or past the dissertation stage included experience with awareness of voice, role, audience, and purpose; with revising; with eliciting and sorting through feedback where and when needed; and with handling criticism. An indication of the value of the peer group work is that peer groups outside of class began to form for seminar papers and for dissertation draft review after the 1994 class, when I began to offer it each fall. Three interviewees from the 1994 and 1995 classes noted that the peer group experience in the course was the direct impetus for these continuing groups and that they were very helpful in their graduate work. One survey respondent wrote that she continues to seek peer feedback on her seminar papers, revises a great deal, and hasn't seen improved grades but she's "happier with the results." Some respondents and interviewees said they found out they were "creative"—which seemed to mean that they could write something besides academic papers.

CARRYOVER TO TEACHING

As is evident in some of the statements cited earlier, GTAs linked their expanded sense and knowledge of writing directly to their teaching. This was a frequent theme in the portfolio prefaces because I had *asked* for such statements. But even the interview and survey comments spoke emphatically about how the expansion of GTAs' own writing was an essential, even indispensable, factor in their own teaching. The reason was the same: they learned *how* writing happens—how chaotic and messy it is at first, how to find significance, how to shape and keep shaping, how to get good feedback, how to write for an audience, how to assess and evaluate from word-level to whole: "We were *doing* what we were learning in the abstract." "This course was the missing link for me. . . . [M]y Master's program [at another university] told me about these things, we read about them, but I didn't understand how to do it in the classroom." Several mentioned their confidence and credibility as teachers of writing, knowing they had done it and knowing how to guide their own students' drafting and revising: "I never say to students now 'this is how you write.'" Other GTAs echoed this learning about the individuality of writing in contrast to *the* writing process as a static model. Barbara Couture has noted how Moffett's program was implemented in the narrow way that process pedagogy took on by the late seventies, attributing its failure to the static, linear way teachers had implemented it. When teachers are writing, rewriting, and working in peer groups, process shows up as individual, varied, nonlinear, and fluid, with one writing growing out of another. The problem in so-called process pedagogy was its detachment from actual writing; otherwise it would not have become a mere linear stage-model. GTAs who found the peer group helpful to their own writing use it in their classes. One forms spontaneous peer groups from among her advanced literature students as needed. She says she now knows how to "coach and articulate purpose, audience, and voice. . . . I can speak from my own experience as a writer of perils and pitfalls." Others mentioned that they make assignments more specific now and include intended audience. They add to the class calendar more deadlines for pieces and stages of students' writing. GTAs say they learned in the pedagogy course how peer groups work and what they offer, so they know how to use them in their own classrooms: "I would never have known how to do it before," one said, and this idea was a refrain running throughout GTA comments, and it was frequent all during the course each time I taught it.

STRUGGLE AND EMPATHY

Another major theme was empathy for what GTAs' students went through. Those who mentioned fear and frustration as an initial reaction to the portfolio assignment said they realized their students were experiencing this too. Many of the GTAs who talked the most about fear had been successful writers in professions or graduate schools. They attributed their fear to having written so long in one genre that they had lost a flexible knowledge of other ways of writing and of what to do to be effective outside narrow, familiar bounds. But all interviewees and survey responders said they were glad to have gone through the experience because they learned so much, and as one said, "I would have hit that point with the dissertation anyway. When I got there, I'd already been through it." This interviewee had taken a tenure-track position the fall before the interview; he had been much sought after on the job market for his excellence in teaching and scholarship. While a GTA, his students raved to everyone about his teaching and invariably ranked the peer groups the most important part of his courses. He and other GTAs put a very high value on empathy; they saw getting in touch with their students' experience as a central part of their own process of learning to teach. One said she had previously seen students in the abstract and without realizing it treated them "rather like machines." After the portfolio experience, she realized that every student is an individual and no one will write exactly the same way, nor be able to do exactly what others do. She said, "Before, I was just expecting them to know how to do it—write a definition, or how to punctuate. But now, because I've felt vulnerable, now I take time to assess where the student is. The students are not just abstract now—they're individuals. I will never see students in the abstract again."

This GTA and many others mentioned how hard it was to learn to take criticism. But they saw one another going through the same thing, and it made them acutely aware of how their students feel. One had this to say about the faculty where she now teaches and gives writing workshops: "If teachers were in the [writing] trenches, they'd probably be more gentle, or positive with students in their writing." One interviewee emphasized that it was "important to have an encouraging professor" during the portfolio project. And another: "I know now what that look of panic on my students' faces is." The lesson of how hard it is to write, the "time and energy it takes," the "struggle" writing is, coupled with knowing how to coach in specific terms as well as to give general encouragement, made for attentive, flexible, strong teaching.

LEARNING COMMUNITY

Not all the peer groups worked well, though most years they did. Two respondents said their groups did not work well because people were unwilling to give criticism. They attributed this to fear and/or introverted personalities. This too, they said, was a lesson in working with their students. But even members of these groups gave encouragement and comfort—"we were all in the same boat," said one former GTA, "and that helped." But experiencing an uncritical peer group did not necessarily deter GTAs from using peer groups in their own classrooms. The "boat" quote came from the former GTA cited earlier whose students raved about his class and the peer groups he established. Even though he himself was at first fearful and his own peer group did not work well, he learned how to make them work extremely well with his students. He claimed he was an "introvert" and so were the other members of his group. But the experience brought him out of "isolation" and got them all involved in discussions of writing and teaching. He talked frequently with other GTAs about day-to-day teaching, sought and gave ideas and advice, and used peer group response in his dissertation. Now in a tenure-track position, he is trying to get a teaching discussion group started in his new department. He is one of three interviewees who took my class in 1995; he is one of two who credits the writing groups for the vital, cooperative GTA community that developed then and continues today. The third interviewee from that year said he could not be sure about the connection since the majority of GTAs were moved to a new office space with a central lounge that year; that new space made daily conversation about teaching and their own writing easier. But the first two, and others in the next two years, claimed that the vital GTA community would not have developed without the peer groups. Most admitted that without the peer groups they would never have discussed their teaching or shown their writing to other GTAs. "Every fall," offered one GTA, "you can go down to Room 19 and groups will be gathered together over their writing project for 723" (the number of my graduate class). Several survey comments mentioned that the peer group experience seemed more valuable once they had taken positions elsewhere, because it helped them work with other faculty more effectively. In all, nine of the sixteen survey comments contained claims for the beneficial impact of the portfolio experience on the GTA community or on respondents' own faculties.

VARIATION IN IMPACT

As I read over the survey and interview responses, I detected the common themes previously discussed, but I also noticed a substantial pattern of variation: students took what they needed and what they could from their various experiences with the writing, revising, and working in peer groups they did in the pedagogy course. Though most perceived clear and strong influences on what they taught and how, as well as on the GTA community, they emphasized most strongly the influence on their own writing; whatever the greatest impact was had the most impact on their teaching. Often the impact was greatest in the areas where GTAs had at first felt inadequate, fearful, lacking in confidence, or introverted, such as expanding their own writing beyond academic formulas; law, business, or technical writing; or journalism. Or it was finding voice or choice of voices and styles. Sometimes it was recognition of the importance of audience, or of the need to design assignments more carefully. Sometimes it was working one-on-one with students in conferences. And sometimes the greatest benefit was claimed for their own writing.

GTAs who stressed learning about voice emphasized their knowledge of how to coach students through developing voice for particular audiences. Other GTAs stressed that they learned the importance of multiple drafts, and others emphasized their understanding of where students are with particular papers and what they may be going through. Two wrote at length about encouraging students to explore different styles, voices, and ways of approaching assignments. Five wrote or spoke about their ability to coach students through difficulties and one about her success with conferencing, which she attributed to her peer group experience. Responses to survey items showed GTAs rating some items higher than others and none rating *all* of them very high or very low. The variation showed that respondents took some care with their ratings, that they tried to weigh relative impact in the different areas. The interviews and end-of-survey comments in particular revealed that GTAs' personalities and previous backgrounds in writing and teaching varied, and the experience filled varying needs and self-chosen and newly discovered directions for teaching and for continued learning.

RHETORICAL SENSITIVITY AND SENSIBILITY

Joseph Petraglia has suggested that what composition teachers need to do in a post-postprocess era is help student writers learn "rhetorical sensibility" and "sensitivity" (62). I think these terms are good ones for the hard-to-specify learning that writing itself is and that these GTAs talked and wrote about. The portfolio assignment could not be done without engaging in rhetorical thinking because students had to move from audience to audience, purpose to purpose, style to style, role to role, on the same topic. They had to engage different genres as well, so they had to learn how language, genres, modes, voice, style, and so on slip, shift, slide into others as one goes along. They had to learn that there is no one "process," that no theory, framework, model, or person could precisely guide them to a successful essay each and every time. Revising with peer feedback, or at least encouragement, helped them to see their writing differently and to figure out how to change it. Staying on the same topic helped them to see how narrative, for example, can be either argument or exposition; how argument includes expository sections; how exposition can slip into argument, often without intention; how significance and purpose develop during revision; and how one draft can branch off into other pieces of writing or dramatically transform. Study subjects commented often on how audience, voice, and purpose go through vast changes in successive revisions: these comments suggest they were learning about the ways in which rhetorical concerns enter and stay in play in specific ways from start to finish. Many comments attested to the individuality and difficulty of each writing task: GTAs came to recognize that there is no single way to write; that students need to be coached out of difficulties; that the teacher needs to be aware of how very difficult writing is for students; that writing is nebulous and hard to "tell" students about. These kinds of comments indicate that GTAs acquired greater rhetorical sensibility and sensitivity. Gaining empathy for students, working with other GTAs on their own writing and on day-to-day teaching issues—these are the results of a greater rhetorical awareness as well. As GTAs became more grounded in actual writing, teaching writing was no longer "abstract." Practice in writing, rewriting, and working in peer groups gave them what they needed to move from a narrow view of process to a broader view of individual writing processes, from rhetoric as concept to practical rhetorical sensibility and sensitivity.

WRITING POWER AND PEDAGOGY

Two GTAs called the portfolio "a rich experience," but all who responded to the survey and all who were interviewed said virtually the same in their emphatic—and often extensive—expressions of the experience's importance to them. The experience had given them the power to give their students more power over their own writing because these new teachers had learned how to write and respond in the ways they were asking of their students, and they had worked with other writers in response groups and seen "what sort of feedback was useful." GTAs from Howard were especially vocal during and after my course that the course content had helped them see how they could guide students to saying what they wanted to say with greater power. The long study of Martin Luther King, Jr.'s essay was especially enlightening and appreciated. But they all maintained they would not know how to guide students to more varied and powerful writing if they hadn't done the writings and worked in peer groups themselves. This was the necessary component that made the knowledge of pedagogy work. It was what they needed to be able to teach writing to *individuals*, not to "*the* student." Writing itself opened out, destroying many misconceptions. The *un*learning was important.

Conclusions

While GTAs were engaging in writing processes in order to teach writing process more knowledgeably, they learned their way into elements that are now regarded as postprocess: awareness of individuality and the social nature of writing (Berlin); using "passing theory"—ad hoc forming of "how to" during actual writing of a piece alongside a general theory (Kent); rhetorical sensibility and sensitivity (Petraglia); fluidity and flexibility of genres; contextual and situational dependence of decision making; empathy; growth of writing and teaching communities; and power from knowing more about how to use language powerfully and how to teach others to use language powerfully. As the authors of the essays in Thomas Kent's collection, *Post-Process Theory: Beyond the Writing-Process Paradigm*, agree, process theory, research, and pedagogy still form the background of postprocess work, which is confined largely to research and theory and has generated little pedagogical change. Tracing the outgrowth of postprocess from process, Lynn Z. Bloom argues that Maxine's Hairston's 1982 prediction in "The Winds of Change"—that "teaching writing as process, not product"—will remain a "significant influence in composition studies . . . with modifications and contemporary upgrades . . . so long as one of the major aims—and responsibilities—of the profession is to continually improve our teaching of writing" ("Great Paradigm" 31). Bloom predicts that the split between "theoretically sophisticated research and process-model composition classrooms will continue, and will probably widen" (41). And perhaps it will. The mandate for pedagogy remains the teaching of writing, and students must have the background in order to recognize and learn the foreground.

Bloom lists and examines new areas of investigation opened and expanded by postprocess research and theorizing: genres as socially constructed and dependent on audience; more complex views of writing process, including "developing 'rhetorical sensitivity' in students" ("Great Paradigm" 41). She suggests that students need "knowledge design" of "situated rhetorical performances," reflective practices, and a widening of writing beyond the classroom audience and concerns. At the end of her essay, Bloom affirms Kurt Spellmeyer's call for a return to learning as an "active *process* with creation rather than criticism as its aim" ("Great Paradigm" 43). By including in GTA pedagogy courses a major emphasis on GTAs' own writing, revision, and peer group work, a large step in that direction can be taken. For the GTAs in this study, the writing portfolio encouraged and assisted integration of process and postprocess ideas while improving their own writing, their teaching, and their participation in professional communities.

Works Cited

Berlin, James A. *Rhetorics, Poetics, and Cultures: Refiguring College English Studies*. Urbana, IL: National Council of Teachers of English, 1996.

Bloom, Lynn Z. "Finding a Family, Finding a Voice: A Writing Teacher Teaches Writing Teachers." *Journal of Basic Writing* 9.2 (1990): 13–14.

———. "The Great Paradigm Shift and Its Legacy for the 21st Century." *Composition Studies in the New Millennium: Rereading the Past, Rewriting the Future*. Ed. Lynn Z. Bloom, Donald A. Daiker, and Edward M. White. Carbondale: Southern Illinois UP, 2003.

Couture, Barbara. "Modeling and Emulating: Rethinking Agency in the Writing Process." Kent 30–48.

Hairston, Maxine. "The Winds of Change: Thomas Kuhn and the Revolution in the Teaching of Writing." *College Composition and Communication* 33.1 (1982): 76–88.

Kent, Thomas, ed. *Post-Process Theory: Beyond the Writing-Process Paradigm*. Carbondale: Southern Illinois UP, 1999.

Moffett, James. *Teaching the Universe of Discourse*. Boston: Houghton Mifflin, 1968.

Petraglia, Joseph . "Is There Life after Process? The Role of Social Scientism in a Changing Discipline." Kent 49–64.

Spellmeyer, Kurt. *Arts of Living: Reinventing the Humanities for the Twenty-First Century*. Albany: State U of New York P, 2003.

Winslow, Rosemary. "Course Syllabi and Critical Statements." *Composition Studies/Freshman English News* 23.2 (1995): 6–10.

INDEX

EDITOR

Sidney I. Dobrin is director of writing programs and associate professor in the Department of English at the University of Florida and also serves on the faculty of the College of Natural Resources and Environmental Studies. He received his PhD in rhetoric and composition in 1995 from the University of South Florida. He is author or coauthor/coeditor of numerous books and textbooks, including *Post-Composition* (forthcoming), *Cracks in the Mirror* (forthcoming), *Technical Communication for the Twenty-First Century* (with Christopher J. Keller and Christian R. Weisser, forthcoming), *Writing Environments* (with Christopher J. Keller, 2005), and *Saving Place* (2005). His articles and essays cover a range of subjects about composition theory and writing from ecocomposition to postprocess theory and have appeared in a variety of journals and books. He is past coeditor of *JAC: Journal of Advanced Composition*, served for two years on the Conference on College Composition and Communication's Scholars for the Dream Travel Award Committee, and is former chair of the CCCC Nominating Committee. He serves on the editorial boards of *Composition Forum* and *WPA: Writing Program Administration*. In his spare time, Dobrin is a PADI dive instructor, a boat captain, and all-around blue water bum. Dobrin lives with his wife and son at Flying Fish Farm in Alachua, Florida. Together, the three spend endless hours searching beaches, rivers, open ocean, and lakes for treasures.

CONTRIBUTORS

Joanne Addison is associate professor at the University of Colorado–Denver. She has directed the department's teaching practicum for the last six years and has been the writing program administrator for the last two. Addison's publications include articles in *Written Communication, Computers and Composition,* and *English Education,* as well as a coedited collection on feminist empirical research. Her current research focuses on the use of the experience sampling method in the study of literacy development.

Anis Bawarshi is associate professor of English and director of the expository writing program at the University of Washington. In addition to teaching the practicum course, he teaches a range of graduate and undergraduate courses in composition theory, discourse analysis, rhetoric, and language policy. His publications include *Genre and the Invention of the Writer: Reconsidering the Place of Invention in Composition* (2003); *Scenes of Writing: Strategies for Composing with Genres* (with Amy J. Devitt and Mary Jo Reiff, 2004); *A Closer Look: The Writer's Reader* (with Sidney I. Dobrin, 2003); and articles in *College English, JAC,* and the *Writing Center Journal.* He is currently working with Mary Jo Reiff on a volume on genre for the Reference Guides to Rhetoric and Composition series edited by Charles Bazerman.

Kelly Belanger is associate professor of English at Virginia Polytechnic Institute and State University, where she teaches courses in composition pedagogy, literacy, and professional writing. She worked in writing program adminstration at Wyoming, Youngstown State University, and The Ohio State University, where she earned her PhD in 1992. She has coauthored (with Linda Strom) *Second Shift: Teaching Writing to Working Adults* and published in journals and books such as the *Journal of Basic Writing,* the *Journal of Business Communication,* the *Writing Instructor, Radical Teacher,* and *Critical Literacy in Action.*

Michael Bernard-Donals is Nancy Hoefs Professor of English and Jewish studies at the University of Wisconsin–Madison, where he directs the English department's first-year writing course. His most recent books include *Witnessing the Disaster: Essays on Representation and the Holocaust* (2003) and *Between Witness and Testimony: The Holocaust and the Limits of Representation* (2001), both with Richard Glejzer. He is currently working on a book on tropes of memory since 1945 tentatively titled *Forgetful Memory.*

Samantha Blackmon is assistant professor in the English department at Purdue University, where she teaches graduate courses in computers and composition theory and minority rhetorics. She is director of technology integration and a mentor of first-year teaching assistants in the introductory composition program. Areas of focus for her scholarship include community building in cyberspace and archival research on writing programs in historically black colleges and universities.

Jonathan Bush is assistant professor of English education at Western Michigan University, where he teaches courses in teacher education and composition studies. He is the coauthor (with Janet Alsup) of *"But Will It Work with REAL Students?" Scenarios for Teaching Secondary English Language Arts* (2003). He is also codirector of the Third Coast Writing Project and coeditor of the *Language Arts Journal of Michigan (LAJM).*

Ruth Overman Fischer has been a member of the English department at George Mason University since 1987. She holds an MA in English: linguistics and a PhD in English with an emphasis in rhetoric and linguistics. She has primarily taught Mason's general education composition courses, English 101: Composition for first-year students as well as English 101: Composition for Non-native Speakers of English and English 302: Advanced Composition for upper-division students in their majors. She was director of composition from fall 1998 through spring 1999. Her current teaching interest is a special section of English 302 for nontraditional adult students in Mason's Bachelor of Individualized Studies Program.

Sibylle Gruber is associate professor of rhetoric and director of the University Writing Program at Northern Arizona University, where she teaches graduate and undergraduate courses in literacy studies, rhetoric and cultures, computers and composition, and the theory and history of composition studies. She is the editor of *Weaving a Virtual Web: Practical Approaches to New Information Technologies* (2000) and coeditor with Laura Gray-Rosendale of *Alternative Rhetorics: Challenges to the Rhetorical Tradition* (2001). Gruber's work on cybertheories, feminist rhetorics, composition, and cultural studies can be found in journals such as *Computers and Composition, Computer Supported Cooperative Work, Jour-*

nal of Basic Writing, Works and Days, Journal of the Assembly on Computers in English, and *The Information Society*, as well as in collections such as *Feminist Cyberscapes: Mapping Gendered Academic Spaces, Global Literacies and the World-Wide Web*, and *Fractured Feminisms*.

Juan C. Guerra is associate professor in the English department at the University of Washington, Seattle, where he co-directs the Washington Center for Teaching and Learning and teaches courses on writing pedagogy, language, literacy, and ethnography. His principal areas of research are highlighted in two books: *Writing in Multicultural Settings* (1997), a collection of original essays coedited with Carol Severino and Johnnella E. Butler, and *Close to Home: Oral and Literate Practices in a Transnational Mexicano Community* (1998). He is currently working on an auto/ethnographic project that examines how the rhetorical practice of transcultural repositioning plays itself out in the contexts of language, schooling, and identity.

Joe Marshall Hardin is composition director and associate professor of English at Western Kentucky University, where he teaches courses in writing, rhetoric, and writing theory. His publications include *Opening Spaces: Critical Pedagogy and Resistance Theory in Composition* (2001) and *Teaching, Research, and Service in the Twentieth-Century English Department: A Delicate Balance* (with Ray Wallace, 2004). He is also coeditor of *Composition Forum*, a journal of composition pedagogy.

Georgina Hill is director of the composition program at Western Michigan University. She supervises graduate and undergraduate mentoring in composition instruction and teaches graduate and undergraduate courses in composition studies, professional writing, and writing teacher education.

Lu Ellen Huntley is associate professor of English at the University of North Carolina at Wilmington, where she has been teaching since 1985. Her background in composition studies began when she was a graduate student at the Bread Loaf School of English, where she received a master's degree in 1984 while teaching high school in rural North Carolina. She received a doctorate from North Carolina State University in literacy studies in 1994 and served as director of composition in the English department at UNCW from 2001 to 2003. She teaches courses in English education, composition, literature, and critical literacy and has published articles in *Arizona English Bulletin, High School Journal, North Carolina English Teacher*, and *Journal of Adolescent and Adult Literacy* and has contributed chapters to various collections.

Stephanie L. Kerschbaum is assistant professor of English at Texas A&M University, College Station. Her dissertation investigated how students in a postsecondary writing classroom engaged with difference in the classroom, and her research interests include writing pedagogy, discourse studies, and rhetorical history.

bonnie lenore kyburz teaches writing in a rhetoric–cultural studies orientation as well as critical theory and twentieth- and twenty-first-century literature. She engages regularly in interdisciplinary research involving rhetorics of science, visual rhetorics, and somatic pleasures associated with intertextual play between music (and other aesthetic/cultural texts) and the ongoing work of theorizing her role as a teacher-scholar. kyburz is coeditor with Elizabeth Vander Lei of *Negotiating Religious Faith in the Writing Classroom* (2005) and author of "Meaning Finds a Way: Chaos (Theory) and Composition" in *College English* (May 2004). Engaging her love of visual rhetorics in the context of what is still—despite laments to the contrary—"independent" filmmaking, kyburz also works for the Sundance Institute as a day actor and manages the Sundance Screening Room for the Sundance Film Festival. In her spare time, she writes screenplays, reads, buys beauty products like a kook, and watches movies and whatnot on cable.

Jeanne LaHaie received her MA in English from Western Michigan University, where she is currently a part-time instructor. She teaches basic writing, first-year composition, and children's literature. She also teaches composition and literature in WMU's Academically Talented Youth Program (ATYP) for high-achieving middle school and high school students.

Anthony J. Michel is assistant professor of English, specializing in composition and rhetoric, at California State University, Fresno, where he teaches the graduate introduction to composition practicum. His areas of interest are composition and rhetorical theory, cultural studies, and the visual rhetorics. He has published articles in the collection *Alternative Rhetorics: Challenges to the Rhetorical Tradition* and in *Black Arts Quarterly* and *Red Cedar Review*.

Susan Kay Miller is a faculty member at Mesa Community College in Arizona, where she teaches writing, linguistics, and ESL. She recently completed her doctorate in rhetoric, composition, and linguistics at Arizona State University, where she both participated in and helped facilitate professional development opportunities for graduate teaching assistants. Her work has appeared in *Composition Studies* and *Computers and Composition*, and she coedited (with Duane Roen, Veronica Pantoja, Lauren Yena, and Eric Waggoner) *Strategies for Teaching First-Year Composition* (2002).

Deborah Murray has been a supervising mentor to graduate students at Kansas State University since 1989 and a teacher of the practicum since 1996 (when KSU began calling it that). In addition to expository writing, she teaches drama and British literature for nonmajors, and in 2002, Murray was recognized by KSU with a Presidential Award for Excellence in Undergraduate Teaching. She has been director of the writing center since 1993 and recently published "Zen Tutoring: Unlocking the Mind" in the *Writing Lab Newsletter* (June 2003). Murray received her MA from KSU in 1986.

Mary Lou Odom is assistant professor of English and assistant director of the Kennesaw State University Writing Center at Kennesaw State University. Her research interests and current projects focus on the identification of theory–practice intersections to facilitate the training of writing teachers and peer tutors.

Veronica Pantoja is currently a full-time faculty member in English at Chandler-Gilbert Community College in Arizona. Her research interests include teaching writing with technology and writing center theory and administration. She is also a doctoral student in English (rhetoric/composition and linguistics) at Arizona State University.

Jeff Rice is assistant professor of English at Wayne State University and a former WPA. His research and teaching focus on the intersection of new media and writing. He is currently finishing a critical examination of composition history and is working on a book-length critique of literacy in relationship to new media.

Rochelle Rodrigo is an English faculty member at Mesa Community College in Arizona and before that co-coordinated Arizona State University's Preparing Future Faculty program (2001–2002) and served as assistant director of ASU's writing programs (2000–2001). She is currently finishing her PhD in rhetoric, composition, and linguistics at ASU. In addition to her recent coauthored essays on teaching portfolios (in *Composition, Pedagogy & the Scholarship of Teaching*) and group portfolio presentations (in *Strategies for Teaching First-Year Composition*), Rodrigo is currently working on a paper and a grant focusing on usability testing of online writing courses.

Duane Roen, professor of English, currently directs the Center for Learning and Teaching Excellence at Arizona State University, where he previously served as writing program administrator. Before that, he directed the writing program at Syracuse University and then served as coordinator of graduate studies in English at the University of Arizona, where he also worked as director of rhetoric, composition, and the teaching of English from 1988 to 1992. In addition to his five previous books and many chapters, articles, and conference papers, his most recent book project is *Strategies for Teaching First-Year Composition* (with Veronica Pantoja, Lauren Yena, Susan K. Miller, and Eric Waggoner, 2002). During the past two decades, Roen has offered a range of professional development experiences for graduate students in the form of workshops, individual conversations, and coauthoring and coediting.

Shirley K. Rose is associate professor in the English department at Purdue University, where she teaches graduate courses in writing program administration. She is director of composition and regularly mentors first-year teaching assistants in the introductory composition program. She is currently ice president of the Council of Writing Program Administrators. Areas of focus for her scholarship include defining the intellectual work of writing program administration, citation studies in composition, and archival theory and practice.

David Stacey is professor of English and composition director at Humboldt State University in Arcata, California. He has published articles and chapters on composition theory, computers and writing, and the future of the profession. He is currently working on a longer study of Kenneth Burke.

Anne Trubek is associate professor of rhetoric and composition and English at Oberlin College. She is the coeditor of *Writing Material: Readings from Plato to the Digital Age* (with Evelyn B. Tribble, 2003) and is currently working on *The Writing on the Wall: Visiting American Authors Houses*. In 2002 she founded the community-based writing program at Oberlin College.

Rosemary (Gates) Winslow is associate professor of English at The Catholic University of America. Her work on rhetoric and composition, style, business and technical communication, and American poetry has appeared in numerous journals, book chapters, and encyclopedias. She has won several grants and awards for writing program work and for her poetry, which has appeared in the *Southern Review*, *Poet Lore*, *Crossroads*, and other places.

This book was typeset in Sabon by BookComp, Inc.
Typefaces used on the cover include Cool Dog Plain and Frutiger.
The book was printed on 50-lb. Williamsburg Offset paper
by Versa Press, Inc.